First World War
and Army of Occupation
War Diary
France, Belgium and Germany

7 DIVISION
20 Infantry Brigade
Devonshire Regiment
8th (Service) Battalion
17 July 1915 - 30 November 1917

WO95/1655/2

The Naval & Military Press Ltd
www.nmarchive.com
Published in association with The National Archives

Published by

The Naval & Military Press Ltd

Unit 10 Ridgewood Industrial Park,

Uckfield, East Sussex,

TN22 5QE England

Tel: +44 (0) 1825 749494

www.naval-military-press.com

www.nmarchive.com

Contents

Document type	Place/Title	Date From	Date To
Heading	WO95/1655/2		
Heading	BEF 7 Division 20 Brigade 8 Bn Devonshire Regt 1915 July-1917 Nov		
Heading	##		
War Diary	Bamptoke	17/07/1915	17/07/1915
War Diary	Aldershot	22/07/1915	25/07/1915
War Diary	Havre	26/07/1915	27/07/1915
War Diary	Wizernes	28/07/1915	03/08/1915
War Diary	Carvin	04/08/1915	17/08/1915
War Diary	Locon	18/08/1915	26/08/1915
War Diary	C.1	27/08/1915	30/08/1915
War Diary	Las Cleuliaux	31/08/1915	31/08/1915
Heading	20th Inf. Bde. 7th Div. 8th Battn. The Devonshire Regiment. September 1915.		
War Diary	Busnes	01/09/1915	02/09/1915
War Diary	Noyalle	03/09/1915	04/09/1915
War Diary	V.2. a	05/09/1915	08/09/1915
War Diary	Les Harisoirs	09/09/1915	13/09/1915
War Diary	Verquin	14/09/1915	14/09/1915
War Diary	Fermelle	15/09/1915	17/09/1915
War Diary	Verquin	18/09/1915	22/09/1915
War Diary	Verquigneul	23/09/1915	23/09/1915
War Diary	Vermelles	24/09/1915	29/09/1915
War Diary	Beuvry	30/09/1915	30/09/1915
War Diary	20th Inf. Bde. 7th Div. 8th Battn. The Devonshire Regiment. October 1915		
War Diary	Cambrin.	01/10/1915	01/10/1915
War Diary	Maison Rouge Dug Outs	02/10/1915	05/10/1915
War Diary	Maison Rouge Burbere	06/10/1915	06/10/1915
War Diary	Cambrian (Trenches)	07/10/1915	09/10/1915
War Diary	Essars	10/10/1915	13/10/1915
War Diary	Cambrin	14/10/1915	15/10/1915
War Diary	Bethune	16/10/1915	17/10/1915
War Diary	Ecleme	17/10/1915	19/10/1915
War Diary	Le. Harisoire	20/10/1915	20/10/1915
War Diary	Givenchy	21/10/1915	23/10/1915
War Diary	Essars	24/10/1915	31/10/1915
Heading	20th Infantry Brigade. 7th Division 8th Battn. The Devonshire Regiment. November 1915		
War Diary	Essars	01/11/1915	01/11/1915
War Diary	B.I. Sector Trenches Guinchey	02/11/1915	03/11/1915
War Diary	Halte	04/11/1915	04/11/1915
War Diary	Bernenchon	05/11/1915	06/11/1915
War Diary	7th Essars	07/11/1915	07/11/1915
War Diary	8th Trenches Givenchy	08/11/1915	09/11/1915
War Diary	Trenches Essars	10/11/1915	10/11/1915
War Diary	Essars	11/11/1915	11/11/1915
War Diary	Trenches B 3, Sector	12/11/1915	13/11/1915
War Diary	Essars.	14/11/1915	14/11/1915
War Diary	Mt Bernenchon	15/11/1915	21/11/1915

War Diary	Mt Bernenchon Lehamel	22/11/1915	22/11/1915
War Diary	Lehamel Festubert	23/11/1915	23/11/1915
War Diary	Trenches at Festubert	24/11/1915	24/11/1915
War Diary	Trenches	25/11/1915	29/11/1915
War Diary	Festubert Village	30/11/1915	30/11/1915
Miscellaneous	Nov 1915		
War Diary	20th Infantry Brigade. 7th Division 8th Battn. The Devonshire Regiment December 1915		
War Diary	Festubert Hingette	01/12/1915	01/12/1915
War Diary	Hingette	02/12/1915	02/12/1915
War Diary	Hingette Contrainne	03/12/1915	03/12/1915
War Diary	Contrainne	04/12/1915	06/12/1915
War Diary	Contrainne Lillers	07/12/1915	07/12/1915
War Diary	Saleux	07/12/1915	07/12/1915
War Diary	Ailly	07/12/1915	21/12/1915
War Diary	Ailly Sur-Somme	21/12/1915	29/12/1915
War Diary	Fourdrinoy	30/12/1915	31/12/1915
Heading	20th Brigade 7th Division. 8th Battalion Devonshire Regiment. January 1916		
War Diary	Fourdrinoy	01/01/1916	03/01/1916
War Diary	Fourdrinoy and Pontremy	04/01/1916	04/01/1916
War Diary	Pont Remy	05/01/1916	28/01/1916
War Diary	Ailly Sur Somme	29/01/1916	31/01/1916
Heading	20th Brigade. 7th Division. 8th Battalion Devonshire Regiment February 1916		
War Diary	Ailly Somme	01/02/1916	01/02/1916
War Diary	Cardonette	01/02/1916	01/02/1916
War Diary	La Houssoye	02/02/1916	02/02/1916
War Diary	Meaulte	03/02/1916	03/02/1916
War Diary	Trenches D 1 J	04/02/1916	09/02/1916
War Diary	Trenches DI. Becordel	10/02/1916	12/02/1916
War Diary	Ville Sur Ancre	13/02/1916	18/02/1916
War Diary	Ville Sur-Ancre	19/02/1916	19/02/1916
War Diary	Ville and D2. Sec.	20/02/1916	20/02/1916
War Diary	Trenches	21/02/1916	28/02/1916
War Diary	Meaute	28/02/1916	29/02/1916
Heading	20th Brigade. 7th Division. 8th Battalion Devonshire Regiment March 1916		
War Diary	Meaulte	01/03/1916	01/03/1916
War Diary	Becordel	01/03/1916	02/03/1916
War Diary	Meaulte	02/03/1916	03/03/1916
War Diary	Becordel	03/03/1916	04/03/1916
War Diary	Meaulte	04/03/1916	04/03/1916
War Diary	Trenches DI	05/03/1916	07/03/1916
War Diary	Becordel Fricourt	08/03/1916	11/03/1916
War Diary	Meaulte	11/03/1916	16/03/1916
War Diary	DI. Trenches	17/03/1916	22/03/1916
War Diary	Meaulte	23/03/1916	24/03/1916
War Diary	2 en Becordel	25/03/1916	26/03/1916
War Diary	Meaulte Becordel	27/03/1916	27/03/1916
War Diary	Meaulte	28/03/1916	28/03/1916
War Diary	DI Subsector	29/03/1916	29/03/1916
War Diary	F3 9/5	30/03/1916	31/03/1916
Heading	20th Brigade 7th Division. 8th Battalion Devonshire Regiment April 1916.		
War Diary	D1.	01/04/1916	06/04/1916

War Diary	Meaulte	07/04/1916	07/04/1916
War Diary	Vaux S Somme	08/04/1916	24/04/1916
War Diary	Bois Des Tailles	25/04/1916	30/04/1916
Heading	20th Brigade. 7th Division. 8th Battalion The Devonshire Regiment May 1916		
War Diary	Brav Crantown	01/05/1916	03/05/1916
War Diary	Trenches B2	04/05/1916	12/05/1916
War Diary	Grantown Crovetown	13/05/1916	17/05/1916
War Diary	B2 Subsector	18/05/1916	24/05/1916
War Diary	Morlancourt	25/05/1916	31/05/1916
Heading	20th Brigade. 7th Division. 8th Battalion Devonshire Regiment. June 1916.		
War Diary	Morlancourt	01/06/1916	10/06/1916
War Diary	Grovetown	11/06/1916	19/06/1916
War Diary	BI. Trenches	20/06/1916	23/06/1916
War Diary	Grovetown	24/06/1916	30/06/1916
Heading	20th Inf. Bde. 7th Div. 8th Battn. The Devonshire Regiment. July 1916		
Miscellaneous			
War Diary	Trenches BI Sector Ref. Montauban Map F.17.a	01/07/1916	04/07/1916
War Diary	Treux	05/07/1916	10/07/1916
War Diary	Minden Post F.17.b	11/07/1916	13/07/1916
War Diary	Bazentin Le Grand Wood	14/07/1916	14/07/1916
War Diary	White Trench Ref Montauban Map S25 Central	15/07/1916	20/07/1916
War Diary	Dernacourt	21/07/1916	21/07/1916
War Diary	Ailly Sur Somme	22/07/1916	31/07/1916
Miscellaneous	Appendices I to IV		
Miscellaneous	War Diary 8th (Ser) Bn Devonshire Regiment. Appendix 1. Containing all Important orders for Operations July 1st, 2nd and 3rd.		
Miscellaneous	Orders Received No. B.M.74	01/07/1916	01/07/1916
War Diary		30/06/1916	01/07/1916
Operation(al) Order(s)	Appendix 111. 20th Infantry Brigade Operation Order No. 74.		
Operation(al) Order(s)	Appendix V. 20th Brigade Operation Order No. 76.	19/07/1916	19/07/1916
Miscellaneous	Appendix IV Report On Recent Operations	14/07/1916	14/07/1916
Miscellaneous	Instructions For Forthcoming Operations. by Major B.C. James Commanding, 8th (Ser) Bn Devonshire Regiment. No 2.		
Miscellaneous	Supply of Water and Food.		
Miscellaneous	20th Infantry Brigade Provisional Order.		
Heading	20th Brigade. 7th Division. 8th Battalion Devonshire Regiment. August 1916		
War Diary	Ailly Sur Somme	01/08/1916	12/08/1916
War Diary	Buire Sur Ancre	13/08/1916	23/08/1916
War Diary	Buire	24/08/1916	31/08/1916
War Diary	20th Brigade. 7th Division. 8th Battalion Devonshire Regiment. September 1916.		
War Diary	Companies of The Battn for The assault.	08/09/1916	08/09/1916
War Diary	Siasco 4 The Attack	09/09/1916	09/09/1916
War Diary	Boundaries of The Area to Be Cleared by Coys of 21 Border Rgt.	10/09/1916	10/09/1916
War Diary	Strong Points To Be Established	11/09/1916	11/09/1916
War Diary	Lewis Guns	12/09/1916	12/09/1916
War Diary	Bondlers	13/09/1916	13/09/1916
War Diary	Grenadum	14/09/1916	14/09/1916

War Diary	Eamlumn	15/09/1916	15/09/1916
War Diary	Special Equipment	16/09/1916	16/09/1916
War Diary	SAA & Very Light	17/09/1916	17/09/1916
War Diary	Water & Rahms	18/09/1916	18/09/1916
War Diary	Medical Communication	19/09/1916	19/09/1916
War Diary	Escort To Pmonir	21/09/1916	21/09/1916
War Diary	Snasslin Port	22/09/1916	22/09/1916
War Diary	Barger	23/09/1916	23/09/1916
War Diary	Miscellaneous	24/09/1916	24/09/1916
War Diary	Bde HQ.	25/09/1916	25/09/1916
War Diary	Buire-Sur-Ancre	01/09/1916	01/09/1916
War Diary	Ancre (Ref Map)	02/09/1916	02/09/1916
War Diary	France 62. D.N.E.	03/09/1916	03/09/1916
War Diary	F.20.a Buire	08/09/1916	09/09/1916
War Diary	Allery	10/09/1916	17/09/1916
War Diary	Allery Le Romarin (Papot)	18/09/1916	18/09/1916
War Diary	Papot Le Bizet	19/09/1916	19/09/1916
War Diary	Le Bizet	20/09/1916	25/09/1916
War Diary	Trenches (Le Toucquet Sector)	25/09/1916	25/09/1916
War Diary	Trenches	26/09/1916	30/09/1916
War Diary	Pont Nieppe	30/09/1916	30/09/1916
Miscellaneous	Report On Recent Operations. Appendix 1. Orders Received.	03/09/1916	03/09/1916
Miscellaneous	Appendix IV Report On Operation from 3-9-16 to 7-9-16	03/09/1916	03/09/1916
Miscellaneous	Appendix IV Report On Operation from 3-9-16 to 7-9-16	03/09/1916	07/09/1916
Miscellaneous			
Miscellaneous	Appendix 11. Report On Operations from 3-9-16 to 7-9-16.	03/09/1916	03/09/1916
Miscellaneous	Report On The Work of A Company 8th Devon Regt During the Operations Before Ginchy	10/09/1916	10/09/1916
Miscellaneous		10/09/1916	10/09/1916
Miscellaneous	To O.C. Fact		
Miscellaneous	A Form. Messages And Signals.		
Miscellaneous	C Form (Duplicate) Messages And Signals.		
Miscellaneous	C Form (Original). Messages And Signals.		
Miscellaneous	The Adjutant 8th Division Ref		
Miscellaneous	C Form (Original). Messages And Signals.		
Miscellaneous	A Form Messages And Signals.		
Miscellaneous	8 Division		
Miscellaneous	Oc B.O.D. Coy	05/09/1916	05/09/1916
Miscellaneous			
Miscellaneous	A Form Messages And Signals.		
Miscellaneous			
Miscellaneous	O.C. Battn on Our Right	05/09/1916	05/09/1916
Miscellaneous			
Miscellaneous	Messages And Signals.		
Miscellaneous	To Adjutant 8th Devons	07/09/1916	07/09/1916
Miscellaneous	Capt HOE of C Coy	07/09/1916	07/09/1916
Diagram etc	Delville Wood		
War Diary	Trenches Pont De Nieppe	01/10/1916	01/10/1916
War Diary	Pont De Nieppe	02/10/1916	06/10/1916
War Diary	Trenches (Le Toucquet Sector)	07/10/1916	12/10/1916
War Diary	Le Bizet	13/10/1916	18/10/1916
War Diary	Trenches (Le Toucquet Sector)	19/10/1916	25/10/1916

War Diary	Pont Nieppe	26/10/1916	31/10/1916
War Diary	Appendix 1 to October War Diary. Report On Gas Attack.		
War Diary	Pont Nieppe (Ref Map Sheet 36 1/40,000)	01/11/1916	01/11/1916
War Diary	La Creche	02/11/1916	02/11/1916
War Diary	Thieushouk	03/11/1916	03/11/1916
War Diary	(Ref Haze Broucr Map 1/40,000	04/11/1916	08/11/1916
War Diary	Lynde	09/11/1916	09/11/1916
War Diary	Serques	10/11/1916	10/11/1916
War Diary	Nortleulinghem	11/11/1916	14/11/1916
War Diary	Int Hazebrook Map. 1/100,000. Setque	15/11/1916	15/11/1916
War Diary	Radinghem	16/11/1916	17/11/1916
War Diary	Verchin (Ref Lens Map 1/100,000. Oeuf.	18/11/1916	19/11/1916
War Diary	Buire Au Bois	20/11/1916	20/11/1916
War Diary	Doullens	21/11/1916	21/11/1916
War Diary	Bertancourt	22/11/1916	22/11/1916
War Diary	Mailly Mallet	23/11/1916	23/11/1916
War Diary	(Trenches) Beaumont Hamiel	24/11/1916	27/11/1916
War Diary	Mailly Mallet.	28/11/1916	30/11/1916
Heading	8th Battalion Devonshire Regiment December 1916		
War Diary	Mailly Maillet	01/12/1916	01/12/1916
War Diary	Trenches Beaumont	02/12/1916	02/12/1916
War Diary	Kariez Sector	03/12/1916	05/12/1916
War Diary	Bertrancourt	06/12/1916	10/12/1916
War Diary	Trenches Beaumont Hamel Sector	11/12/1916	20/12/1916
War Diary	Beaumont Hamel Sector	21/12/1916	22/12/1916
War Diary	Mailly Maillet	23/12/1916	25/12/1916
War Diary	Trenches Beaumont Hamel Sector	26/12/1916	31/12/1916
Heading	8th Devonshire Regiment. January 1917.		
War Diary	Trenches Beaumont Hamel Sector	01/01/1917	06/01/1917
War Diary	Louvencourt	06/01/1917	14/01/1917
War Diary	Trenches Beaumont Hamel Sector	15/01/1917	19/01/1917
War Diary	Bus.	20/01/1917	22/01/1917
War Diary	Beauval	23/01/1917	30/01/1917
War Diary	Pernois	31/01/1917	31/01/1917
Miscellaneous	8th Devonshire Regiment February 1917		
Heading	War Diary 8th Bn The Devonshire Regt February 1917		
War Diary	Pernois	01/02/1917	15/02/1917
War Diary	Beauval	16/02/1917	17/02/1917
War Diary	Beauquesne	18/02/1917	20/02/1917
War Diary	Bertrancourt	21/02/1917	25/02/1917
War Diary	Mailly Mallet	26/02/1917	28/02/1917
War Diary	8th Devonshire Regiment March 1917.		
War Diary	Mailly Mallet	01/03/1917	01/03/1917
War Diary	Puisieux-Au-Mont	02/03/1917	04/03/1917
War Diary	Puisieux	04/03/1917	05/03/1917
War Diary	Mailly Maillet	06/03/1917	16/03/1917
War Diary	Mailly Puisieux	18/03/1917	19/03/1917
War Diary	G Leger	20/03/1917	20/03/1917
War Diary	Ervillers	21/03/1917	25/03/1917
War Diary	Mory	26/03/1917	28/03/1917
War Diary	Ervillers	29/03/1917	29/03/1917
War Diary	Courcelles	30/03/1917	31/03/1917
War Diary	Courcelles Le-Comte	01/04/1917	01/04/1917
War Diary	Ecoust	02/04/1917	02/04/1917
War Diary	Courcelles Le-Comte	03/04/1917	03/04/1917

War Diary	Ablainzeville	04/04/1917	11/04/1917
War Diary	Courcelles	12/04/1917	12/04/1917
War Diary	Ablainzevelle	13/04/1917	19/04/1917
War Diary	Scoost St-Mein	20/04/1917	30/04/1917
Miscellaneous	8th Ser Battalion The Devonshire Regt. Report On Operations At Ecoust		
Heading	8th Devonshire Regiment. May 1917.		
War Diary	Ablainseville	01/05/1917	03/05/1917
War Diary	Trenches Near Bullecourt	04/05/1917	09/05/1917
War Diary	Mary	10/05/1917	10/05/1917
War Diary	Courcelles	11/05/1917	14/05/1917
War Diary	Ablainseville	15/05/1917	31/05/1917
Miscellaneous	8th (Service) Battalion The Devonshire Regiment. Report on Operation In and around Bullecourt between the dates of 4th May to 10th May 17	04/05/1917	10/05/1917
Miscellaneous	8th S. Bn The Devonshire Regiment. Casualties For Period 5th May 1917 To 9th May 1917		
Heading	7th Division. 20th Inf Bde. 8th Devonshire Regiment. June 1917.		
War Diary	Ablainseville	01/06/1917	13/06/1917
War Diary	Mory	14/06/1917	14/06/1917
War Diary	Gcoust	15/06/1917	16/06/1917
War Diary	Trenches Bullecourt	17/06/1917	21/06/1917
War Diary	Ecoust	22/06/1917	25/06/1917
War Diary	Hery	26/06/1917	26/06/1917
War Diary	Eivillers	27/06/1917	30/06/1917
Map			
Heading	7th Division. 20th Inf Bde. 8th Devonshire Regiment. July 1917.		
War Diary	Ervillers	01/07/1917	05/07/1917
War Diary	Ecoust	06/07/1917	09/07/1917
War Diary	Trenches Bullecourt	10/07/1917	14/07/1917
War Diary	Scourt	15/07/1917	17/07/1917
War Diary	Camp near Ervillers	18/07/1917	29/07/1917
War Diary	Ecoust	30/07/1917	31/07/1917
Heading	7th Division 20th Inf Bde. 8th Devonshire Regiment August 1917.		
War Diary	May Trenches Bullencourt	01/08/1917	07/08/1917
War Diary	Eervillers	08/08/1917	09/08/1917
War Diary	Bailleulval	10/08/1917	28/08/1917
War Diary	Busseboom	29/08/1917	30/08/1917
War Diary	Steenvoorde	31/08/1917	31/08/1917
Heading	7th Division. 20th Inf Bde. 8th Devonshire Regiment. September 1917.		
War Diary	Buss Boom	01/09/1917	01/09/1917
War Diary	Steenvoord	02/09/1917	04/09/1917
War Diary	Hazeorouck	05/09/1917	12/09/1917
War Diary	Rennescure	13/09/1917	14/09/1917
War Diary	Tatinghem	15/09/1917	27/09/1917
War Diary	Bayenghem	28/09/1917	30/09/1917
Map	Becelaere		
Heading	7th Division. 20th Inf Bde. 8th Devonshire Regiment. October 1917. Appendices Attached.		
War Diary	Camp Near Reninghelst	01/10/1917	01/10/1917
War Diary	Trenches Near Polygon Wood	02/10/1917	07/10/1917
War Diary	Zillebeke	08/10/1917	08/10/1917

War Diary	Chateau Sigard	09/10/1917	09/10/1917
War Diary	Camp Near Westoutre	10/10/1917	23/10/1917
War Diary	Camp Near Vierstmat	24/10/1917	24/10/1917
War Diary	Dugouts S. of Zillebeke to be & Trenches W of Gheluvelt	25/10/1917	26/10/1917
War Diary	Camp Near Veerstraat	27/10/1917	27/10/1917
War Diary	Camp Near Veerstraat	28/10/1917	28/10/1917
War Diary	Camp Near Laclytte	29/10/1917	29/10/1917
War Diary	Billets Near Blairinghem	30/10/1917	31/10/1917
Miscellaneous	8th (Service) Battalion The Devonshire Regt.	02/10/1917	02/10/1917
Miscellaneous	8th (Service) Battalion The Devonshire Rgt.	02/10/1917	02/10/1917
Miscellaneous	8th (Service) Battalion The Devonshire Regiment. Report On Operations	26/10/1917	26/10/1917
Miscellaneous	8th (Service) Battalion Devonshire Regiment. Total Casualties	26/10/1917	26/10/1917
Heading	7th Division. 20th Inf Bde. 8th Devonshire Regiment November 1917		
War Diary	Blaringhem	01/11/1917	02/11/1917
War Diary	La Beth Croix	03/11/1917	12/11/1917
War Diary	St Pierre	13/11/1917	13/11/1917
War Diary	Therouanne	14/11/1917	14/11/1917
War Diary	Fruges	15/11/1917	15/11/1917
War Diary	Wavrans	16/11/1917	23/11/1917
War Diary	Legnago	25/11/1917	25/11/1917
War Diary	Vo	26/11/1917	30/11/1917
Heading	7th Division 20th Infy Bde 2nd Bn Border Regt Oct 1914 Nov 1917		

WO95/1655/2

BEF

7 DIVISION

20 BRIGADE

8 BN DEVONSHIRE REGT

1915 JULY - 1917 NOV

TO ITALY DEC 1917

20th Infantry Brigade.

7th Division.

(Battn. disembarked at Havre 26.7.15. Posted to 20th Bde. 4.8.15)

WAR DIARY

8th BATTN. THE DEVONSHIRE REGIMENT.

JULY and AUGUST

1 9 1 5

(17.7.15 - 31.8.15)

Feb. 1919

Instructions regarding War Diaries and Intelligence Summaries are contained in F. S. Regs., Part II. and the Staff Manual respectively. Title pages will be prepared in manuscript.

WAR DIARY
or
INTELLIGENCE SUMMARY.
(*Erase heading not required.*)

Army Form C. 2118.

8th (Service) Bn: Devon Regt.

Place	Date	Hour	Summary of Events and Information	Remarks and references to Appendices
Basingstoke	17th July	6-30 PM.	Battalion ordered to prepare for service in France, returned to Aldershot on following day.	
Aldershot	22nd July		Train Transport arrived Bn: completely mobilised	
"	25th July		Bn: left in two trains at 7.20 + 8.55 for Southampton. Left Southampton in evening in 2 ships	
Havre	26th July		arrived 2.30 am. Disembarked at 7.30 am + went to Rest Camp	
"	27th	"	Left Havre at 5.30 in one train for Wizernes.	
Wizernes	28th	"	arrived 10.30 am + went into billets.	
"	30th	"	Inspected by B.G.C. G.H.Q. Troops + highly complimented	
"	3.8.15		Left by Route March at 8.30 for Cavrin to join 20th Brigade of 7th Division vice 2nd Grenadier Guards going to form Guards Division, marched via Aire + halted at Molinghem for the night.	
Cavrin	4.8.15		Left Molinghem at 2.30 reached Cavrin at 5. PM – Comfortable billets.	
"	16.8.15		A Coy (followed by remainder at 48 hour intervals) went for 48 hours tour to trenches attached to 21st Brigade	
"	17.8.15		Left Cavrin for Locon being now in Divisional Reserve. Halted for the night at Pacaut	
Locon	18.8.15		arrived 10.30. am – fair billets.	
"	19.8.15		2 casualties in B Coy – Pte: Pearcey being killed + Pte Oak wounded.	
"	21.8.15		C.O., ~~Adjt~~ M.O. + self went to trenches for a tour of inspection, returned same night; things seem very quiet. Sandbags innumerable.	

Army Form C. 2118.

WAR DIARY
or
INTELLIGENCE SUMMARY.
(Erase heading not required.)

Instructions regarding War Diaries and Intelligence Summaries are contained in F. S. Regs., Part II. and the Staff Manual respectively. Title pages will be prepared in manuscript.

Place	Date	Hour	Summary of Events and Information	Remarks and references to Appendices
LOCON	22nd Aug:		General Trefusis came to Church Parade with us. Draft of 50 men arrived from XI Bn. after lunch. D Coy went up to the Trenches in Evening	
"	24th		D Coy returned no casualties, Has 1 casualty on a working party which was out all night.	
"	25th		Bn: was going up to Trenches to take over sector B.3 & B.O. & self was to have gone up this afternoon to prospect but this was cancelled & I heard at 3.20 that we were going up to occupy sector C.1. (The line our Coy: had been in for instruction) tomorrow 26th. This was short notice.	
"	26	6.50	Bn moved to go into C.1 sector of Trenches in relief of 2nd Bedfords. Fine light night. Relief completed at 10.20 pm	
C.1	27		A very quiet day – These Trenches were made by 1st Bn last Oct: which is curious. Shelled enemy Transport heard by A Coy at RUE DU MARAIS – success uncertain	
"	28	3am	Snipers busy	
		3pm	Very hot, no activity.	
"	"	11pm	Shelled enemy working party – success unknown	
"	29	noon	very very quiet & still	

1577 Wt. W10791/1773 500,000 1/15 D. D. & L. A.D.S.S./Forms/C. 2118.

Army Form [illegible]118.

Instructions regarding War Diaries and Intelligence Summaries are contained in F. S. Regs., Part II. and the Staff Manual respectively. Title pages will be prepared in manuscript.

WAR DIARY
or
INTELLIGENCE SUMMARY.

(*Erase heading not required.*)

Place	Date	Hour	Summary of Events and Information	Remarks and references to Appendices
C. 1	29	3 Pm	Got shelled this afternoon. Otherwise quiet. Lt Machachlan [?] reports German working parties in front of our 2 front Coys Cdrs. Turned on Company's machine guns. All telephone wires mysteriously cut at about 10.30 – unable to get touch with R.A. Flank Bns: or Coys: looked bad but nothing happened	
"	30th	~~9~~	Not much doing, a little shelling. Relieved by 9th W. Fusiliers. to billets at Les Choquaux. Reached billets at 2.30 am	
Les Choquaux	31st	9.30	Left by Route march for billets near BUSNES. All ranks rather tired	

1577 Wt. W10791/1773 500,000 1/15 D. D. & L. A.D.S.S./Forms/C. 2118.

20th Inf.Bde.
7th Div.

WAR DIARY

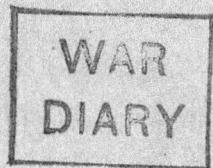

8th BATTN. THE DEVONSHIRE REGIMENT.

S E P T E M B E R

1 9 1 5

Instructions regarding War Diaries and Intelligence Summaries are contained in F. S. Regs., Part II. and the Staff Manual respectively. Title pages will be prepared in manuscript.

WAR DIARY
or
INTELLIGENCE SUMMARY.
(Erase heading not required.)

8th Devon Regt.

Army Form C. 2118.

1

Place	Date	Hour	Summary of Events and Information	Remarks and references to Appendices
BUSNES	1915		Rested morning to 6.11.b. to 2nd Brigade Temporarily. Arrived at NOYELLE	
"	2nd		at about 10.30 P.M. & had to get into uninviting billets when one got cold. — marched some 15 miles.	
Noyelle	3rd		Very wet. Working parties went out in the evening	
"	4th		Got orders at noon to go into Sector Y.2.A of the trenches relieving 2nd Borders. Moved at 2 P.M. Relief complete by 5.20 P.M. Trenches in a fearfully wet & muddy condition; not so comfortable as the last sector & little room. Not a sandbag line like C.1 but literally Trenches. A lot of digging required.	
Y.2.a	5th		Went round the line in morning. Very sticky & muddy. Very quiet time.	
"	6th		Warm — Quiet on the whole. M.G emplacement spotted by 2/Lt Phipps & shelled by Howitzer who claim direct hit. The Patrols last night reports large working party of enemy in front of some wire we want to reconnoitre between our lines & German lines.	
"	7th		Patrols went out last night & by their information, machine gun fire was brought to bear on enemy. A quiet day & warm. These trenches have improved a lot since we have been here but a lot of work is required for what they want—	

1577 Wt. W10791/1773 500,000 1/15 D. D. & L. A.D.S.S./Forms/C. 2118.

Instructions regarding War Diaries and Intelligence Summaries are contained in F. S. Regs., Part II. and the Staff Manual respectively. Title pages will be prepared in manuscript.

WAR DIARY
or
INTELLIGENCE SUMMARY.
(Erase heading not required.)

Army Form C. 2118. 2

Place	Date	Hour	Summary of Events and Information	Remarks and references to Appendices
8th Sept		Sect. V.2.9(?)	East wind & warm. Some rumours of German attack. Relieved by 2nd Warwicks 3-5 P.M. — Returned to billets at VERQUIGNEUL got there at 7 P.M. & onwards — Had 1 man killed & 1 wounded during last 24 hrs. which was bad luck — All 3 men killed have had name beginning with P. — Ptes. Pearcey — Punch & Pretty, John	
LES HARISOIRS			Left VERQUIGNEUL at 8-9 am got here at 11-12; A restful place after the Trenches	
"	9th		The attack which was to have come off on 11th is apparently postponed	
"	10th		Fine & warm	
"	11th		Major Story detailed to command 9th Bn. vice Col Davies.	
"	13th		Left billets unexpectedly at 8am for VERQUIN. Dirty billets.	
VERQUIN	14th		Left again suddenly for VERMELLES. Arrived there about 11 am. There are not billets at all, the entire Town being in ruins. Our guns do not add to the restfulness of the place	
VERMELLES	15th		warm. Our artillery active. It now looks as if the attack would take place about Sat. or Sun.	
"	16th		Germans shelled our billets at 9am M.O. had a very narrow escape with 2 stretcher bearers on way to aid one man of Sec B the shell pitching next off him. Capt Ballwood(?) developed appendicitis. 8 of 'B' Coy got hit outside their billet by a shell — real bad luck.	
"	17th		Left for billets at VERQUIN & very crowded they are too & not clean	
VERQUIN	18th		Warm & cloudless	

Army Form C. 2118.

Instructions regarding War Diaries and Intelligence Summaries are contained in F. S. Regs., Part II. and the Staff Manual respectively. Title pages will be prepared in manuscript.

WAR DIARY
or
INTELLIGENCE SUMMARY.
(Erase heading not required.)

Place	Date	Hour	Summary of Events and Information	Remarks and references to Appendices
VERQUIN	19th Sept	– 21st Sept	Wind East, weather fine. Preparing for the attack to take place	
"	22nd		1st day of concentration. Left billets at 6 pm for VERQUIGNEUL	
VERQUIGNEUL	23rd		Leave billets at 6.30 pm. for VERMELLES + go into Trenches at 9.15 pm on 24th for the attack which is due to take place on 25th. —	
VERMELLES	24th		At 9.15 pm. moved up into trenches for the attack in early morning - 'C' Coy in new front line, 'A' in no 2 support, 'D' in no 1 support and 'B' and Headquarters in old front line. Trenches very muddy and bad to move about in. Capt Roberts, Capt Jordan, Lt. Sheepshanks, 2Lt. Pepys and 2Lt. Drew were left behind with the transport as a reserve of officers	
	25th		As soon as our guns started the intensive bombardment the German guns - scenting what was in the wind - replied with heavy and light artillery and caused some casualties though not many. On the signal being given 'C', 'A' and 'B' companies seemed to all go forward together in one line, this happened probably because A & D companies started too soon. The result was great crowding towards the gaps in the wire and consequent increase in casualties - most of which occurred just outside or in the midst of the wire in front of the BRESLAU TRENCH. Another result of the excessive speed with which the attack was started was that the front 3 companies seem to have caught up "Accessory no. 1" - and casualties occurred from the effects of this. During the advance from our own trenches to the BRESLAU TRENCH every officer - save 3 - was either wounded or killed. Col Grant, shot and killed; Major Carden, shot and killed; Captain Kenrick, shot through the head dying soon afterwards; Lt Windle, Lt Carver & 2Lt Ashcroft all killed, the first and last by bullets & 2Lt. Carver by a shell; Lt Dodgson apparently killed by "Accessory no 1" in the BRESLAU TRENCH. Capt James shot in the stomach, wounded: Capt Pryor shot 6 times in the ankles & legs, wounded; Lt Macmichael shot in the leg, wounded, Lt. Hulm shot in the knee, wounded, Capt Broadbridge arm broken by a shell, wounded, 2Lt. Nixon shot in leg and arm, wounded; 2Lt Bridson, shot in stomach, wounded, 2Lt Cracroft, taken to hospital suffering	

Army Form C. 2118.

Instructions regarding War Diaries and Intelligence Summaries are contained in F. S. Regs., Part II. and the Staff Manual respectively. Title pages will be prepared in manuscript.

WAR DIARY
or
INTELLIGENCE SUMMARY.
(Erase heading not required.)

Place	Date	Hour	Summary of Events and Information	Remarks and references to Appendices
	September 25th (Continued)		from effects of "accessory no 1". As soon the attack reached the German trench the few Germans therein put their hands up and surrendered. The attackers then bore to the SE. and crossed the HULLUCH ROAD. No opposition was met with and GUN TRENCH was reached: the German gunners put their hands up & surrendered and so the Battn. captured 4 field guns. These guns by their over heated state bore witness to the intensity of the German artillery fire. The charge towards the guns was led by Sgt. Northam 'A Coy' and "8th Devons" was chalked upon them.	
		8 am.	Then the advance proceeded to the X roads W of HULLUCH. The battn. here was about 100 strong. in charge of Capt Gwynn and 2 Lt Trott. All the machine guns were gone - 2 knocked out in the first advance and the other 2 seem to have been lost on the outskirts of HULLUCH owing to a section getting too far forward and getting cut off. No advance from these crossroads was possible during the day for 2 reasons:- (i) At first the artillery were still firing only just beyond the position. (ii) No troops came up to reinforce So the battn. dug themselves in just to W of road with their right on the X roads: the 2nd Gordons were on the right and no one at all on the left. At this place Sgt. Northam (mentioned above) was killed by a sniper. At this time there seems to have been very few of the enemy in HULLUCH or CITE ST ELIE and lack of support alone kept the German line unbroken.	
		6.15pm.	All day this position was held and at 6.15 pm ration parties started off to draw rations at X roads CHAPELLE NRE DAME de CONSOLATION. At about 9.30 pm. the enemy coming from CITE ST ELIE got behind our position	
		9.30pm.	in estimated strength of a company and the first known of this was the interception of the ration parties. A retirement was then made to GUN TRENCH in the course of which many losses were sustained owing partly to rifle fire & bombing by the enemy and partly from rifle & machine gun fire from the Bedfords in gun trench who in the dark mistook friend for foe. Here Capt Gwynn & 2 Lt Trott who had led so gallantly during the day were both wounded and CSM Bryant who had prevented a panic from setting in was stunned by a German bomb when attempting to rescue Sgt. Hansford who got cut off in the retirement. The remnants of the battn. occupied GUN TRENCH and then dug themselves in - finding themselves with 2nd Borders on their left with their left on HULLUCH Rd. and the 6th Gordons on the right. Mixed up with the battn. were many of the 9th Devons & a few of other units. There was no more infantry action during the night. During the course of the evening QMS Davey was on the HULLUCH Rd with the ration waggons about ½ mile from firing line when he met some men of another unit flying in disorder. Borrowing a rifle and bayonet he rallied them, led them back to the firing line and stayed there until arrival of staff officer.	

Army Form C. 2118.

Instructions regarding War Diaries and Intelligence Summaries are contained in F. S. Regs., Part II. and the Staff Manual respectively. Title pages will be prepared in manuscript.

WAR DIARY
or
INTELLIGENCE SUMMARY.
(Erase heading not required.)

Place	Date	Hour	Summary of Events and Information	Remarks and references to Appendices
	Sept 26		During night GUN TRENCH was improved and by daybreak it afforded sufficient protection from rifle fire. The position was as follows:- from HULLUCH ROAD to 200 yards S were the 2nd Borders about 250 strong; then a mixture of 9th & 8th Devons - the latter about 50 strong with no officers; and on our right were the 1/6th Gordons. About 5.30 am. the reserve officers Capt Roberts, Capt Jordan, Lt Sheepshanks, 2Lt Drew and 2Lt Pepys joined the Battn in the trench: Captn Roberts took command. The rest of the day was passed in this trench as (verbal) orders were received from Brigade to hold on about 8 am. There was no infantry action; the German guns were active but did not shell us at all. Very likely they didn't know where we were. There was a little sniping but most disconcerting was the maxim fire & stray bullets coming from the direction of FOSSE 8, which was practically 'reverse' fire. Owing to this 1 man was shot thro' back of head and killed. Our guns were very busy shelling CITÉ ST. ELIE and PUITS 13 and it was a pleasant spectacle. We were relieved by 2nd RSF at 10 p.m. and received orders to occupy CURLEY CRESCENT: found this occupied by 2nd Gordons and reported this to S.C. who told us to get in where we could. Eventually got into OLD SUPPORT LINE with right on HULLUCH ROAD and left on CHAPEL ALLEY.	
	Sept 27 28 29		Restored organisation as far as possible: Bn. now 130 strong as many stragglers came in and about 50 men had spent yesterday in trench on N of road. Spent 3 very uncomfortable days: all ranks very tired and very dirty and weather was very bad. There was continuous fighting for FOSSE 8 and also below the LOOS ridge, the first of which could be plainly seen. German artillery very active indeed and they had got up some of their bigger guns. Got orders to move out at 7pm. 29th inst. to billets but these immediately cancelled by an order "to stand to arms and be ready to move at once": then verbal orders that we were to move up to front line and be ready to attack to the N as HOHENZOLLERN REDOUBT had been retaken. So moved up to NEW FRONT LINE and then received orders that position was normal, no truth in above statement and that we were to march back to Billets at BEUVRY. Got there about 2 am. [illegible] Draft of 50 arrived on Sept. 28th and these men were very tired and could hardly march the distance but all ranks were the same.	

Army Form C. 2118.

WAR DIARY
or
INTELLIGENCE SUMMARY.
(Erase heading not required.)

Instructions regarding War Diaries and Intelligence Summaries are contained in F. S. Regs., Part II. and the Staff Manual respectively. Title pages will be prepared in manuscript.

Place	Date	Hour	Summary of Events and Information	Remarks and references to Appendices

6.

Army Form C. 2118.

WAR DIARY
or
INTELLIGENCE SUMMARY.
(Erase heading not required.)

Instructions regarding War Diaries and Intelligence Summaries are contained in F. S. Regs., Part II. and the Staff Manual respectively. Title pages will be prepared in manuscript.

Place	Date	Hour	Summary of Events and Information	Remarks and references to Appendices
BEUVRY	Sept 30		Men cleaned themselves up as well as possible. During the afternoon General Trefusis went round billets and congratulated them on their conduct in action.	

20th Inf.Bde.
7th Div.

8th BATTN. THE DEVONSHIRE REGIMENT.

O C T O B E R

1 9 1 5

Instructions regarding War Diaries and Intelligence Summaries are contained in F. S. Regs., Part II. and the Staff Manual respectively. Title pages will be prepared in manuscript.

Army Form C. 21

WAR DIARY
or
INTELLIGENCE SUMMARY.
(Erase heading not required.)

October 1915 — 8/Devonshire Regiment.

Place	Date	Hour	Summary of Events and Information	Remarks and references to Appendices
CAMBRIN.	~~Nov~~ Oct 1		In morning battalion paraded and roll call held from which Casualty list roughly got. At 1.15 received verbal orders to proceed to trenches E of CAMBRIN at once to take over:- MAISON ROUGE dug outs, and garrison ARTHURS KEEP and RUSSEL KEEP each with 25 men and 1 sergeant. Met guide at Bde H.Q. but he was quite as strange to trenches as I. Battalion marched in at 5 p.m. disposition:- 'A' Coy under 2Lt Drew in the 2 keeps, B C & D in the dug outs. Very quiet night.	
(MAISON ROUGE Dug Outs)	Oct 2		Quiet day. At night the following officers arrived :- Capt. Graham 2Lt Horne 2Lt. Heyward 2Lt. Moore Capt Graham senior to me, but received order over the telephone from the Bde. Major that I was to remain in temporary command	
	Oct 3		2Lt Horne took over duties of Adjutant from 2Lt Pepys.	
	Oct 4		~~[illegible]~~ P.M. The Bn was employed in clearing the field of arms ammunition & constructing fire trenches at CAMBRIN. Very Quiet day.	
	Oct 5		Quiet day: at night the following officers arrived :- 2nd Lt. Trefellis " Mansel-Carey " Notley " Duff " Catling " Borden " Roper.	[illegible] 2Lt Adjt.

1577 Wt. W10791/1773 500,000 1/15 D. D. & L. A.D.S.S./Forms/C. 2118.

T2134. Wt. W708—776. 500000. 4/15. Sir J. C. & S.

Instructions regarding War Diaries and Intelligence Summaries are contained in F. S. Regs., Part II. and the Staff Manual respectively. Title pages will be prepared in manuscript.

WAR DIARY
or
INTELLIGENCE SUMMARY.
(Erase heading not required.)

Army Form C. 2118.

Place	Date	Hour	Summary of Events and Information	Remarks and references to Appendices
MAISON ROUGE	1915 Oct		Quiet day. Evacuated all the Boyaus of arms accoutrements etc.	
BURBERE	6th		The following Officers joined in the evening 2Lt Hinton & Lewis with a draft of 50 NCOs & men.	
CAMBRIAN (Trenches)	7th	1PM	Relieved the 2/Gordons in front line Trenches & garrisoned Arthurs Keep. A Draft of Three hundred (300) N.C.Os & Men joined & were sent to BEUVRY. Captain H. J. Graham & 2Lt Notley proceeded with this party to train them in bombing etc.	
-do-	8th		Quiet day. 2Lt Williams joined the Bn.	
-do-	9th		Quiet day. The following Officers joined Capt. Scaife D.S.O. 2Lt Savill, Lock & Ephraums.	
ESSARS	10th		Relieved from Trenches by 2nd Bn Yorkshire Regt & marched to billets at ESSARS. C.O inspected billets	
ESSARS	11th	8-12	Bn cleaned up their personal Kit etc. Shelled fields in the vicinity	
		2-4	Coys did Coy drill, bombing etc.. 4PM. Divisional Band played selections	
ESSARS	12th	10AM	Inspection of recent drafts by Brigadier Genl J. F. Trefusis D.S.O complimented on their smartness & soldierly bearing. Coy Drill etc was carried out during the day.	

Instructions regarding War Diaries and Intelligence Summaries are contained in F. S. Regs., Part II. and the Staff Manual respectively. Title pages will be prepared in manuscript.

WAR DIARY
or
INTELLIGENCE SUMMARY.
(Erase heading not required.)

Army Form C. 2118.

Place	Date	Hour	Summary of Events and Information	Remarks and references to Appendices
ESSARS	1915 Oct 13th		a F.G.C.M was held at H.Q. The Bn marched to CAMBRIN & relieved the 2nd Bedfords, Garrisoned the following defensive positions. S.P. & fortified houses on the LA BASSE Road.	
CAMBRIN	14th		very heavy bombardment by our artillery lasting the whole of the night & well on into the day. Bn found a fatigue party of 4 Officers & 200 men to improve Trenches.	
CAMBRIN	15th		Quiet day. Draft of 18 men joined here very late in the night. These had taken part in the attack 25/26 being the first of the Casualties to rejoin.	
BETHUNE	16th	9AM	Marched from CAMBRIN to BETHUNE there to be billeted in the Tobacco Factory, a draft of 50 joined here during the afternoon.	
BETHUNE	17th do		The Bn was formed up in 3 sides of a square & Capt. Roberts Comdg, gave R.QMS Davey & C.S.M. Bryant cards of recognition of service in the field on the 25/26th	
BETHUNE	17th do		& made a glowing speech to all ranks, who greatly appreciated same. Notification was received that Capt. Gwynn had been made a Companion of the D.S.O	
ECLEME	17th		Bn was inspected by C.O. & then marched to ECLEME to billets.	
ECLEME	18th		C.O. inspected billets, 2 platoons went to the rifle range & fired 10 rounds. Close & Extended drill was carried out by companies.	

Instructions regarding War Diaries and Intelligence Summaries are contained in F. S. Regs., Part II. and the Staff Manual respectively. Title pages will be prepared in manuscript.

WAR DIARY
or
INTELLIGENCE SUMMARY.
(Erase heading not required.)

Army Form C. 2118.

Place	Date 1915	Hour	Summary of Events and Information	Remarks and references to Appendices
ECLEME	19th Oct.	9 AM	Bn did a 9 mile route march in the morning. Bt Lt Col J.D. Ingles 2/Devons reported his arrival & took over command from Capt G.D. Roberts.	
		9PM	Bn marched to billets at LES HARISOIRE.	
LE HARISOIRE	20th Oct	3AM	Issued Operation orders re march to Trenches at to relieve 3/Middlesex Regt.	
		7AM	C.O. adjt & 2 Coy Comdrs proceeded to reconnoitre this sector. Capt Acaix D.S.O met with an accident by his horse running away & was not discovered during the day. B Coy had 3 casualties. Officially notified: [struck out] that R.Q.S. DAVEY & C.S.M. BRYANT & Sgt HOLLAND awarded D.C.M. for gallantry in the field, 25/26th SEPT. 1915.	
GIVENCHY	21st Oct		Quiet day. Cookers brought up food to VAUXHALL BRIDGE, one cook was wounded in leg.	
do	22nd		Quiet day. ENEMY shelled us occasionally. Improved parapets & parados & made foot steps.	
do	23rd		Quiet day, except for a few rifle grenades which wounded 5, we retaliated with shrapnel & all was quiet again.	
do	24th		Brigadier General F. J. Tufnis C.B. D.S.O was mortally wounded.	
ESSARES		3PM	Bt Lt Col J.D. Ingles assumed tempy command of 20th Inf Bde. Capt A.J. Graham assumed Tempy command of the Bn. Pte Pragne was killed. The Bn was relieved by 2/Bedfords, & marched to billets at ESSARS.	

Instructions regarding War Diaries and Intelligence Summaries are contained in F. S. Regs., Part II. and the Staff Manual respectively. Title pages will be prepared in manuscript.

WAR DIARY or INTELLIGENCE SUMMARY.

(Erase heading not required.)

Army Form C. 2118.

Place	Date	Hour	Summary of Events and Information	Remarks and references to Appendices
ESSARS	1915 Oct 25th	11 AM	Inspection of Billets by C. O. Inspection of Kits by Coy Commanders.	
		2 PM	Funeral of the late Brigadier General Hon[?] J. F. Trefusis C.B. D.S.O. Lt Col J. D. Ingles. Capts Jordan & Graham, Lts Ashurst[?] & Goldsmith & 22nd Regt attended at WINDY CORNER.	
ESSARS.	26th		Inspection by Bt Lt Col J. D. Ingles temporary Commandant 20th Infantry [Brigade]. Voluntary Church Service was held in the evening.	
ESSARS	27th		Commanding Officer Coy Officers & Adjutant reconnoitred defensive position	
ESSARS	28th		Comdg Officer inspected "C" Coy. ~~300~~ A party of 4 Officers & 200 Men embussed at E6a.3.8 for work under R.E. at Canadian Farm. "C" Coy carried out Musketry (target practice) at BETHUNE. The Bn had baths allotted to	
ESSARS	"		them at W.30.c. Very wet day had fires lighted to dry their clothing.	
ESSARS	29th		Comdg Officer inspected Transport B and D Coys also Bombers & made a short speech with reference to the Bns name, discipline etc.	
ESSARS	30th		Bn found Working Party for R.E. consisting of 1 Capt. all Platoon Officers available & 300 Men, this party proceeded to [illegible]. A lecture by Rev. Abbott[?] was given to the Bn subject the present War. Divisional Band played selections to the troops outside Parish Church.	

1577 Wt. W10791/1773 500,000 1/15 D. D. & L. A.D.S.S./Forms/C. 2118.

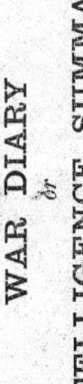

Instructions regarding War Diaries and Intelligence Summaries are contained in F. S. Regs., Part II. and the Staff Manual respectively. Title pages will be prepared in manuscript.

WAR DIARY
or
INTELLIGENCE SUMMARY.
(Erase heading not required.)

Army Form C. 2118.

Place	Date	Hour	Summary of Events and Information	Remarks and references to Appendices
ESSARS	31/10/15		The Bn paraded for Church. The Commanding Officer & all Coy Officers proceeded to (B 1 sector) CUINCHY to reconnoitre trenches	
			E M Hore Capt & Adjt, 8th Devon Regt.	

20th Infantry Brigade.

7th Division.

WAR DIARY

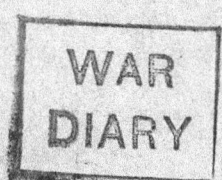

8th BATTN. THE DEVONSHIRE REGIMENT.

NOVEMBER

1 9 1 5

Instructions regarding War Diaries and Intelligence Summaries are contained in F. S. Regs., Part II. and the Staff Manual respectively. Title pages will be prepared in manuscript.

WAR DIARY
or
INTELLIGENCE SUMMARY.
(Erase heading not required.)

8th Bn Devonshire Rgt — Army Form C. 2118.

1st to 30th Novr 1915.

20

Place	Date	Hour	Summary of Events and Information	Remarks and references to Appendices
~~ESSARS~~			~~[illegible]~~	EMH
ESSARS	1/11/15		C. O. proceeded to Pont Hinges to meet Brigadier	
		11AM	Bn marched to Trenches (B1 Sectn) at Cuinchy	
B.1. Sectn Trenches, CUINCHEY	2/11/15		Trenches, rained very heavy. Parapets & paradoes fell in	
-do-	3/11		In Trenches, A Coy was relieved in front line by B Coy & marched to PONT FIXE.	
HALTE	4/11		Hd Qrs billeted at Halte, also A Coy. B Coy billeted at AVELLETE C Coy at HINGETTE D Coy at Hinges. Bn marched to BERNENCHON at 3 PM. Great coats were carried on lorries on a/c of their wet & muddy state	
BERNENCHON	5/11		Comdg Officer inspected billets, Coys were employed cleaning their kits etc, also showed kits.	
BERNENCHON	6/11		Voluntary Church Parade. Drying Great coats. Officers Conference.	

1577 Wt. W10791/1773 500,000 1/15 D. D. & L. A.D.S.S./Forms/C. 2118.

Army Form C. 2118.

WAR DIARY
or
INTELLIGENCE SUMMARY.
(Erase heading not required.)

Instructions regarding War Diaries and Intelligence Summaries are contained in F. S. Regs., Part II. and the Staff Manual respectively. Title pages will be prepared in manuscript.

Place	Date	Hour	Summary of Events and Information	Remarks and references to Appendices
7th ESSARS	1915 Nov 7th		The Bn marched from Mt BERNENCHON to ESSARS there to be billeted. Coy Commanders recconnoited (B3 Sector)	
8th Trenches GIVENCHY	Nov. 8th		The Bn paraded at 9 A.M. and marched to the trenches relieving the 2nd Queens. The R E exploded a mine, the 2 Gordons were on our right & the Lancs on our left	
Trenches GIVENCHY	Nov 9th		Rained very heavily. ENEMY shelled Pont Fixe.	
Trenches ESSARS	Nov 10th		The Bn spent a very wet night, the parapets & paradoes falling in in places, repaired same, Casualties during this time 2 Killed & 4 wounded relieved by 9th Devons.	
ESSARS	Nov 11th		Comdg Officer held a conference, which Coy Comdrs attended. All Comdg Officers attended at Bde H. Qrs holding new line of trenches	
Trenches B3 Sector	Nov 12th		The Bn marched to the trenches from ESSARS. The R. E exploded a mine at 9 PM, on our Right were the N. Lancs. & left Gordon Highlanders	

Instructions regarding War Diaries and Intelligence Summaries are contained in F. S. Regs., Part II. and the Staff Manual respectively. Title pages will be prepared in manuscript.

WAR DIARY
or
INTELLIGENCE SUMMARY.
(Erase heading not required.)

Army Form C. 2118.

Place	Date	Hour	Summary of Events and Information	Remarks and references to Appendices
Trenches B3. section	1915 Nov. 13th		Enemy shelled Vauxhall Bridge.	
ESSARS.	Nov. 14th		Bn was relieved from B3. Sector by 9th Devon Regt. & marched to ESSARS. Left at Garrison consisting of 1 Platoon, B Coy & 2 Machine Guns at HERTS Redoubt & Mole Farm.	
Mt — BERNENCHON	Nov 15th		Bn marched to Mt Bernenchon, arrived at 4. P.M	
Mt — BERNENCHON	Nov. 16th		Bn carried out a short march, Kits were inspected by Coy Comdrs. Formed a new Regtl. Grenade class under 2Lt. Goldsmith.	
Mt — BERNENCHON	Nov. 17th		Bn had the 7th Div. Baths allotted, The N.C.Os. & men enjoyed same which consisting of a warm spray bath.	
Mt BERNENCHON	Nov. 18th		Bn attended a "Gas Demonstration", all available Officers N.C.Os. & men attended & went through a trench filled with Gas. The test was very successful & useful, especially to those who had not experienced Gas before.	

1577 Wt. W10791/1773 500,000 1/15 D. D. & L. A.D.S.S./Forms/C. 2118.

Instructions regarding War Diaries and Intelligence Summaries are contained in F. S. Regs., Part II. and the Staff Manual respectively. Title pages will be prepared in manuscript.

WAR DIARY
or
INTELLIGENCE SUMMARY.
(*Erase heading not required.*)

Army Form C. 2118.

Place	Date 1915	Hour	Summary of Events and Information	Remarks and references to Appendices
Mt BERNENCHON	Nov. 19th		Bn carried out a route march under Coy arrangements. Distance 5 miles. C.O. inspected billets.	
Mt BERNENCHON	Nov 20th		Bn carried out a route march. C.O. went to a conference at Bde H.Q. at HALTEDGAM. Bombers were exercised in throwing live bombs.	
Mt BERNENCHON	Nov. 21st		Coys at the Disposal of Coy Officers. Voluntary church parade at 2.30 PM.	
Mt Bernenchon.	Nov	8 AM	Bn marched to LE HAMEL at 8 AM. & took over	
LE HAMEL	22nd	10.30 AM	billets from South Lancashire Regt.	
LE HAMEL	Nov 23rd			
FESTUBERT			Bn relieved 7th Bn North Lancashire Regt. & 7th Bn East Lancashire Regt.	
Trenches at FESTUBERT	Nov. 24th		Bn worked in the trenches, day & night building up a new breastwork & razing ~~the Parapet~~ snd. Parados to the ground to fill in trench ~~and~~ & make ground habitable.	

1577 Wt. W10791/1773 500,000 1/15 D. D. & L. A.D.S.S./Forms/C. 2118.

Army Form C. 2118.

Instructions regarding War Diaries and Intelligence Summaries are contained in F. S. Regs., Part II. and the Staff Manual respectively. Title pages will be prepared in manuscript.

WAR DIARY
or
INTELLIGENCE SUMMARY.
(*Erase heading not required.*)

Place	Date	Hour	Summary of Events and Information	Remarks and references to Appendices
TRENCHES	1915 NOV. 25th.		Bn carried on with the work vigorously in spite of the inclement weather in many instances Officers & men worked in water	
TRENCHES	26th.		Work proceeding as above the 6th Gordons were on our left	
TRENCHES	27th		& the 7/Camerons on our right.	
TRENCHES	28th		Work still in progress, during the 7 days in the trenches we were shelled daily –	
TRENCHES	29th.		A & B Coys were relieved by A & B Coys 9th Devons. & proceeded to garrison FESTUBERT EAST & CENTRAL & the village	
FESTUBERT VILLAGE	30th.		C & D Coys & H.Q. 2nd were relieved by 9th Devons & proceeded to FESTUBERT in Reserve.	
			E M Hore Lt. adjt. 8th Devons	

NOV 1915

20th Infantry Brigade.

7th Division.

WAR DIARY

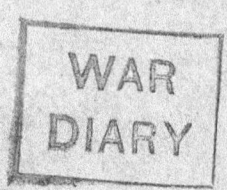

8th BATTN. THE DEVONSHIRE REGIMENT.

DECEMBER

1 9 1 5

Instructions regarding War Diaries and Intelligence Summaries are contained in F. S. Regs., Part II. and the Staff Manual respectively. Title pages will be prepared in manuscript.

WAR DIARY
or
~~INTELLIGENCE SUMMARY.~~
(Erase heading not required.)

8th (S) Bn Devon Regt
7th Bn.

Army Form C. 2118.

Place	Date 1915	Hour 1915	Summary of Events and Information	Remarks and references to Appendices
FESTUBERT	1st December	4 PM	Bn was relieved by the 6th Gordon Highlanders & marched into Hingette	
HINGETTE		6 PM	arrived at HINGETTE, Comdg Officer went round the billets & saw that everyone was settled.	
HINGETTE	2nd Dec	10 AM	Comdg Officer held Orderly Room the first time for 8 days owing to the Bn being in the trenches. Inspection of Kits etc by Co Comdrs.	
HINGETTE	3rd	9.15 AM	Bn marched to CANTRAINNE there to be billeted.	
CONTRAINNE	Dec		arrived here at 12 noon. C.O. inspected billets.	
CONTRAINNE	4th Dec		Brigadier General Deverell inspected the Billets. G.O. had a conference of Officers at 2 P.M. & lectured the Sergts at 3.15 P.M. Adjutant had a parade of NCOs; Drill etc.	
CONTRAINNE	5th Dec.		Comdg Officer reconnoitred the road to LILLERS Station adjt Transport officer & Qr Mr -do- re entraining the Bn.	
CONTRAINNE	6th Dec		Bn commenced close order drill, saluting etc in accordance with programme issued by Brigadier.	
CONTRAINNE LILLERS	7th Dec	3.51 AM	Bn entrained for SALEUX there to be billeted	
SALEUX	7th Dec.		Bn arrived here at 12-45 P.M. 25 Officers & 695 O.Ranks constituted the Bn. Tea was served to the men at 1.15 PM in a field adjoining the station. Bn paraded at 3 PM & marched to AILLY-sur-SOMME.	
AILLY	7th Dec.			

1577 Wt. W10791/1773 500,000 1/15 D. D. & L. A.D.S.S./Forms/C. 2118.

Instructions regarding War Diaries and Intelligence Summaries are contained in F. S. Regs., Part II. and the Staff Manual respectively. Title pages will be prepared in manuscript.

WAR DIARY

or

~~INTELLIGENCE SUMMARY.~~

(Erase heading not required.)

8th (S) Bn Devon Regt.

Army Form C. 2118.

Place	Date 1915	Hour	Summary of Events and Information	Remarks and references to Appendices
AILLY	7th Dec.		Length of March was 11 miles, everyone marched in with the Bn. The G. O. C. complimented the Bn on its smartness in training & detraining	
AILLY	8th Dec.		Colonel inspected the billets, Bn started a programme of Training, Drill,	
AILLY	9th Dec.		Brigadier General Deverell inspected the whole of the billets & was pleased with the arrangements etc of above.	
AILLY	Dec 9th		Programme of work continued	
AILLY	Dec 10th		Programme of work continued. Major Genl. L. J. Bols C.B. D.S.O., paid a visit to H.Q.	
AILLY	Dec 11th		Programme of work continued. A lecture was given at the schoolroom to the Officers of this Bn & the 9th (S) Bn Devon Regt. by Brigadier General Deverell	
AILLY	Dec 12th		Joint Church Parade with 9th (S) Bn Devon Regt. at Cross Roads N. W of AILLY. Brigadier General DEVEREL was present. The Divisional band was also present.	

1577 Wt. W10791/1773 500,000 1/15 D. D. & L. A.D.S.S./Forms/C. 2118.

Instructions regarding War Diaries and Intelligence Summaries are contained in F. S. Regs., Part II. and the Staff Manual respectively. Title pages will be prepared in manuscript.

WAR DIARY
or
~~INTELLIGENCE~~ SUMMARY.
(Erase heading not required.)

Army Form C. 2118.

8th (S) Bn Devon Regt.

Place	Date	Hour	Summary of Events and Information	Remarks and references to Appendices
AILLY	Decr 13th		Programme of Training for week ending Decr 18th commenced	
AILLY	"		Divisional band in attendance and played Selections to troops billeted here	
AILLY			Lecture given by Comdg Officer to Officers & Sergts of Bn. Subject - Advance, Rear & Flank Guards	
AILLY	14th		Programme of training continued	
AILLY	"		Lecture given by Comdg Officer to Officers & Sergts of Bn. Subject :- Outposts	
AILLY	"		Comdg Officer inspected billets.	
AILLY	15th		Programme of training continued	
AILLY	"		Inspection of Transport by Comdg Officer	
AILLY			A & B Coys & Machine Gunners had use of baths ~~[illegible]~~ (Hot) & washed underclothing	
AILLY	"		A draft of 69 Other Ranks arrived from Base and were inspected by Brigadier General Dwerk & Comdg Officer. The Comdg Officer made a short address to them.	

Instructions regarding War Diaries and Intelligence Summaries are contained in F. S. Regs., Part II. and the Staff Manual respectively. Title pages will be prepared in manuscript.

WAR DIARY
or
~~INTELLIGENCE SUMMARY.~~
(Erase heading not required.)

8th (S) Bn Devon Regt

Army Form C. 2118.

Place	Date 1915	Hour	Summary of Events and Information	Remarks and references to Appendices
AILLY	Dec 16		C & D Coys made use of the hot spray baths: also washed underclothing at Baths	
AILLY	16		Blankets of A, B & D Coys, Transport &c cleansed by Brigade Machine which was in attendance	
AILLY	17		Programme of training continued	
AILLY	17		Remainder of Bns blankets cleansed. "A" Coy at Range at BREILLY	
AILLY	18		Battalion Route March. From Level Crossing at AILLY to St SAUVEUR.	
AILLY	19		St VAST; La CHAUSSE, PICQUIGNY and back to billets - distance about 10 miles (every man completed march) B Coy at the Range.	
AILLY	20		A & C Coys attended Divine Service in A Coy's Billet & D & B in D Coy's Billet	
			The Mayor of Exeter visited the Battalion	
AILLY-SUR-SOMME	Dec 21st		Programme of training continued D Coy carried out a Musketry programme ~~on~~ BREILLY range.	
AILLY-SUR-SOMME	Dec 22nd		Commanding Officers parade as strong as possible	

Instructions regarding War Diaries and Intelligence Summaries are contained in F. S. Regs., Part II. and the Staff Manual respectively. Title pages will be prepared in manuscript.

WAR DIARY ~~or INTELLIGENCE SUMMARY.~~ 8th (S) Bn Devon Regt.

(Erase heading not required.)

Army Form C. 2118.

Place	Date	Hour	Summary of Events and Information	Remarks and references to Appendices
AILLY-SUR SOMME	1915 Dec. 23		Programme of training was continued.	
	24th		— do —	
— do —	Dec. 25th		N. C. Os. & Men of each Company dined together at 2-30 P.M. of which there was a plentiful supply of Turkey, plum puddings &c. The C. O. visited each Coy during their dinner.	
— do —	Dec 25th		(~~2nd~~) W. Os. & Sergeants had the School kindly placed at their disposal & dined together at 7 P.M. The Comdg Officer, with several other Officers paid them a visit during the dinner.	
— do —	Dec. 26th		Divine Service. A draft 120 O Ranks arrived & were posted to Coys.	
— do —	Dec. 27th		Programme of Training continued	
— do —	Dec 28th		— do —	
	Dec. 29th		— do — including Commanding Officers parade as strong as possible	
FOURDRINOY	Dec. 30th	11 AM	Bn marched from AILLY-SUR-SOMME to FOURDRINOY there to be billeted	
— do	Dec. 31st		D Coy carried out musketry at BREILLY remainder of Bn was placed at the disposal of their respective Commanders. A draft of 21 other ranks arrived & were taken on strength of the Bn. The Brigadier & D.A.D.M.S. inspected the billets.	

J. D. Ingles. Lt Colonel
Commanding 8th (S) Bn Devon Regt

20th Brigade.
7th Division.

8th BATTALION

DEVONSHIRE REGIMENT.

JANUARY 1 9 1 6

Army Form C. 2118.

8th Devon Regt

Instructions regarding War Diaries and Intelligence Summaries are contained in F. S. Regs., Part II. and the Staff Manual respectively. Title pages will be prepared in manuscript.

WAR DIARY
or
INTELLIGENCE SUMMARY.

(Erase heading not required.)

Place	Date 1916	Hour	Summary of Events and Information	Remarks and references to Appendices
FOURDRINOY	1st Jany		a draft of 19 O Ranks arrived & were posted to companies. Comdg Officer inspected draft.	
-do-	2nd Jany		Brigadier General Deverell inspected recent drafts consisting of 160 O Ranks.	
-do-	3rd Jany		"A" & "C" Coys were BREILLY } Ranges Target Practice "B" & "D" do - were at PICQUIGNY } Comdg Officer attended a lecture at VIGNACOURT.	
FOURDRINOY and PONTREMY	4th Jany		The Bn marched from FOURDRINOY at 9 A.M to PONT REMY a distance of 15 miles, 9 men fell out, 5 of which fell out near their billets at PONT REMY	
PONT REMY	5th Jany		Brigadier inspected the billets & was pleased with the arrangements made by the Comdg Officer & complimented the Bn on its splendid march from FOURDRINOY	
PONT REMY	6th Jan.		Training Continued - Bn carried out a tactical exercise Advance Guard.	
PONT REMY	7th Jan		Training Continued - Bn carried out an attack - Dress marching Order.	
PONT REMY	8th Jan		Companies at the disposal of Coy Officers. Gas & Tube helmets, boots, ammunition inspections.	
PONT REMY	9th Jan		Divine Service in Cinema at 9-30 & 10 A.M.	

Instructions regarding War Diaries and Intelligence Summaries are contained in F. S. Regs., Part II. and the Staff Manual respectively. Title pages will be prepared in manuscript.

WAR DIARY
or
INTELLIGENCE SUMMARY.
(Erase heading not required.)

Army Form C. 2118.

8th Devon Regt.

Place	Date	Hour	Summary of Events and Information	Remarks and references to Appendices
PONT REMY	Jan. 10th.		Battalion carried out an attack on SOREL	
PONT REMY	Jan. 11th.		Battalion carried out an attack near BUIGNY	
PONT. REMY	Jan. 12th.		Coys at the disposal of Coy Commanders.	
PONT REMY	Jan. 13th.		Bn carried out a programme Inf in the attack ~~Grenadiers~~, Signallers, etc under their respective Comdrs.	
PONT REMY	Jan 14th.		Bn carried out a route march from PONT REMY to SOREL to X roads 1½ miles S. of Sorel to LONGPRE to LONG - COCKEREL to PONT Remy, a draft of 40 O Ranks arrived & were posted to Coys at 7 A.M.	
PONT REMY	Jan 15th.		Continuation of Battalion Training	
PONT REMY	Jan. 16th.		Divine Service 9 - 10 A.M. in the Cinema.	
PONT REMY	Jan 17th.		Continuation of training, which included night outpost 4 - 30 P.M. — 8 P.M.	
PONT REMY	Jan. 18th.		do —, Cross Country Race, Lt. SAVILL took 2nd place, our team won the 3rd prize i.e. 50/-	
PONT REMY	Jan. 19th.		Battn in the attack, area, WANEL	

1577 Wt. W10791/1773 500,000 1/15 D. D. & L. A.D.S.S./Forms/C. 2118.

Instructions regarding War Diaries and Intelligence Summaries are contained in F. S. Regs., Part II. and the Staff Manual respectively. Title pages will be prepared in manuscript.

WAR DIARY

~~or~~

~~INTELLIGENCE SUMMARY.~~

(Erase heading not required.)

Army Form C. 2118.

8th Devon Regt.

Place	Date 1916	Hour	Summary of Events and Information	Remarks and references to Appendices
PONT REMY	Jan 20th		Bn Training continued	
[PONT] REMY	Jan 21st		Brigade Operations, Advanced Guards,	
Pont REMY	Jan 22nd		Coys at the Disposal of Coy Comdrs.	
do	Jan 23rd		Divine Service.	
do	Jan 24th		Route March to BELLANCOURT — PONT REMY	
do	Jan 25th		Disposal of Coy Comdrs.	
do	Jan 26th		Brigade operations attended by the Corps Comdr. Divisional Comdr. & in the neighbourhood of BELLANCOURT.	
do	Jan 27th		Coys at the Disposal of Coy Comdrs.	
PONT REMY	Jan 28th	9AM	Bn moved to AILLY-SUR-SOMME by march route 17 miles. arrived AILLY 5 P.M.	
AILLY SUR SOMME	Jan 29th		Coys at the disposal of Coy Comdrs. Feet Inspection	
AILLY SUR SOMME	Jan 30th		Divine Service.	
SOMME	Jan 31st		Attack on Trenches at AILLY/SOMME	

J. S. Ingles. Lt Colonel
Comdg 8th (S) Bn Devon Regt.

1577 Wt. W10791/1773 500,000 1/15 D. D. & L. A.D.S.S./Forms/C. 2118.

20th Brigade.

7th Division.

8th BATTALION

DEVONSHIRE REGIMENT

FEBRUARY 1 9 1 6

8th Devon Regt.

Army Form C. 2118.

7th Div

WAR DIARY
or
~~INTELLIGENCE SUMMARY.~~

(Erase heading not required.)

Instructions regarding War Diaries and Intelligence Summaries are contained in F. S. Regs., Part II. and the Staff Manual respectively. Title pages will be prepared in manuscript.

Place	Date 1916	Hour	Summary of Events and Information	Remarks and references to Appendices
AILLY SOMME	1st Feby		Bn marched from AILLY/Somme &	
CARDON-NETTE	-do-		to CARDONNETTE there to be billeted. Grenade Coy was formed under the command of 2/Lt W. J. Bowden.	
LA HOUSSOYE	2nd		Bn was billeted at LA HOUSSOYE. C.O. gave a limited number of passes, for all ranks to visit the 1st Devonshire Regt at MONTIGNY	
MEAULTE	3rd		Bn marched to MEAULTE there to be billeted	
Trenches D 1 1	4th		Trenches. Bn marched from MEAULTE to take over D 2 Sec. at BECORDEL relieving the 6th Bn NORTHAMPTONS.	
do	5th		Trenches. on our right were the Manchester Regt, on our left the 2/ Border Regt. occupying D 1 - and 3 respectively	
do	6th		Trenches -do-	
do	7th		Trenches. -do-	
do	8th		Trenches -do-	
do	9th		Trenches. -do-	

1577 Wt. W10791/1773 500,000 1/15 D. D. & L. A.D.S.S./Forms/C. 2118.

Instructions regarding War Diaries and Intelligence Summaries are contained in F. S. Regs., Part II. and the Staff Manual respectively. Title pages will be prepared in manuscript.

WAR DIARY

~~or~~

~~INTELLIGENCE~~ SUMMARY.

(*Erase heading not required.*)

Army Form C. 2118.

8th Devon Regt.

Place	Date 1916	Hour	Summary of Events and Information	Remarks and references to Appendices
Trenches D1. Becordel	FEB. 10th		Trenches.	
do	11th		Trenches. on our left the 2nd Borders were relieved by the 2nd Gordons.	
-do-	12th		Bn was relieved by 6th Cheshires & marched by Companies to VILLE-SUR-ANCRE there to be billeted arriving at 4-30 P.M.	
VILLE SUR ANCRE	13th		Bn found working parties for the Trenches & for road making consisting of 264 O.R & 5 Officers.	
-do-	14th		Bn found a working party of 120 O.R & 2 Officers to work in the trenches D2 & Road making. 2nd Lt [illegible] proceeded to FLIXECOURT. Capts Graham, Roberts [illegible] joined [illegible]	
-do-	15th		— do — 370 Capt H. J. Graham 3/Dorsets took Command of the Bn. Capt Roberts took over Command of D Co. Capt [illegible] B Coy.	
-do-	16th		— do — 420	
do	17th		— do — 420 working in D2. Becordel	
do	18th		— do —	

1577 Wt. W10791/1773 500,000 1/15 D. D. & L. A.D.S.S./Forms/C. 2118.

Instructions regarding War Diaries and Intelligence Summaries are contained in F. S. Regs., Part II. and the Staff Manual respectively. Title pages will be prepared in manuscript.

WAR DIARY

~~or~~

~~INTELLIGENCE SUMMARY.~~

(*Erase heading not required.*)

Army Form C. 2118.

Place	Date Feb.	Hour	Summary of Events and Information	Remarks and references to Appendices
VILLE SUR-ANCRE	19th		Bn found working parties consisting of 5 Officers and 324 O Ranks	
VILLE and D2. Sec	20th		Bn marched from VILLE-SUR-ANCRE to BECORDEL to take over Trenches from 6th Bn Cheshire Regt at 8.30 A.M.	
Trenches	21st		Trenches D.2. BECORDEL - FRICOURT - MAP Ref. E.9a.7.8 to E 9 d 8.3. On our right were the 20th MANCHESTERS on the LEFT 2/BORDER REGT,	
do	22nd		About 5.30 P.M. on the 22nd inst the enemy bombarded Kingston Road	
do	23rd		Trenches D2 — Heavily with Shrapnel and high explosive. Retaliation was called for by Lt Col J.D. Ingles, the ENEMYS bombardment increased and was directed on the TAMBOUR the left of D2 and KINGSTON ROAD, North of RUNDLE AVENUE	
do	24th		Trenches D2, — the Right half of D2, and KINGSTON ROAD was also shelled, though not severely. The parapet in front line trench was blown in on left in 2 places and a traverse was blown down. RUNDLE	
do	25th		Trenches D2. — AVENUE was also blown in in one place and 85 Street suffered slightly. While the bombardment was going on the enemy kept up a very heavy M.G fire on our parapet most of which appears to have been high. At 6.45	
do	26th		Trenches D2. — p.m. we opened with rifle and machine gun fire on FRICOURT and EAST of TAMBOUR by special request. At 6.45 fire slackened on both sides considerably and at 8.30 PM all was quiet. Our Casualties were 1 killed & 6 wounded, 3 of the Trench MORTAR Battery in my sector	
do	27th		Trenches D2. — were wounded. No advance was made by the ENEMY in front of D.2. A draft of 41 arrived from Base, posted to Coys.	
do and MEAULTE	28th		Trench D2. — Relieved by 9th Bn Devon Regt. & 20th Manchesters which took over [illegible] right sub sectn D2. Bn marched [illegible] there to be relieved.	

Instructions regarding War Diaries and Intelligence Summaries are contained in F. S. Regs., Part II. and the Staff Manual respectively. Title pages will be prepared in manuscript.

WAR DIARY

~~or~~

~~INTELLIGENCE SUMMARY.~~

(Erase heading not required.)

Army Form C. 2118.

8th Devon Regt.

Place	Date Feb. 16	Hour	Summary of Events and Information	Remarks and references to Appendices
MEAUTE	29th		Comdg Officer & 2nd in Command inspected draft billets & arranged for men not on duty to have a bath. Battalion stood to arms & marched to Battle position at 6.15 P.M, on account of S.O.S. being received from O.C. D2. Sub. Sector, after our artillery bombarded the sector occupied by the Enemy opposite D2, situation became normal & the battalion returned to billets at 8.15 p.m.	

In the Field
29-2-16.

E. McHone(?) Lt. adjt.
for. Lt. Colonel
Comdg 8th (S) Bn Devon Regt.

1577 Wt. W10791/1773 500,000 1/15 D. D. & L. A.D.S.S./Forms/C. 2118.

20th Brigade.
7th Division.

8th BATTALION

DEVONSHIRE REGIMENT

MARCH 1 9 1 6

Instructions regarding War Diaries and Intelligence Summaries are contained in F. S. Regs., Part II. and the Staff Manual respectively. Title pages will be prepared in manuscript.

20/7

WAR DIARY

~~or~~

~~INTELLIGENCE SUMMARY.~~

(Erase heading not required.)

Army Form C. 2118.

Place	March 1916 Date	Hour	Summary of Events and Information	Remarks and references to Appendices
MEAULTE	1st		H.Q. C. & D Coys billeted in MEAULTE	
BECORDEL	1st		A & B marched from MEAULTE to BECORDEL there to be billeted ~~Yorking mining fatigue & Redoubt housemaiding parties, Guards etc~~	
do	2nd		— do —	
MEAULTE	2nd		H.Qrs C. & D. Coy.	
do	3rd		— do — G.O.C. 7th Div. inspected billets.	
Becordel	3rd		A & B continuing fatigue work for Mining Co.	
~~M~~ do	4th		— do — returning to H.Q MEAULTE about noon there to be billeted	
MEAULTE	4th		C. & D. found every available man for RE Fatigue.	
Trenches D I	5th		Bn marched from MEAUTE to take over D I. Sub sector FRICOURT relieving 9th Devonshire Regt. On our Right in C 2 were the 24th Manchesters on left 2/ Border Regt in D 2.	6
	6th		Trenches. D. I.	46

1577 Wt. W10791/1773 500,000 1/15 D. D. & L. A.D.S.S./Forms/C. 2118.

Instructions regarding War Diaries and Intelligence Summaries are contained in F. S. Regs., Part II. and the Staff Manual respectively. Title pages will be prepared in manuscript.

WAR DIARY

~~or~~

~~INTELLIGENCE SUMMARY.~~

(Erase heading not required.)

Army Form C. 2118.

8th Devon Regt.

Place	Date 1916 MARCH	Hour	Summary of Events and Information	Remarks and references to Appendices
D1. Trenches	7th		Bn holding D I.	
BECORDEL — FRICOURT	8th		— do — Lt. F R BRADFORD was wounded	
do	9th		— do —	
do	10th		— do —	
do	11th		— do — Relieved by 9th Bn Devon Regt. Gordon Highlanders on the left — 24th MANCHESTERS on our Right.	
MEAULTE	11th		Battalion was billeted in MEAULTE.	
do	12th			
do	13th		C & D Coys were on detachment at BECORDEL finding mining fatigues	
do	14th		— do —	
do	15th		— do —	

Instructions regarding War Diaries and Intelligence Summaries are contained in F. S. Regs., Part II. and the Staff Manual respectively. Title pages will be prepared in manuscript.

WAR DIARY

or

~~INTELLIGENCE SUMMARY.~~

(*Erase heading not required.*)

Army Form C. 2118.

8th Devon Regt.

Place	Date	Hour	Summary of Events and Information	Remarks and references to Appendices
MEAULTE	16th		C & D Coys returned to MEAULTE	
D1. Trenches	17th		Bn relieved 9th Devonshire Regt in D1 Sub Sector on our right were the 24th Manchesters on left 2/ Border Regt. 1st Sheepshanks killed	
-"-	18th		Trenches D1. SUB SECTOR. } F 3/9 France (ALBERT.)	
-"-	19th		— do — } Combined Sheet 57 d SE, 57 c SW, 62 d NE, 62 c NW } 1/40000	
-"-	20th		— do —	
-"-	21st		— do —	
-"-	22nd		— do on our left 2nd Bn Gordon Highlanders. Capt G H Graham 3/DORSETS took over Command whilst C.O. proceeded to ENGLAND on leave.	
MEAULTE	23rd		Relieved by 9th Devon Regt. - proceeded to MEAULTE to billets	
-do-	24th		— do —	
-do- 21st BECORDEL	25th		do } A & B Coys proceeded to BECORDEL to relieve 2/Border Regt. finding mining fatigue etc.	
-do-	26th		— do — — do —	

1577 Wt. W10791/1773 500,000 1/15 D. D. & L. A.D.S.S./Forms/C. 2118.

Instructions regarding War Diaries and Intelligence Summaries are contained in F. S. Regs., Part II. and the Staff Manual respectively. Title pages will be prepared in manuscript.

WAR DIARY

~~or~~

~~INTELLIGENCE SUMMARY.~~

(Erase heading not required.)

8th Devon Regt.

Army Form C. 2118.

Place	1916 Date MARCH	Hour	Summary of Events and Information	Remarks and references to Appendices
MEAULTE			H.Q. C and D Coys –	
BECORDEL	27th		A and B Coys –	
MEAULTE	28th		A and B Coys returned from BECORDEL.	
D1. SUB.SECTOR F3 9/5	29th		Battalion ~~was~~ relieved 9th Devon Regt, 20th MANCHESTERS on our right 2nd BORDERS left.	
	30th		Trenches.	
– do –	31st		Trenches.	

E W Hone Lt Col. Major.
Comdg 8th (S) Bn Devon Regt

1577 Wt. W10791/1773 500,000 1/15 D. D. & L. A.D.S.S./Forms/C. 2118.

20th Brigade.

7th Division.

8th BATTALION

DEVONSHIRE REGIMENT

APRIL 1 9 1 6.

Instructions regarding War Diaries and Intelligence Summaries are contained in F. S. Regs., Part II. and the Staff Manual respectively. Title pages will be prepared in manuscript.

WAR DIARY

~~or~~

~~INTELLIGENCE SUMMARY.~~

(Erase heading not required.)

Army Form C. 2118.

8th Devon Regt.

Place	Date 1916 April	Hour	Summary of Events and Information	Remarks and references to Appendices
D1.	1st		Trenches. On our right were the 20th MAN. and on our left the 2/BORDER Regt	
"	2nd		Trenches.	
"	3rd		Trenches.	
"	4th		Trenches.	
	5th		Trenches.	
"	6th		~~Trenches~~ ~~[illegible]~~	
MEAULTE	7th		(MEAULTE) Bn was relieved by the 9th Kings Own Yorkshire Light Inf. and marched to MEAUTE there to be billeted	
VAUX s SOMME	8th		Battalion training at VAUX	
-do-	9th		Divine Service do	
-do-	10th		do	
-do-	11th		do	
-do-	12th		do	
-do-	13th		do.	

Instructions regarding War Diaries and Intelligence Summaries are contained in F. S. Regs., Part II. and the Staff Manual respectively. Title pages will be prepared in manuscript.

WAR DIARY

~~or~~

~~INTELLIGENCE SUMMARY.~~

(Erase heading not required.)

8th Devons

Army Form C. 2118.

Place	Date 1916	Hour	Summary of Events and Information	Remarks and references to Appendices
VAUX S SOMME.	April 14th		Battalion training	
"	15th		— do —	
"	16th		Divine Service	
"	17th		Battalion training	
"	18th		do	
"	19th		do	
"	20th		do	
"	21st		C and D Coys marched on detachment to GROVETOWN Camp.	
	22		C and D Coys at GROVETOWN H.Q and A and B at VAUX	
	23		do	
	24		do	
BOIS DES TAILLES	25	9.0 AM	marched to BOIS DES TAILLES Camp (A and B Coys & H.Q. C & D Coys at GROVETOWN	

Instructions regarding War Diaries and Intelligence Summaries are contained in F. S. Regs., Part II. and the Staff Manual respectively. Title pages will be prepared in manuscript.

WAR DIARY

or

INTELLIGENCE SUMMARY.

(Erase heading not required.)

Army Form C. 2118.

Place	Date 1916 April	Hour	Summary of Events and Information	Remarks and references to Appendices.
	26		A & B and HQ at BOIS DES TAILLES. C & D at GROVETOWN.	
	27		H.Q., C and D marched to BRAY, A & B to GRANTOWN } morning	
	28		H.Q. C and D at BRAY A & B GRANTOWN } Working parties	
	29		do	
	30		do.	

A Graham Major
for Adjutant

20th Brigade.

7th Division.

8th BATTALION

THE DEVONSHIRE REGIMENT

M A Y 1 9 1 6

Instructions regarding War Diaries and Intelligence Summaries are contained in F. S. Regs., Part II. and the Staff Manual respectively. Title pages will be prepared in manuscript.

WAR DIARY

or

~~INTELLIGENCE SUMMARY.~~

(Erase heading not required.)

Army Form C. 2118.

VII 8th Devons. Vol 1

Place	Date 1916 MAY	Hour	Summary of Events and Information	Remarks and references to Appendices
BRAY GRANTOWN	1st		H.Q. C. and D Coys. at BRAY in billets } Working parties formed A and B coys. at GRANTOWN in huts }	
—"—	2nd		Do.	
—"—	3rd		Do.	
Trenches B2	4th		Battalion relieved 2nd GORDONS in B2 Sub-sector. on our ~~left~~ ~~[illegible]~~ 21st MANCHESTER REGT on ~~right~~ the 1 S. Staffords	
"	5th		B2 sub-sector MAP Reference Meaulte. 62 D N.E 2. Scale 1/10000. F.11.	
"	6th		Do.	
"	7th		Do	
"	8th		Do	
"	9th		Do.	
"	10th		Do. on right 1/ Queens on Left 1/ W. Fusiliers	
"	11th		Do.	
" GRANTOWN GROVETOWN	12th		Do relieved by 2/ Gordon Highlanders. ~~B~~ & D Coys GRANTOWN HQ - A & B Coys GROVETOWN	

1577 Wt. W10791/1773 500,000 1/15 D. D. & L. A.D.S.S./Forms/C. 2118.

Instructions regarding War Diaries and Intelligence Summaries are contained in F. S. Regs., Part II. and the Staff Manual respectively. Title pages will be prepared in manuscript.

WAR DIARY

~~or~~

~~INTELLIGENCE SUMMARY.~~

(Erase heading not required.)

Army Form C. 2118.

8th Devons

Place	1916 Date MAY	Hour	Summary of Events and Information	Remarks and references to Appendices
GROVETOWN GRANTOWN	13th		H.Q. A & B Coys in BIVOUACS very wet weather prevails. C. & D Coys in Dug Outs.	
do	14th		—do—	
do	15th		—do— 2 officers joined =	
do	16th		Lt Col J.D. INGLES appointed Temp. Brigadier General Comdg 93rd Bde 31st Division.	
do	17th		Capt B.C. JAMES to be T/MAJOR & appointed to Command 8th Devon Regt.	
B2. SUBSECTOR	18		Bn relieved 2/GORDON HIGHLANDERS — on our right — on left 20th MANCHESTERS.	
do	19th		Trenches. Map Ref. MEAULTE 62.D.NE2 10/2 — 11/4	
do	20th		do —do—	
do	21		do —do—	
do	22		do —do—	
do	23		do —do—	
do and MORLANCOURT.	24		Bn relieved by 1/South Staffords & marched to MORLANCOURT there to be billeted for training.	

Instructions regarding War Diaries and Intelligence Summaries are contained in F. S. Regs., Part II. and the Staff Manual respectively. Title pages will be prepared in manuscript.

WAR DIARY
~~or~~
~~INTELLIGENCE SUMMARY.~~
(Erase heading not required.)

Army Form C. 2118.

8th Devon Regt.

Place	Date 1916	Hour	Summary of Events and Information	Remarks and references to Appendices
MORLANCOURT.	25th May.		Coys carried ~~out~~ training, under Coy Comdrs.	
-do-	26th		-do-	
-do-	27th		-do-	
-do-	28th		-do-	
-do-	29th		-do- Under Bn Commander - Coys in the attack	
-do-	30th		-do- Outposts by day 9 - 1 P.M. by night 7 P.M. to 11.30 P.M.	
-do-	31st		-do Route march 8 miles.	

31/5/16

E. M. Horn 2Lt Adjt
for Major Comdg 8th (S) Bn Devon Regt.

T2134. Wt. W708—776. 500000. 4/15. Sir J. C. & S.

20th Brogade.

7th Division.

8th BATTALION.

DEVONSHIRE REGIMENT.

J U N E 1 9 1 6.

WAR DIARY
or
~~INTELLIGENCE~~ SUMMARY.
(Erase heading not required.)

Army Form C. 2118. 7

Instructions regarding War Diaries and Intelligence Summaries are contained in F. S. Regs., Part II. and the Staff Manual respectively. Title pages will be prepared in manuscript.

8th Devon Regt.
Vol 9

Place	Date	Hour	Summary of Events and Information	Remarks and references to Appendices
MORLANCOURT	1916 June			
"	1st.		Bn in the attack – Training	
"	2nd		Outpost – scheme – do –	
"	3rd		Bn Drill – Night operations – do –	
"	4th		Divine Service	
"	5th		Route march Training.	
"	6th		Working Parties – Every available N.C.O & man	
"	7th		– do –	
"	8th		– do –	
"	9th		– do –	
"	10th		– do –	
GROVETOWN	11th	8 AM	Battalion moved into Bivouac, Finding working parties etc.	
	12th		– do – – do –	
	13th		do	
	14th		do –	
	15th		– do –	
	16th		– do –	
	17th			

Instructions regarding War Diaries and Intelligence Summaries are contained in F. S. Regs., Part II. and the Staff Manual respectively. Title pages will be prepared in manuscript.

WAR DIARY ~~or~~ ~~INTELLIGENCE SUMMARY.~~

(Erase heading not required.)

Army Form C. 2118.

8th Devons

Place	Date 1916	Hour	Summary of Events and Information	Remarks and references to Appendices
GROVETOWN	June 18th		Bn found the usual mining fatigues & working parties	
-do-	19th		—do—	
B1. Trenches	20th		Bn relieved the 9th Devon Regt. in this Sector Map Ref	
"	"		On the Right were the 6th R. BERKS and on the Left 2/GORDONS.	
"	21st		—do—	
"	22nd		—do—	
"	23rd		Bn was relieved by the 10th Lancashire Regt. & marched to GROVETOWN	
GROVETOWN	24th		Bn had a days rest.	
" "	25th		Bn resting at GROVETOWN [illegible]	
"	26th		—do—	
"	27th		Lt. E.W. Horne to England. Lt C Pepys appointed Adjutant. —do—	
	28th		Bn resting at GROVETOWN 2 platoons detached to hold C1 subsector	
	29th		— — —	
	30th		Bn moved at 11.35 pm to assembly trenches B2 Subsector.	

20th Inf.Bde.
7th Div.

WAR
DIARY

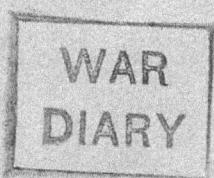

8th BATTN. THE DEVONSHIRE REGIMENT.

J U L Y

1 9 1 6

Attached:

Appendices I to V.

JULY 1916

Instructions regarding War Diaries and Intelligence Summaries are contained in F. S. Regs., Part II. and the Staff Manual respectively. Title Pages will be prepared in manuscript.

WAR DIARY
or
~~INTELLIGENCE SUMMARY~~
(Erase heading not required.)

Army Form C. 2118.

8th Devon Reg

Vol 10

Place	Date	Hour	Summary of Events and Information	Remarks and references to Appendices
Trenches 87 Section Ref. MONTAUBAN MAP F.17.a	July 1st	3.45 am	Battalion in Assembly trenches. The orders received dealing with subsequent operations are attached in Appendix I, the report on operations in Appendix II. The weather & the condition of the ground were favourable for operations. The following are the names of officer casualties Killed; Capt Tregelles 2nd Lt Rew. 2nd Lt Davidson. Wounded; Capt Mahaffy. 2nd Lts Roper, Cameron, Hinton, Lockyer, Chapman, & Lewis.	Appendix I Appendix II
	2nd		Ref Appendix II	
	3rd		Ref Appendix II	
—	4th		Bat in same position, holding BUNNY TRENCH, SUNKEN RD, ORCHARD TR. N. & the ORCHARD. Consolidation, burying the dead & clearing the battle field continued. Men of Devon Reg were buried in a cemetery consecrated by Capt Crosse C of E at MANSEL COPSE Ref S11 C 4 5	
TREUX	5th	4pm	The Battalion marched to TREUX into billets	
—	6th		Battalion resting & refitting. Companies reorganizing	
—	7th		Battalion training. The G.O.C. 7th Div, Major Gen Watts C.B. inspected the battalion at 3 pm	
—	8th		Divine services	
—	9th		~~Battalion training~~. Route marching. Extended order drill, advance & rear guards	
—	10th		Battalion training	
MINDEN POST F.17.b	11th	2pm	Battalion marched to MINDEN POST & bivouaced. Arrived 7 30 pm	
	12th		Battalion resting. C.O. & officers made a reconnaissance of the SNOUT (S 14 d)	
—	13th		Battalion resting. 5 casualties from shell fire	
		11 25pm	Battalion left for assembly position. Orders received dealing with the subsequent attack are attached in Appendix III, the report on the operation in Appendix IV	Appendix III Appendix IV
BAZENTIN LE GRAND WOOD	14th		Ref Appendix IV. The weather & condition of the ground were favourable for operations. Names of officer casualties Killed; Capt Billcoe, 2nd Lt Lewis, 2nd Lt Boyd, 2nd Lt Gainey, 2nd Lt Carter. Wounded 2nd Lts Scott, & Perritt Richardson	

127

Army Form C. 2118.

WAR DIARY
or
~~INTELLIGENCE~~ SUMMARY

(Erase heading not required.)

8th Devon Reg

Instructions regarding War Diaries and Intelligence Summaries are contained in F. S. Regs., Part II. and the Staff Manual respectively. Title Pages will be prepared in manuscript.

Place	Date	Hour	Summary of Events and Information	Remarks and references to Appendices
WHITE TRENCH	July 15th		Ref Appendix IV Battalion moved from BAZENTIN LE GRAND WOOD to WHITE TRENCH.	
Ref MONTAUBAN MAP S25 central	16th		Battalion resting	
	17th		Battalion resting. C.O. & officers made a reconnaissance of HIGH WOOD S 14.4	
	18th		Battalion resting	
	19th	9 pm	Battalion moved to assembly position S of HIGH WOOD. Orders received dealing with subsequent operations are attached in Appendix V & the report on the operation in Appendix VI	Appendix V
	20th		Officer casualties. Killed 2nd Lt Hayward. Missing 2nd Lts Joseph & Rundle. Wounded Lt Saville 2nd Lts Gay, Hewitt & Perkins.	Appendix VI
ERNACOURT		10.30 pm	Bn. relieved by 14th WARWICK REG & marched to DERNACOURT & bivouaced	
	21st		Battalion resting	
AILLY SUR SOMME	22nd	2.45 am	Bat marched to MERICOURT. Entrained at 9.30 am. Departed at 10 am. Detrained at HANGEST at 2 pm. Reached AILLY SUR SOMME at 6 pm. Battalion bivouaced. Divine Service at 11 a.m. Battalion marched into billets at 2.30 pm.	
—	23rd		Battalion resting & refitting	
—	24th		Battalion training. Rifle exercises, musketry. Coy drill	
—	25th		Battalion training G.O.C 7th Division inspected drafts joined since July 1st	
—	26th		Battalion training Drill & route marching.	
—	27th		Battalion training Route march & musketry	
—	28th		Battalion training Coy outposts. G.O.C. 7th Division inspected the transport.	
—	29th		Divine service at 10 am. G.O.C 20th Inf Bde inspected billets	
—	30th		Battalion training. Musketry on BREILLY Range	
—	31st			

2449 Wt. W14957/M90 750,000 1/16 J.B.C. & A. Forms/C.2118/12.

A P P E N D I C E S

I to IV

W A R D I A R Y.

8th (Ser)Bn Devonshire Regiment.

A P P E N D I X 1.

Containing all important orders for operations July 1st,2nd and 3rd.

Instructions for forthcoming Operations No 2.

20th Infantry Brigade Provisional Order.

Subsequent Orders.

Orders Received

No B.M.74 dated 1-7-1916.

O.C.8th Devons.

The b igade will at once occupy the objective orignally assigned to it and will occupy the line in the following order from the right AAA Gordons AAA Two companies Warwicks AAA 8th and 9th Devons AAA Borders AAA In brigade reserve in DANTZIG ALLEY,Warwick two companies AAA All battalions to be in close touch with one another and with brigade right and left AAAMachine Gun Coy to take up positions as ordered AAA Report when in position.

20th Infantry Brigade.

B.M. 82 dated 2-7-1916.

O.C. 8th Devons.

The 17th Division is attacking FRICOURT to-day 2nd July 1916 The boundary between 7th and 17th Divisions is as follows:- BECORDEL BECOURT-PERONNE Road as far as THORN LANE,thence to WILLOW AVENUE STREAM at F.4.c.4.6. thence WILLOW AVENUE STREAM.

The objectives of the 17th Division are as follows:

1st objective; FRICOURT VILLAGE from F.4.c.4.6. ROSE COTTAGE-RED COTTAGE.

2nd objective. The road running from FRICOURT CHURCH to FRICOURT FARM inclusive,capture FRICOURT FARM and join up with 21st Divisn near the POODLES.

3rd objective. Capture RAILWAY ALLEY and join up with 7th Division about X.29.d.0.6.

7th Division are co-operating.

(a)in first objective by capturing ORCHARD ALLEY,THORN LANE and ROSE TRENCH as far as WILLOW AVENUE.

(b) in the third objective they will join up with 17th Division about X.29.d.0.6.

The 22nd Infantry Brigade have orders to capture ROSE TRENCH from ORCHARD ALLEY to WILLOW AVENUE STREAM.

20th Infantry Bde.

B.M.No 89 dated 2-7-16.

O.C.8th Devons.

17th Division have occupied FRICOURT and they are about to advance on each side of FRICOURT WOOD AAA 8th Devons will occupy and consolidate ORCHARD TRENCH NORTH and the ORCHARD as soonas 17th Division have passedAAA 2nd Gordons will similiarly occupy and consolidate BUNNY TRENCH

20th Infantry Brigade.

B.M.No 96.
O.C.8th Devons.

1. The Xlll Corps on the right remain in their position on the line of the final objective. On the left 17th Division is holding FRICOURT FARM and eastern and north eastern edge of FRICOURT WOOD. They are consolidating the East end of the WOOD,WILLOW TRENCH and a line joining the latter to FRICOURT FARM. They will form a junction with the 20th Infantry Brigade at the ORCHARD.

2. Today the 17th Division will capture RAILWAY ALLEY,RAILWAY COPSE and BOTTOM WOOD,and will join up along the line of the hedge running between BIRCH TREE and BOTTOM WOOD,with the 21st Division who will capture SHELTER WOOD and BIRCH TREE WOOD.The attack will be preceded by an intensive bombardment beginning at 8-40 am.The attack will be launched at 9-0 am.

3.(a)The 91st Infantry Brigade will remain holding their present position. (b)2nd Gordon Highlanders will hold BUNNY TRENCH from present left of the 1st S.Stafford regt to the MAMETZ-FRICOURT Road exclusive.

8th Devon Regt will hold from junction of BUNNY TRENCH and MAMETZ-FRICOURT Road inclusive along the MAMETZ-FRICOURT Road and ORCHARD TRENCH NORTH to the ORCHARD(inclusive) where a strong point has been established.

9th Devon Regt will concentrate about HIDDEN WOOD and PLUM LANE. Head Quarters remaining in their present position in DANTZIG TRENCH.

2nd Broder Regt will concentrate in BOIS FRANCAIS and BOIS FRANCAIS SUPPORT. Head Quarters remaining as at present in 75 STREET.

20th Machine Gun Company will remain in its present position and look out for targets.

20th T.M.Battery will remain concentrated in DANTZIG TRENCH as at present.

The 2 Companies 2nd Warwick Regt will rejoin their Battalion which will come under the orders of G.O.C.,22nd Infantry Brigade.

All moves to be complete by 9-0 am.

4. Completion of all moves to be reported to Brigade Head Quarters which will remain at ESSEX AVENUE.

5. ACKNOWLEDGE.

3-7-1916. 20th Infantry Brigade.

No B.M. 215.dated 3-7-1916.

O.C.8th Devons.

1. 91st Infantry Brigade will take over the line as far as the N.W.corner of BOTTOM WOOD tonight.Dividing line between 91st Infantry Brigade and the Division on the left will be from that point along West edge of BOTTOM WOOD to WILLOW AVENUE just North of BUNNY WOOD thence along WILLOW AVENUE.

The strong point at X.28.d.7.2. will be completed by the neighbouring division to-night.

22nd Infantry Brigade are moving 1 battalion to the HALTE.

2. The 8th Devon Regt will remain in their present position holding ORCHARD TRENCH NORTH and the ORCHARD.
20th Machine Gun Coy will remain in their present positions.
The 9th Devon Regt,2nd Border Regt and 2nd Gordon Highlanders and 20th T.M.Battery with its mortars,will move back at once to the CITADEL.
Billeting parties will be sent on at once to meet the Staff Captain at the CITADEL.

3. Battalions will bring back their empty petrol tins.

3-7-1916. 20th Infantry Brigade.

APPENDIX II

Instructions regarding War Diaries and Intelligence Summaries are contained in F. S. Regs., Part II. and the Staff Manual respectively. Title Pages will be prepared in manuscript.

WAR DIARY
or
~~INTELLIGENCE SUMMARY~~
(Erase heading not required.)

Army Form C. 2118.

8th Devon Reg

Place	Date	Hour	Summary of Events and Information	Remarks and references to Appendices
	30-6-16.		Battalion paraded at 11-0 pm and marched into trenches in the following order of companies:- B,D,A and C Company less two platoons. The battalion arrived in trenches and were in the following positions at 3-45 am,1-7-1916. B Company in PERONNE AVENUE. D Company LUDGATE CIRCUS. A and C Company in LUCKNOW REDOUBT. Two Platoons of C Company rejoined the Battalion at 6-25 a.m.	
	1-7-16.		At ZERO hour 7-30 a.m.,B Company moved from PERONNE AVENUE to RESERVE TRENCH via 68 STREET their left on 69 STREET,their right in touch with D Company. D Company occupied 67 SUPPORT. A and C Company moved from LUCKNOW REDOUBT to LUCKNOW LANE,C Company picking up their Two platoons at ESSEX AVENUE. A Company withntheir right on LUCKNOW AVENUE. This was the situation at ZERO hour.	
			At 8-40 am A Company moved up into RESERVE TRENCH having B Company in touch with their right. This made Two Companies in RESERVE TRENCH,One Company in 67 SUPPORT and One Company in LUDGATE LANE. AT 8-6 am O.C."B" Company reports 91st Brigade are on East of MAMETZ.Parties of GORDONS can be seen in MAMETZ but seemed to be bearing off to the East of our objective.	
			10-30 am "B" Company were moved from RESERVE TRENCH and sent forward to support the left of the GORDONS and right of the 9th DEVONS.O.C."B" Company moved his troops via MANAEL COPSE in-to the hollow on the BRAY-FRICOURT Road. This Company did not move again as a whole until 4-0 pm when all its Officers had been wounded and C.S.M.? Holwill assumed command.	
			10-40 am."C" Company took up position in reserve trench vacated by "B" Company at 10-15 am. O.C.GORDONS was lent "D" Company 8th DEVON REGT to use as support to his battalion if required.	
			10-45 am.Officer Commanding "D" Company reports two of his platoons sent forward to support the right of the GORDONS. (O.C. 9th Devon Reg)	
			10-20 am.Colonel STOREY,ordered the advance of "A" Company to support the right of the 9th DEVONS. This Company was in position in RESERVE TRENCH. No information of this move was given to Battalion head quarters.They moved in the direction of the HALTE.The four officers of this Company were either killed or wounded and I got no information as to the whereabouts of this Company until late in the evening when 2/Lieut DUFF reported to me he had picked this company up.	
			3-30 pm. "C" Company my last company in RESERVE TRENCH were given orders to proceed to HIDDEN WOOD via MANSEL COPSE. This company sent Two Platoons over the top of RESERVE TRENCH but Lieut SAVILE seeing numerous casualties took remainder of the company of company via 70STREET and proceeded to his objective with practically no casualties at all.	
			4-0 pm. I sent out 2/Lieut Duff to collect "B" Company and push on in support of "C" Company to HIDDEN WOOD.	
			4-20 pm 2/Lieut DUFF report having found remnants of "B" Company in MAMETX TRENCH and working	

2449 Wt. W14957/M90 750,000 1/16 J.B.C. & A. Forms/C.2118/12.

APPENDIX II

Instructions regarding War Diaries and Intelligence Summaries are contained in F. S. Regs., Part II. and the Staff Manual respectively. Title Pages will be prepared in manuscript.

WAR DIARY
or
INTELLIGENCE SUMMARY
(Erase heading not required.)

Army Form C. 2118.

Place	Date	Hour	Summary of Events and Information	Remarks and references to Appendices

through trench with GORDONS in direction of DANTZIG SUPPORT and HIDDEN WOOD.
5-10 pm. This same Officer reported "having joined up with 2/Lieut JOSEPH of "C" Company also "A" C company men under C.S.M. MELHUISH also some 9th DEVONS, we have worked under the bank to HALTE and beyond, are now working round to HIDDEN WOOD. I have taken and sent back many prisoners from under the bank including four Officers." (Bank referred to is F.11.c.2.9. MONTAUBAN MAP.)
At 8-6 am 91st Brigade were reported to have reached their objective E of MAMETZ. On the left of Brigade no advance was made.
The nature of the engagement waw affected by mopping up parties not clearing the trenches, leaving Machine Guns and Snipers who caused practically all their casualties.
The Bank by the HALTE was entirely disregarded and all dug-outs in DANTZIG TRENCH were found occupied; the enemy using the bank above could concentrate an enfilade fire on troops advancing to HIDDEN WOOD or MAMETZ. Also the traverses being firestepped, they could shoot down the valley to our lines. A machine gun was found at the Halte which had fired a great quantity of rounds.
The enemy had taken advantage of this high bank to make it an impregnable position advanced on by a bombing party down to COMBE ALLEY or along the bottom of the bank.
The result of the engagement was entirely successful.
In the aid post in DANTZIG TRENCH the O.C. 109th RESERVE REGT was found wounded on a stretcher with a broken thigh.
At night fall the brigade occupied the original objective assigned to it.
2-7-16. In the morning the 8th Devons advanced up ORSHARD TRENCH NORTH and established a strong point in the ORCHARD and consolidated the position. Touch was established with the 17th Division in WILLOW TRENCH.
3-7-16. In the evening the 8th Devons occupied all the Brigade frontage.
The 8th Devons suffered the following casualties.

OFFICERS

3	Killed
7	Wounded

O'Ranks

37	Killed
153	Woundedd
7	Missing.

The 8th DEVON REGT captured a great deal of German Arms and equipment. They had a Lewis Gun Damaged. Only a small quantity of S.A.A., was used.

(Sd) B.C. JAMES. Lieut Colonel
Commanding, 8th Devon Regt.

2449 Wt. W14957/M90 750,000 1/16 J.B.C. & A. Forms/C.2118/12.

APPENDIX 111.

20th Infantry Brigade Operation Order No 74.

Ref:Trench Maps 1/20,000
and MONTAUBAN and MARTINPUICH
Sheets.

Information Regarding the enemy.

The enemy has been greatly disorganised by our attacks. The LEHR Regiment (3rd Guards Division) held the line in front of BAZENTIN LE GRAND WOOD, with the 122nd Reserve Regiment (163rd Division) on its right, and the 16th Bavarian Regiment (10th Bavarian Division) on its left.

Dividing Lines.

(a). The dividing line between the 7th Division and XIII Corps will run from point S.20.d.90.35.- junction of roads S.14.d.90.15. to east edge of BAZENTIN LE GRAND WOOD to the North East corner of the CEMETERY inclusive.

(b). Between the 7th and 21st Division - S.19. central, road running from the East corner of MAMETZ WOOD S.20.a.1.8. to road junction S.14.b.1.5. - Road along East of BAZENTIN LE PETIT WOOD to MARTINPUICH (road inclusive to 7th Division).

N.B. The hammer headed portion of MAMETZ WOOD in S.19.a. is allotted to 7th Division.

Objectives.

(a) The attack will be delivered with the 20th Infantry Brigade in the front followed by the 22nd Infantry Brigade with the 91st Infantry Brigade in reserve.

(b) Objectives of the 20th Infantry Brigade.

1st Objective. The enemy's front line trenches between point S.15.c.15.40. and the road at S.14.a.70.35.

2nd Objective. The enemy's support line from point S.15.a.25.10 to the point in BAZENTIN LE GRAND WOOD where CIRCUS Trench turns North ward, thence straight to the western edge of the WOOD.

3rd Objective. The whole of BAZENTIN LE GRAND WOOD.

The 20th Infantry Brigade will not abvance beyond their 3rd Objective.

(c) Objectives of the 22nd Infantry Brigade.

T o capture BAZENTIN LE PETIT Village East of the MARTINPUICH Road (road inclusive) and the CEMETERY, and to establish from S.15.a. 20.95. (where a junction will be made with 13th Corps) through the CEMETERY to the Northern exit of BAXENTIN LE PETIT Village where a junction will be made with the 21st Division. The 22nd Infy Brigade will be prepared to attack the houses West of the MARTINPUICH Road should the 21st Division be delayed.

Advances will be timed in accordance with the times shown on the barra ge map attached, the Infantry moving as close up to the forward line of the barrage as possible just before the time when the fire will lift.

Distribution of Battalions.

The attack will be carried out by the 8th Devon Regt on the right and the 2nd Border Regt on the left. 2nd Gordon Hrs will be in the hammer head portion of MAMETZ WOOD in S.19.a. North East portion and 9th Devon Regt in CATERPILLAR WOOD. The two latter battalions will be in brigade reserve.

O.C. 2nd Gordon Hrs will closely watch the course of operations of the two assualting Battalions and will re-inforce at once should the situation demand it.

Formation of Assualting Battalions.

The two assualting battalions will be deployed one hour before the ZERO hour in the following formations:-

2nd BORDER REGT, left in the valley 100 yards West of FLAT IRON COPSE - along the bank of small shrubs to the bend at S.20. b.1.9.

8th DEVON REGT left in touch with 2nd Border Regt at S.20. b.1.9.- thence due East across MALBOROUGH Trench to the track inclusive in S.20.a.8.8.

The dividing line between the two battalions will be the western face of the SNOUT. 8th Devon Regt will be responsible for MALBOROUGH TRENCH and for the western face of the SNOUT, but 2nd Border Regt will maintain touch with them on that face.

Outposts.

The O.C. Assaulting Battalions will arrange that their

respective lines of deployment are occupied by an outpost line as their battalions move up into the positions ordered.

BOMBERS.

MARLBORO Trench will be held by a strong bombing party of the 8th Devon Regt, and a block established in advance of the leading line at the point of deployment.

SILENCE.

Absolute silence must be maintained when moving into position.

ZERO HOUR.

ZERO Hour is 3-25 am on the 14th July 1916.

REPORTS.

Reports will be sent to Brigade Head Quarters at POMMIERS REDOUBT.

(Sgd) C.C.FOSS., Major.
Brigade Major.
20th Infantry Brigade.

APPENDIX V.

20th Brigade Operation Order No 76. 19th July 1916.

MARTINPUICH Sheet 1/20,000.

The enemy counterattacked Xlll Corps yesterday and again regained possession of a portion of DELVILLE WOOD and the Northern portion of LONGUEVAL.

To relieve presser on the Xlll Corps and to assist their attack, to recover the lost ground, XV Corps will to-morrow attack HIGH WOOD and the roads leading thence to LONGUEVAL.

The 5th Division will first occupy the road from S.17½a.4.2. to S.10.d.7.8. and secondly form a junction with the right of the 7th Division at S.11.a.5.8.

The 7th Division will capture the road from S.11.c.5.8. to Eastern corner of HIGH WOOD.

The 33rd Division will capture HIGHWOOD and the enemys trench running from the switch trench at S.4.a.1.7. round the western corner of the WOOD.

The attack of the 7th Division will be carried out by the 20th Infantry Brigade.

The Infantry will assualt at 3-35 am.

Boundaries.

The dividing line between the 5th and 7th Division will be from S.16.a.3.9. to S.10.d.8.8. thence to road junction S.11.c.5.8.

Between the 7th and 33rd Division from S.9.c.0.0. to S.10.a. 5.3. junction of track, thence by the track to S.4.d.8. Western corner of the WOOD.

The bombardment of objectives has already commenced and continues all night. At 2-55 a.m. heavy bombardment will start.

At 3-35 am bombardment lifts off WOOD and road S.4.d.2.8. - S.11.c.5.8.

The Brigade will assault with 8th DEVONS on the right objective from S.11.a.5.8. to S.10. b.9.9. ie. a distane of 600 Yards joining up with the 2nd GORDONS on their left. The objective of the 2nd GORDONS is the road from S.10.b.9.9. to the Eastern most corner of the WOOD when they will join up with 33rd Division.

At 2-30 am the two assualting battalions will be deployed in assualt formation ready to move forward.

Position of deployment - The Valley in S.10.a. The battalion will assualt each with two companies extended in the leading two lines distance between lines 100 Yards. One company of each battalion in support and one in reserve.

The battalions will advance so as to occupy the road from the South corner of the WOOD as the barrage lifts off it at 3-25 am and will then continue so as to occupy the Brigade objectives as the barrage lifts off it at 3-35 am.

Brigade Reserve.

9th DEVONS in trenches North of BAZENTIN LE GRAND WOOD ready to afford immediate support th either of the assualting battalions os required.

2nd BORDERS in CATERPILLAR WOOD.

Consolidation.

The position when gained will be consolidated at once. The assualting companies willat once dig themselves in on the objective the supporting companies will dig themselves in about the road from South corner of the WOOD to form the second line, subsequently be assisted by two companies 24th MANCHESTER REGT.

Strong points will be established at both ends and in the centre of two lines to be consolidated

Green flares will be lit on objectives at 10 am.

Reports will sent to Brigade headquarters at S.14.b.2.2. West corner of BAZENTIN LE GRAND WOOD.

Sd C.C.FOSS Major.
Brigade Major., 20th Infantry Brigade.

WAR DIARY 8th Devon Reg

APPENDEX VI

REPORT ON OPERATIONS ON JULY20TH 1916.

The objective of he Battalion was to take hold and consolidate the part of the road from S.11.b.3.8. to S.10.b.9.9. Information received from a patrol stated this road was not held by the enemy.

The Battalion went in 20 Officers and 564 Other Ranks Strong.

Assembly March. The Battalion moved from WHITE TRENCH at 9-0 pm on July 19th.
At 10-50 pm the Briga de Major reported to the Commanding Officer that the Companies were in position.
The Battalion took up the following positions:-
The two assaulting companies extended under a bank running from S.10.c.8.9. to S.10.c.5.9.
One Company in Suppoet dug in under a bank running along the road at S.10.c.4.8.
One Company in reserve dug in under a bank along the road at S.9.5.0.
Battalion Headquarters were at S.9.c.9.1.
At 2-30 a m the 2 assaulting Companies deployed and moved forward and extended on a line from S.10.d.4.8. to S.10. b.0.3.,

Attack. A t 3-15 am the 2 assaulting Companies started to move forward and at 3-25 am occupied the road running through S.10.b.4.4.
The leading Platoons then pushed forward to the second road running through S.11.a.2.5.
The two Platoons in support occupied the road at S.10.b.4.4.
During the advance to the second road our artillery caused many casualties.
The enemy were found to be holding the second road and opened a heavy fire from Machine Guns and Rifles.
Our barage was falling short of the road.
The 2 Platoons suffered very heavy casualteis and sterted to dig in about 25 yards from the road. They stayed here about an hour.
Green flares were used freely but our guns did not lift and continued to fire short. Finding they were not in touch on either flank the they then commenced to crawl back in twos to the first roadat S.10.b.4.4. Here they dug in.

Reports. At 4-30 am no information had reached Battalion Headquarters and an Officer was sent forward to report on the situation.
A message reached Battalion Headquarters at 7-0 am timed 5-0 am reporting that we had gained both objectives but that our artillery w ere shelling both roads.
Position of Battalion a t 7-0 am was as follows ;-
The remainder of the two assaulting Companies holding the first road at S.10.b.4.4. in touch with K.O.S.B., on right and 2ND GORDANS on left.
The support and reserve companies in their original position.
At 11-30 am strong posts were being made on the right and the left of the line, held by the Battalion.
At 11-40 am our report was received saying the enemy were shelling the road heavily.
At 12-15 pm orders were issuued to the support company to reinforce the front line. To move in small groups and to keep out of view as much as possible.
Orders were then issued to the reserve company to occupy the line previously held by the support compnay with two platoons.
At 5-0 pm 2 Lewis Guns were sent forward with snipers to deal with enemy snipers or any patrols that might be sent forward.
At 11-0 pm the Battalion was releived by the 14th WARWICKS and marched back to DERNACOURT.
The operation was greatly hindered by the barage falling short and in so doing causing casualties in our ranks and allowing the enemy to man his trenches and keep up a heavy fire. The high standing corn made it hard to see the enemys position, though it conversely afforded good cover from view to our troops consolidating the first road.
The Lewis Guns proved of great value in keeping the enemy down in his trench and also caused him a good many casualties among those

those retiring.
The Battalion lost 8Officers and193 Other Ranks in casualties.

(Ref. MARTINPUICH MAP 1/20,000

In the Field. (Sd) B.C. James. Lieut-Colonel,

2-8-16. Commanding 8th (Service) Battalion Devonshire Regiment .

WAR DIARY 8th Devon Reg.

APPENDIX IV.

REPORT ON RECENT OPERATIONS . 14th. JULY, 1916.

The objective of the battalion was to capture BAZENTIN-LE-GRAND WOOD. The battalion went into action Officers and 637 O'ranks strong.

Assembly March.

The battalion marched from MINDEN POST at 10-25 p.m. Owing to the necessity of crossing trenches by bridges, the battalion moved in single file. Several obatacles, wire and open trenches, were encount-ered, which greatly delayed troops. Only one casualty occurred before the Companies were deployed which was caused by a fuse-cap from our own guns. At 2-25 a.m. Companies reported that they were in position. The battalion then deployed as follows :-

Two companies formed the assaulting line in column on half companies, with the two leading platoons of each extended at 3 paces, the remaining 2 platoons of each in a 2nd line 100 yards in rear, similarly extended. One company in support in small column formation 150 yards in rear again.

One Company in battalion reserve close to MARLBORO WOOD. The left of the leading company was in touch with the 2nd. BORDER REGT at S.20.b.1.9.; the right on a track at S.20.b.8.8. in touch with 3rd. DIVISION (WEST YORKS). This deployment was completed by 2-25 a.m. The battalion then commenced to crawl forward. Owing to the thick wire on WEST side of MARLBORO TRENCH, a good many of the BORDER REGT became mixed with the battalion during the movement.. During this time left company suffered a certain amount of casualties near MARLBORO TRENCH. Included in them were the bombing section under orders to clear MARLBORO TRENCH. Orders were then issued to the battalion bombing Officer to clear MarlBORO TRENCH with the battalion Bombers. During the intense bombardment the leading line crept further forward and at ZERO hour were within 25 yards of the enemy's line.

Attack.

Battalion Head Quarters were in Marlboro Trench at S.20.d.5.9.

At 3-26 a.m. the battalion entered enemy's line.

Right Company.

The right company met verym little resistance in front line. They cleared it easily and bombed a few dug-outs. They remained in it for 10 minutes and reached the second line at 3-45 a.m. which appeared to be upheld.

Two strong posts were then made at S. 15. a. 40. 65.and S. 15. a.l. 2. Patrols were also pushed forward to the NORTH EAST part of the WOOD and captured and sent back 60 prisoners. The post in NORTH EAST end of wood accounted for a good many of the enemy retiring from BAZENTIN LE GRAND village with Lewis Machine Gun fire. Both posts were heavily shelled during the morning causing many casualties. The Company maintained touch with and was given excellen support by troops on right.

Left Company.

Owing to the accuracy of the barrage, the right of the company entered the enemy line with little difficulty. On the left i.e. the WEST face of the SNOUT, the barrage did not lift properly till 3-30 and allowed some of enemy to man trenches and get an automatic rifle into action which caused casualties. This party was soon accounted for by Bombers. Dug outs were bombed as the enemy in several cases would not surrender and fired from the dug outs.

One bomber and a Lewis gun team co-operated with great success. A long tunnel dug out contained ma ny of the enemy. The bomber threw in at one entrance, while the lewis gun accounted for the enemy attempting to retire from the far entrance.

Very little remained of the trench which formedmthe second objective The company finally advanced to the NORTH ed ge of WOOD and dug in. At 4-10 am a report wa s sent to Bde Hd Qrs that this company had reached its final objective. This company only took a very few prisoners.

Support Company. At ZERO hour this Company was 450 Yards from the SNOUT. At 3-45 am it advanced and took up a position in the SNOUT and trenches to the right of it. During this advance it suffered a certain ammount of casualties and a light barrage was put on these trenches by the enemy.
It remained here a few minutes and then advanced to the part of CIRCUS TRENCH in the west portion of BAZENTIN LE GRAND WOOD where their appeared to be none of our Troops. It then advanced according to the barrage time table, and lined the bank facing NORTH WEST looking on to BAZENTIN LE PETIT VILLAGE. It remained here it cleared the enemy of that part of the wood, taking a few prisoners in doing so.
It suffered a certain amount of casualties here. Itnthen advanced to final objective.

Reserve Company. 1 platoon advanced to support the supporting company on the left at 4-0 pm and lost heavily while advancing. Remaining 3 platoons were kept in reserve.
At 2-0 pm 2 platoons were sent up to the SOUTH end of BAZENTIN LE GRAND WOOD. Owing to heavy casualties sustained by the company holding this line,1 platoon and 2 Lewis Guns were kept in reserve the whole time in TRENCH near MALBOROUGH WOOD.

Reports. At 5-45 am a report was sent to Brigade saying the Battalion was holding all BAZENTIN LE GRAND WOOD and was consolidating 2nd and 3rd objectives.
at 6-25 a report was sent that the Battalion held and was consolidating the final objectives.
Between 4-30 am and 5-30 am a heavy barrage was put n the WOOD.

Subsequent dispositions. Between 10 and 11-0 a m enemy heavily bombarded the WOOD and made a counter attack which was repulsed. During this time an urgent request for support came from the CEMETERY. The O.C. Support Company in position on the left, sent forward an Officer and a platoon. It was reported that this party gave valuable assistance during the enemys counter attack.
The position of the Battalion in the afternoon was-
3 Companies less 1 small party dug in from S.14.b.5.6. to S.14. b.8.8. 1 Comapny dug in 100 yards in rear in Support. A small detached partyin strong post at S.15.a.4.7. with the 20th Machine Gun Company.
The Battalion remained in this position till 1-0 pm on July 15th when it was withdrawn, leaving 1 platoon in Strong post at NORTH Corner of BAZENTIN LE GRAND WOOD.
The Battalion suffered 7 Officers casualties and 164 in O'Ranks.
One Lewis gun was damaged, none were lost.

The Battalion captured an 8" Howitzer with ammunition, some Trench Morters,an d Automatic Rifle and a great many rifles and much ammunition and equipment.

In the Field. (Sd) B.C. James. Lieut-Colonel,

2-8-1916. Commanding 8th (Service) Battalion Devonshire Regiment.

INSTRUCTIONS FOR FORTHCOMING OPERATIONS.
by
Major B.C. JAMES.
Commanding, 8th (Ser) Bn Devonshire Regiment. No 2.

Map Refeerence FRICOURT 1/5,000.
Brigade Trench Map 1/5,000.

No 1. Instructions RE-BOMBARDMENT.

(A). If any point or part of the enemys lines holds up our infantry advance to such an extent that it is necessary to bombard again that portion of the enemy defence, application for re-bombardment must be made to Brigade H.Q., and the sanction of of the G.O.C. Division obtained. This application will only be entertained in most urgent necessity, owing to the general disarrangement caused thereby.

(B). The Divisional Commander will fix the zero hour at which the Bombardment will commence. The normal re-bombardment will last 30 minutes, of which the last 5 minutes will be intense. The Bombardment will lift at 0'30, at which hour the infantry will assault.

This is to be thoroughly understood by all ranks, that the only orders regarding re-bombardment that will be issued, will be a message naming the hour fixed for zero (i.e. the hour at which the re-bombardment will commance)

(C). In the event of it being found impossible by the Artillery to begin the re-bombardment at the hour fixed as zero, either the re-bombardment will begin as early as possible after the zero hour, and cease 30 minutes after zero, the last 5 minutes being intensive, or a fresh zero hour will be fixed.

No 2. Preliminary Moves.

On the day previous to the Assault, one company of each of the three assaulting battalions will take over the areas allotted to them, and the battalion of the 17th Division holding the line will be withdrawn prior to the remainder of the Brigade moving up.

Orders a nd march tables for these moves will be issued sepperately.

No 3. Cutting of our own Wire.

Our wire will be cut during the bombardment on the night before the assembly march, Each battalion will detail parties to cut the whole of the wire in their areas. The work should be thoroughly completed that night.

O.C. Companies on again going into the trenches will satisfy themselves that the work has been thoroughly done, and if not complete will complete it immediately it is dark and will report completion to Battalion Head Quarters.

No 4. Method of Assault.

The assault will be carried out steadily behind the Artillery Barrage. At the hour named for the barrage to lift, the leading line will be as close to the hostile position as possible, and on the barrage lifting will at once move forward steadily keeping touch, and only halt and lie down when next compelled to do so by awaiting the lift of the artillery barrage.

The leading line will be strong enough for the purpose required, and will move straight forward to the final objective of the Brigade.

Succeeding lines will follow at a distance of not less than one hundred yards, and not more than one hundred and fifty yards - will halt when the line in front of them halts, and will reinforce only when the line in front requires reinforcements to carry out its task, or to cover the whole frontage allotted as it increases in length

The lines must not be allowed to become prematurely merged into one another.

One Company.........

One Company will be kept in Battalion Reserve, moving as the last line.

The assaulting Battalions on arrival at their final objective, will consolidate it. It is not intended to consolidate each line as captured.

Should some part of the assaulting lines be held up, the remainder will render them the best assistance by advancing to their final objective. The flanks so exposed must however be specially guarded until these parts which have been held up have come into the line.

The position of leading line of assaulting troops will be denoted by smoke candles.

Battalions will move in immediate touch with each other, with the exception that there will be a gap, in the valley through which the road and railway runs, between 2nd GORDON HIGHLANDERS and 9th DEVON REGIMENT.

This gap will be closed on reaching SHRINE ALLEY by the O.C. 9th DEVON REGIMENT, extending to his right until close touch is gained.

2nd GORDON HIGHLANDERS will advance in touch with left of 1st SOUTH STAFFORDSHIRE REGIMENT of 91st INFANTRY BRIGADE.

No 5. Mopping up parties.

Special parties will be detailed by each battalion to "mop up" each hostile trench passed over. This party will consist in each case of a bombing section with an infantry section attached. It is imperative that immediately the barrage lifts these parties commence work so that no machine guns or snipers are allowed to get into action.

No other men are to be allowed to enter or remain in the hostile trenches passed over. The "mopping up" parties will work inwards until touch is gained with the next "mopping up" parties, so as to ensure that no part of the trench is left unsearched.

No 6. Action of Reserve Battalion.

At the zero hour the 8th Devon Regt will commence to move as follows:-

"B" Coy via 69 STREET to reserve Trench WEST of 69 STREET.
"D" Coy via 68 STREET to reserve Trench between 68 and 69 STREETS.
"C" Coy, via SUFFOLK AVENUE and 67 SUPPORT to QUEENS ROAD.
"A" Coy, via SUFFOLK AVENUE to 67 SUPPORT.

Head Quarters 8th DEVON REGT will be at Junction of RESERVE TRENCH and 69 STREET.

Another Battalion will at zero hour move up LUCKNOW AVENUE from LUCKNOW REDOUBT to the forming up trenches vacated by the 8th DEVONS

No 7. Consolidations of positions captured.

Immediately the objective is reached, the infantry will commence to consolidate the position. In addition to the ordinary consolidation to be carried out, the following points will be at once established.

2nd GORDON HIGHLANDERS.
F.5.c.35.90.
F.5.c.0.7.
F.4.d.80.35.i.e. Point at which BUNNY TRENCH crosses the sunken road.

9th DEVON REGT.
Junction of ORCHARD TRENCH and ORCHARD ALLEY.
Junction of ROSE TRENCH and ORCHARD ALLEY.
Point at which ORCHARD ALLEY crosses SUNKEN ROAD.
Junction of APPLE and ORCHARD ALLEYS.

2nd Border Regt.
TRENCH Junction F.10.a.51.11.
Junction of BOIS FRANCAIS SUPPORT and APPLE ALLEY
JUNCTION of BOIS FRANCAIS TRENCH and APPLE ALLEY.

In addition, the 95th FIELD COY R.E. less One Section, and One Company Divisional Pioneer Battalion, will move forward subsequently under orders from Divisional Hd Qrs to place MAMETZ VILLAGE in a state of defence.

O.C. Battalions will arrange to send up any material that they may require for making the strong points allotted to them. In the first instance, pick and shovel only will be required.

In each strong point there will be at least one Lewis Gun.

No 8. Artillery Bombardment.

TIME	AREAS TO BE BOMBARDED.
0'30 - 0'0	The whole area to be attacked by the two Divisions.
0'0 - 0'15.	Area within line running from F.4.b.2.7. along S.E. edge of FRICOURT WOOD to F.3.d.9.9. - thence along curved road to F.3.b.7.2. - North along edge of wood to F.3.b.9.8. - thence in a straight line to re-entrant at X.28.c.98.15. - thence to F.4.b.2.7.
0'15 - 1'45.	Area with line running from F.4.b.2.7. along S.E. edge of FRICOURT WOOD to F.4.a.20.05 - direct to F.3.b.9.6. along trench to road at F.4.a.02.80 - thence East to re-entrant at X.28.c.98.15, - thence to point F.4.b.2.7,

The infantry and machine guns of the brigade will be ready to co-operate and take advantage of any targets presenting themselves during this bombardment.

No 9. Concluding Operation.

When the 22nd Infantry Brigade has captured and occupied ORCHARD TRENCH NORTH and the ORCHARD, where it will be in touch with the 50th Infantry Brigade on the left occupying WILLOW TRENCH, the line ORCHARD TRENCH NORTH - ORCHARD will be taken over and strongly consolidated by a Battalion of the 20th INFANTRY BRIGADE to be named at the time - 8th DEVON REGIMENT if available.

For this consolidation, one section 95th FIELD COY R.E. will be employed.

The ORCHARD will be made into a strong point.

The position of the Brigade will then be -

2nd GORDON HIGHLANDERS	holding and consolidating their original objective, with a strong point in BUNNY WOOD.
A Second Battalion -	prolonging the line via ORCHARD TRENCH NORTH and the ORCHARD to the WILLOW AVENUE STREAM near the ORCHARD where it will be in immediate touch with 50th Infantry Brigade prolonging the line along WILLOW TRENCH through FRICOURT WOOD. The right of the 2nd GORDONS will be in touch with a Battalion of the 91st Infantry Brigade. (SOUTH STAFFORD REGIMENT).

The whole will then form a second line behind the objective assigned to the XV CORPS for the first days operations, with a line of strong supporting points between the first and second lines.

Two Battalions of the Brigade will be withdrawn to form a Brigade reserve in trenches, to be named at the time.

No 10. SMOKE ATTACK.

Provided the wind is favourable, a smoke attack will be made on the portion of the front which is not being attacked by infantry, with the object of:-

(1) Preventing the enemy in the isolated area from observing the progress on either flank, or from impeding our infantry advance.

(2). Drawing the attention of the enemy artillery away from the points in our front line from which our Infantry will issue.

The attack will be made from the junction of trenches F.9.1. and F.9.2. to the left flank of the Division. The smoke must however be arranged so that no smoke drifts east of the line ORCHARD ALLEY, or NORTH of the line joining FRICOURT CHURCH and the N.E. corner of FRICOURT WOOD.

This attack will be made on the day of the assault at five minutes before zero, and will last one hour.

No 11GAS

On the day of assault provided the wind is favourable whiffs of Gas will be turned on at 15 minutes XXXXXXXX before zero, from the portions of the front line lying between the junction of the TRENCHES F.9.1. and F.9.2. and the TAMBOUR.

No whiffs will be discharged after Five minutes before zero, nor will gas be discharged from other portions of the front.

No 1-2.FLARES.

Two flares will be carried by every Cou Officer and N.C.O. The remainder will be carried one per man as far as the issue will allow.

No 13.Periscopes.

Periscopes will be carried by all Coy Officers and N.C.O's as far as the supply will admit.

No 14.Water6

During the march to the assembly trenches the water in water bottles will not be drunk under any circumstances.

No 15.Reports.

Supply of Water and Food.

Every man will carry an Iron Ration, and every animal an extra days ration of oats to be counted as an Iron Ration.

It must be impressed on all ranks that the Iron Ration is NOT to be eaten, except on the order of a Commanding Officer.

If Iron Rations are consumed, the fact must be reported to Brigade Head Quarters immediately.

On the night before the assault, and on each subsequent night rations for consumption will be issued to the men, instead of being kept in the cookers.

This ration will be in addition to the Iron Ration.

Each man will also be given a sandwich, under battalion arrangements, to be eaten shortly before the assault, for which purpose 1/4 lb bread per man will be issued in addition to the normal ration.

Each Battalion is allotted 100 Petrol tins, and will be stored in the left store with the 2nd BORDER REGIMENT.

Battalions will send back for their tins as circumstances permit after reaching their objectives.

Each Unit will send guides to the BRAY - MAMETZ ROAD at the WESTERN point of the GREAT BEAR, to be there by 10-30 p.m. and await the arrival of the Transport, which will be conducted as far as circumstances permit where ration parties must be arranged.

Replacement of Ordnance.

The quick replacement of lost or damaged ordnance is of great importance, especially in the case of Lewis Guns or Vickers.

Units will at once report any such loss or damage to Brigade Hd Qrs whereupon the Staff Captain will telegraph to the D.A.D.O.S., repeating the message to Divisional Head Quarters.

Prisoners of War.

Three Brigade Prisoner Collecting Stations will be formed at:-

CITADEL in charge of Officer 2nd Border Regiment.
LUDGATE CIRCUS - do - 9th Devon Regiment.
MINDEN POST - do - 2nd Gordon Highlanders.

Prisoners captured will be sent back to these Officers with as small an escort as possible, and receipt obtained for prisoners handed over.

AMENDMENT.

In para 4 of 20th Brigade Instructions for forthcoming Operations, No 1, the DOWN TRENCHES for the 2nd BORDER REGIMENT should read "75 and 76 STREET and OLD KENT ROAD".

SECRET

Copy No......

20th INFANTRY BRIGADE PROVISIONAL ORDER.

Ref:Maps FRICOURT 1/5,000.
Brigade Trench Map 1/5,000.

1. The Brigade will take a principal part in an attack on the German Trenches.

OBJECTIVE OF BRIGADE. 2. The objective of the Brigade is the line from bend in BUNNEY TRENCH,F.5.c.35.90. (road inclusive) along BUNNEY TRENCH, to M in BM 90.0. - thence along sunken road to junction of ORCHARD TRENCH NORTH with ORCHARD ALLEY - ORCHARD ALLEY to junction with APPLE ALLEY then along APPLE ALLEY to the small salient in our present line at F.10.c.7.4.

On arrival at this line patrols will be sent forward to the ORCHARD and BUNNY WOOD and to the Eastern Corner of FRICOURT WOOD. The altter together with the trench running from the edge of FRICOURT WOOD across RAILWAY ALLEY to BOTTOM WOOD will be occupied by one Company of the right Battalion so as to protect the left of the 91st Infantry Brigade on our right, and also to assist the advance of the right of the 21st Division on our left.

OBJECTIVES OF OTHER UNITS. 3. The objectives of the 91st Infantry Brigade on the immediate right of this Brigade is:-

(i) To capture the line from point where the track from MAMETZ crosses FRITZ TRENCH in F.6.a. along FRITZ TRENCH to its junction with BRIGHT ALLEY (F.5.b.35.80) thence along BRIGHT ALLEY - then along BUNNY TRENCH to bend F.5.c.35.90.

(ii) To capture the whole of FRITZ TRENCH as far as WILLOW AVENUE STREAM and a line running along the Southern edge of BOTTOM WOOD to point 2392.

The 1st objective for the 21st Division is a line Point 2392 - RAILWAY COPSE - THE POODLES - ROUND WOOD. The right flank of this Division have orders to advance and capture FRICOURT FARM, after which the advance will be continued along RAILWAY ALLEY to their 1st objective.

The capture of FRICOURT VILLAGE and FRICOURT WOOD will be treated as a separate operation, and further orders will be issued regarding it.

BOMBARDMENT. 4. A very heavy bombardment of the hostile trenches by guns and mortars of all calibres will take place for "X" days previous to the assault.

PRELIMINARY MOVES. 5. The Brigade will be withdrawn previous to the bombardment and the line will be held by another Brigade. The troops taking part in the assault will be moved up to their forming up trenches on the night previous to the assault.

FORMING UP POSITIONS. 6. The 2nd Gordon Highlanders will move up by LUCKNOW and SUFFOLK AVENUES and will form up in

Fire trenches, F.11.4. F.11.5.
STAFORD STREET North. LONDON ROAD.
QUEENS ROAD and 67 Support.
Battalion H.Q. junction of 66 STREET and 67 Support.

The boundary on the right is the present boundary of B.2.Subsector. The boundary on the left is the Railway.

The 9th Devon Regiment moving in rear of 2nd Gordon Highlanders to SUFFOLK AVENUE and thence via 68 and 69 Streets will form up in

Fire trenches F.11.7. F.11.8.
Reserve trench from DALE STREET to 70 STREET.
DUKE STREET.
Battalion H.Q. at junction of 69 STREET with RESERVE TRENCH.

FORMING UP POSITIONS. (continued)

The 2nd Border Regiment moving via WELLINGTON AVENUE - ESSEX AVENUE - 70 and 71 STREETS will form up in
Fire trenches F.10.1. F.10.2.
Support line to F.10.1.F.10.2.
Reserve Trench 70 STREET to ALBERT STREET.
Battalion H.Q. junction of 71 STREET and SUPPORT LINE.

The 8th Devon Regiment moving in rear of 2nd Border Regiment will form up in
LORD STREET.
BOLB STREET.
SUFFOLK AVENUE.
PERONNE AVENUE.

95th Field Company and Pioneers moving in rear of all Infantry.
Work No 2. INTERMEDIATE LINE.
N.B. Pioneers will consist of a detachment from a Divisional Pioneer Battalion.

PREPARING OUR WIRE.

7. Gaps in our wire will be cut under arrangements to be made later. This will be done on the night prior to the assaulting troops moving into the trenches.

COMPOSITION OF ASSAULTING COLUMNS.

8. The assault will be carried out by three Battalions, 2nd Gordon Highlanders on the right, 9th Devon Regiment in the centre, and 2nd Border Regiment on the left; 8th Devon Regiment, 95th Field Company R.E. and detachment Pioneers will be in Brigade Reserve.

METHOD OF ASSAULT.

9. Each battalion will advance in four successive lines of four platoons each. The objective of the first line will be:-

DANUBE and MAMETZ Support trenches.

The objective of the second line will be:-
CEMETERY Trench - DANTZIG ALLEY South of its junction with CEMETERY Trench - SHRINE ALLEY - ~~KEI~~ KIEL LANE.

The objective of the third line will be the final objective of the Brigade.

The fourth line will be held in reserve at the disposal of the Battalion Commander.

The second line will halt a few moments at the objective of the first line to gain breath and to allow for the raising of the Artillery, trench mortars,and machine gun barrage. It will then go on carrying the first line with it.
A similar procedure will be followed by the third line halting at the second line, and carrying the first and second lines on with it.

With the third and fourth lines will be complete bombing sections ready to deal with the protection of flanks and blocking of trenches leading into the captured objective.

With the third line will also move parties detailed to deal with shelters and prisoners in each line of trenches passed over.

The assaulting lines will advance direct on to their objectives and consolidate them. It is not intended to consolidate each line as captured.

Should some parts of the assaulting lines be held up, the remainder will render them the best assistance by advancing to their final objective. The flanks so exposed must however be specially guarded until those parts which have been held up have come into line. The position of assaulting troops will be denoted by smoke candles.

BOUNDARIES BETWEEN ASSAULTING BATTALIONS.

10. The boundaries between assaulting battalions are as under;- each of the assaulting battalions being responsible for the capture and clearing of all trenches within its boundaries

Special bombing parties must be told off to advance on the flanks of each line of the assaulting battalions, and will be allotted definite tasks of working outwards until touch is gained with the bombers of the battalion on the flank.

Dividing line between Left Battalion, 91st Infantry Brigade and 2nd Gordon Highlanders.

From our front trenches at the junction of F.11.3. and F.11.4. a straight line to the road junction in MAMETZ immediately South of the Church - thence along the road running Northwards past the Church to the Northern outskirts of the village (road inclusive to 2nd Gordon Highlanders) - thence to the Eastern edge of BUNNY WOOD - thence to Point 2392 on the Southern edge of BOTTOM WOOD and along the railway to point where it crosses the road on the Eastern edge of BOTTOM WOOD.

Between 2nd Gordon Highlanders and 9th Devon Regiment.

From our front line at junction of F.11.5. and F.11.6. along the railway as far as HALT at point at which SHRINE ALLEY cuts the railway (Railway to 2nd Gordon Highlanders) thence to junction of CEMETERY TRENCH and DANTZIG ALLEY. (DANTZIG ALLEY to 9th Devon Regiment) - thence along DANTZIG ALLEY to junction in the ORCHARD TRENCH SOUTH (both to 9th Devon Regiment)- thence to road at B in BM.

Between ~~2nd Border~~ 9th Devon Regiment and 2nd Border Regiment.

From our front line at junction of F.11.5. and F.10.1. - a straight line to the bifurcation of SWAG LANE - along SWAG LANE (SWAG LANE inclusive to 2nd Border Regiment) - thence a straight line from junction of SWAG LANE and TIRPITZ TRENCH to junction of APPLE and ORCHARD ALLEYS.

STRONG POINTS TO BE ESTABLISHED.

11. In addition to consolidating the whole of the Brigade objective, the assaulting battalions will arrange to establish strong points at:-

2nd Gordon Highlanders.

~~East end of FRICOURT WOOD.~~ Cancelled by I.F.C No 2
F.5.c.35.90.
F.5.c.0.7.
Point at which BUNNY TRENCH crosses SUNKEN Road (F.4.d.80.35)

9th Devon Regiment.

Junction of ORCHARD TRENCH North and ORCHARD ALLEY.
Junction of ROSE TRENCH and ORCHARD ALLEY.
Point at which ORCHARD ALLEY crosses SUNKEN Road (F.10.a.95.90)
Junction of APPLE and ORCHARD ALLEYS.

2nd Border Regiment.

Trench junction F.10.a.51.11.
Junction of BOIS FRANCAIS SUPPORT and APPLE ALLEY.
Junction of BOIS FRANCAIS TRENCH and APPLE ALLEY.

Working parties of R.E. and Pioneers will be sent forward as soon as ~~possible~~ practicable to assist in the consolidation ~~of these strong points~~ and wiring of these points but the consolidation of these strong points must be commenced at once, after that portion of the Brigade objective in which they lie, is in our hands. At least one Lewis Gun is to be in each strong point.

ACTION OF BRIGADE RESERVE.

12. The 8th Devon Regiment will not advance immediately in rear of assaulting battalions but will remain in their forming up trenches.

O.C. 8th Devon Regiment will report at Brigade H.Qrs as soon as his battalion has arrived in its forming up trenches, and will remain there to receive the orders as to the future movements of his battalion from the Brigadier.

Officer Commanding 95th Field Company R.E. will also report personally at Brigade H.Qrs as soon as his Company and attached Pioneers are in their forming up trenches. He will have parties detailed in readiness to proceed to work as described in para 11 above. These parties will not move forward until orders to that effect are issued by the Brigadier.

MACHINE GUN COMPANY.

13. 10 guns of this Company will cover the advance from strong shell proof emplacements which have been specially sited.

To cover 2nd Gordon Highlanders.
- 2 Emplacements in CAFTET WOOD.
- 2 do in DALE STREET.
- 2 do in RESERVE TRENCH.

To cover 9th Devon Regiment and 2nd Border Regiment.
- 2 Emplacements in CROSS STREET.
- 1 do in OLDHAM STREET.
- 1 do in OXFORD STREET.

To sweep up WILLOW AVENUE STREAM
- 4 Emplacements below BONTE REDOUBT (1 Section 22nd Infantry Brigade M.G.Coy)

The remaining six guns will be held in Reserve in WELLINGTON REDOUBT ready to move up to the strong points in the captured line. Guns used to cover the attack will also be moved up.

TRENCH MORTAR BATTERIES.

14. Special instructions and detailed programme for Trench Mortars will be issued ~~shortly~~ separately.

TIME OF ASSAULT.

15. The exact hour at which the assault will take place will be arranged by higher authority.

ARTILLERY PROGRAMME.

16. The Artillery programme will be notified later. Arrangements will be made for senior officers of the assaulting battalions to watch the effect of the wire cutting operations opposite the front their battalions will assault.

EQUIPMENT.

17.(a) Greatcoats and spare kits will be left in the man's pack, which will be clearly marked and stacked in a store under Divisional arrangements which will be notified later.

(b) Every man, with the exception of certain specialists will carry:-
- (i) Rifle and equipment less pack.
- (ii) Two bandoliers of S.A.A. in addition to ammunition carried in his equipment (220 rounds in all
- (iii) Haversack on back containing two tins of meat and 8 hard biscuits, and canteen packed with emergency grocery ration.
- (iv) Waterproof cape or mackintosh sheet, with jersey rolled inside, fixed on to waist belt, in the small of the back by supporting straps from the pack.
- (v) 3 sandbags carried under the flap of the haversack.
- (vi) 2 Mills grenades carried in lower jacket pockets.
- (vii) 2 Smoke helmets.

EQUIPMENT. (continued).

(c) Bombers will be equipped as follows:-

	Mills.	Rifle Grenades.	Smoke Grenades.	S.A.A
N.C.O.	6	4	2	50
2 Bayonet men.	12	-	4	50
2 Leading bombers	24.	-	4	50.
2 Reserve Bombers	24	-	4	50
2 spade men.	8	20	-	50

(d) Carriers will be equipped as in (b) with the exception of two bandoliers.

SPECIAL EQUIPMENT.

18. All battalions will be issued with -
100 wire cutters to be carried on the man.
250 shovels do
100 picks do
Smoke candles.

For distribution among bombing sections in addition to hand grenades
384 Rifle grenades.
96 smoke bombs.

Assaulting battalions will also be issued with -
100 hedging gloves to be carried on the man.
100 billhooks do

S.A.A. and VERY LIGHTS.

19.(a) Advanced stores of S.A.A. will be available for battalions as under. Each store will contain

S.A.A. 94,000 rounds for rifles.
5,000 rounds for Lewis Guns.
VERY LIGHTS. 135 rounds 1 inch.
70 rounds 1½ inch.

No 1. STAFFORD ROAD North.
No 2. Loop near junction of RESERVE TRENCH and 70 STREET.
No 3. ALBERT STREET near foot of 73 STREET.

(b) Brigade Ammunition Store junction LUDGATE CIRCUS and WELLINGTON AVENUE, containing

S.A.A. 280,000 rounds for rifles.
8,000 rounds for Lewis Guns.
32,000 rounds for Vickers Guns.
VERY LIGHTS. 500 rounds 1 inch.
250 rounds 1½ inch.

GRENADES.

20.(a) Grenade stores will be formed at the following points:-

	No 5 Mills.
No 1. Right Battalion. Junction of LONDON ROAD and 66 STREET.	1,000.
No 2. Centre Battalion. Junction of F.11.6 -F.11.7.	2,000.
No 3. Left Battalion. 71 STREET junction with Support line.	1,000.
No 4. Reserve Store. Company H.Q. in 76 STREET.	2,000.
No 5. Advanced Brigade Store. LUDGATE CIRCUS.	10,000.

(b) Each grenade section of 1 N.C.O. and 8 men will carry
74 Mills.
24 Rifle Grenades.
14 Smoke Grenades.

(c) A separate memorandum has already been issued (20/BM/471 of 19th April, 1916) dealing with the whole question of the supply and organization of bombing sections during an attack.

<u>R.E.STORES.</u> 21.(a) Four dumps of R.E.Stores will be formed at the following points -

67 Support.
70 STREET. 2 dumps.
TRAFALGAR SQUARE.

which will each contain the following stores -

2,000 sandbags in bundles of 25 for slinging.
125 shovels.
90 picks.
40 French wire coils with staples.
25 skiens of 50 yards each barbed wire.
5 mauls.
150 - 4 ft pickets (wood).

(b) A Brigade Dump near LUDGATE CIRCUS containing

8,000 sandbags.
500 shovels.
240 picks.
20 crowbars.
50 wire cutters.
90 coils French wire with staples.
50 skiens of 50 yards each barbed wire.
30 mauls.
30 billhooks.
400 pickets (wood)
50 pairs hedging gloves.

(c) O.C. 95th Field Company R.E. will draw 1,000 ladders and 1,000 bridges, and arrange to place them in the trenches at suitable points. The ladders will be put in position on the night previous to the assault.

<u>BADGES.</u> 22. (a) Every Officer and man in the Brigade will wear a distinguishing mark, to be worn on the back and to be provided under Divisional arrangements.

(b) Special distinguishing badges will be worn as follows:-

(i) For men carrying wirecutters = A white band 2" wide on right forearm

(ii) For all men employed as "carriers" = A red patch, 2" deep on right shoulder strap.

(iii) For Bombers (who are not badge men) = A white grenade 2½" in length on right sleeve just below the shoulder.

<u>LEWIS GUNS.</u> 23. Lewis Gun Detachments will move up the captured communication trenches preceded by bombing sections.

<u>WATER.</u> 24. 100 petrol tins, full of water, will be stored near each S.A.A. Store.

<u>RATIONS.</u> 25. 2,300 tins of preserved meat will be stored near each S.A.A. Store.

N.B. As soon as these stores are in position, O.C. Battalion holding the Subsector will place guards over them.

MEDICAL. 26. Regimental Aid Posts will be established at
79 Support. Right Battalion.
WELLINGTON REDOUBT. Centre and Left Battalions.

COMMUNICATION. 27. All Battalions will send to Brigade H.Qrs on the day previous to the assault, 6 runners in addition to the present 2. These men will work in pairs. Officer Commanding 95th Field Company R.E. will also send 2 men.

Telephone Signalling Stations will be established in the Battalion H.Qrs. Officer Commanding Battalions will arrange that at least two light wires are run out from their battle H.Qrs to their positions in the captured trenches.

Further instructions regarding pigeons and signalling to the Aerial Contact Squadron will be issued.

POLICE and ESCORTS. CIVILIANS. 28. Battle police will be arranged by the A.P.M.. Prisoners will be sent back under the smallest possible escort (1 man to 10 prisoners is ample) to Prisoners of War Collecting Station. Any civilians found in MAMETZ should be evacuated at once.

MISCELLANEOUS. 29. (a) MAPS. All papers, official or private, are to be destroyed, or left behind before the advance.

The following maps only will be taken forward, and these are not to be marked in any way except for denoting the names of German trenches.

MEAULTE, 1/10,000, Edition 2b.
FRICOURT, 1/5,000.

All messages and reports will refer to one or other of these maps.

(b) No man is to fall out to bring back wounded.

(c) Grenades are not to be thrown indiscriminately.

(d) Only 20 officers are to accompany a battalion in the assault, the remainder are to remain with 1st line transport until required.

BRIGADE H.QRS. 30. Brigade Headquarters will be in ESSEX AVENUE.

20th Brigade.

7th Division.

8th BATTALION

DEVONSHIRE REGIMENT.

AUGUST 1 9 1 6.

Instructions regarding War Diaries and Intelligence Summaries are contained in F. S. Regs., Part II. and the Staff Manual respectively. Title pages will be prepared in manuscript.

WAR DIARY
or
~~INTELLIGENCE SUMMARY.~~
(Erase heading not required.)

Army Form C. 2118.

8th Devon Reg

Vol XI

Place	Date	Hour	Summary of Events and Information	Remarks and references to Appendices
	Aug.		8th Devon Regt August 1916	
AILLY-SUR-SOMME	1/8/16	7.30am	Battalion training. Route march AILLY-FERRIERES-SAVEUSE-AILLY. Short-time: full marching order. Very hot.	
			Strength of battalion 21 officers; 980 O.R. 5 officers (2nd Lts) reported for duty from 11th Devons.	
— — —	2/8/16	2.30pm	Regimental Sports. Very good entries from other units of the Division. Most successful day. Very hot & fine.	
— — —	3/8/16	8 am	Battalion training. Musketry on BREILLY & PICQUIGNY ranges. Continued firing Table A. Shooting moderate.	
— — —	4/8/16	10 am	The Bn, with the other units of 20th Inf Bde, was inspected at PICQUIGNY by Gen Sir Henry Rawlinson G.O.C. IV Army.	
			This General said the 7th Div had been in nearly every fight since it came out, has always done what was expected of it & had a finer fighting record than any other. He congratulated the Bde & thanked them for the work they had done in the last 3 actions which he said was magnificent.	
		2 pm	Brigade ~~H~~ Gymkhana at PICQUIGNY. Bat entered water cart (3rd) Limber driving (1st Pte BAKER) mtd. officers jumping team M.I. race. 4 horses in open jumping. Tug of war team (beaten by 2nd Gordons in final). Very successful day.	
— — —	5/8/16	7.30am	Battalion training. Route march AILLY-ST SAVEUR-cross Rds 1 mile N.E. of VAUX-FREMONT-ST VAST-AILLY (12 miles)	
— — —	6/8/16	10 am	Divine Service.	
— — —	7/8/16	8 am	Battalion training. Musketry BREILLY range. Fired Practices 1 & 2 of Table A with bayonet fixed. Shooting better.	
	8/8/16	6.30am	Battalion training. Physical, Company & Battalion drill. Outposts.	
			Brig Gen H. C. Green DSO (60th Rifles) taken over command of 20th Bde, vice Brig Gen Deverell promoted (to 3rd Div)	
	9/8/16	8 am	Battalion training. Musketry on PICQUIGNY range. 2 practices. Rapid with bayonet fixed. Shooting fair	

T2134. Wt. W708—776. 500000. 4/15. Sir J. C. & S.

Instructions regarding War Diaries and Intelligence Summaries are contained in F. S. Regs., Part II. and the Staff Manual respectively. Title pages will be prepared in manuscript.

WAR DIARY
or
~~INTELLIGENCE SUMMARY.~~
(Erase heading not required.)

Army Form C. 2118.

8th Devon Reg

Place	Date	Hour	Summary of Events and Information	Remarks and references to Appendices
	August 1916			
AILLY SUR SOMME	10/8/16	8 am	Battalion training. Musketry on BREILLY Range. Rapid practices. Shooting good.	
— —	11/8/16	9.30 am	Battalion training. Coys practising advancing under barrage, digging & pushing out strong posts.	
— —	12/8/16	3.40 am	Bn left AILLY & marched to VIGNACOURT. Entrained at 9.15 am. Left at 9.30 am. Route CANAPLES-	
BUIRE-SUR-ANCRE		3.30 pm	FLEXICOURT - HANGEST - AILLY - AMIENS - MERICOURT. arrived 2.30 pm. Marched to billets at BUIRE.	
— —	13/8/16	11 am	Brigade paraded for Divine service. 1 Officer & 65 O.R. on detachment at Corps Cage. VIVIER MILL.	
— —	14/8/16	9 am	Battalion training. Kit inspection & drill.	
— —	15/8/16	9 am	Battalion training. Extended order drill & out posts.	
— —	16/8/16	8 am	Battalion training. Drill & wiring. Night operations at 9.30 pm. Bat in the attack.	
— —	17/8/16	9 am	Bat. training. Route march. BUIRE - TREUX - SAILLY-LE-SEC - VAUX - MERICOURT - BUIRE.	
— —	18/8/16	7 am	Bat training. Physical drill. Bayonet fighting. Bat in attack advancing under barrage.	
— —		3 pm	20th Bde Gymkhana. 3 hurdle & 3 flat races. The C.O. rode 1 winner.	
— —	19/8/16	7 am	Physical drill. Bayonet fighting. Platoon drill. Musketry. G.O.C 7th Div inspected billets at 6 pm.	
— —	20/8/16	10 am	Divine Service.	
— —	21/8/16	8 am	Musketry on 50x range. 9.30 pm Night operations. the Battn in the attack.	
— —	22/8/16	9 am	Coy. drill. Extended order drill. Battalion drill.	
— —	23/8/16	8 am	Batt. bathing in VILLE BATHS. Drill & digging trenches.	

Instructions regarding War Diaries and Intelligence Summaries are contained in F. S. Regs., Part II. and the Staff Manual respectively. Title pages will be prepared in manuscript.

WAR DIARY
or
~~INTELLIGENCE SUMMARY.~~
(Erase heading not required.)

Army Form C. 2118.

8th Devon Reg.

Place	Date	Hour	Summary of Events and Information	Remarks and references to Appendices
	August 1916			
BUIRE	24/8/16	9am	Brigade ceremonial parade. Company & platoon drill	
— —	25/8/16	10.45am	The Brigade & the Corps mounted troops took part in the ceremony of the presentation of decorations to the officers, N.C.Os & men of the French Artillery who had been covering the Corps during the offensive by the G.O.C 4th Army. Parade took place at RIBEMONT. After the ceremony the brigade marched past the G.O.C.	
— —	26/8/16	7am	Physical Drill. Platoon & extended order drill. Wiring.	
— —	27/8/16	11am	Divine Service. Officers & N.C.Os attending course of instruction in bayonet fighting & physical	
— —	28/8/16	7am	Physical Drill. Coy Drill & musketry. 9pm Night operations. drill under Sgt Instructor from Base.	
— —	29/8/16	8am	Musketry on range & trench & strong point digging.	
— —	30/8/16	8am	Baths at VILLE. Lectures & bayonet fighting	
— —	31/8/16	8am	Battalion on duty for the day. 260 men on fatigue. Remainder trench digging & bayonet fighting.	

C Pepys Capt
Adjutant 8th (S) Bn Devon Reg.

T2134. Wt. W708—776. 500000. 4/15. Sir J. C. & S.

20th Brigade.
7th Division.

WAR DIARY

8th BATTALION.

DEVONSHIRE REGIMENT.

SEPTEMBER 1 9 1 6.

Report on Operations at GINCHY 4th-7th September

Compo[redacted] of the Battn for the assault 8. The Battalion will advance in four lines of 4 platoons each at 100ˣ distance between lines:-

1st & 2nd Lines { "A" Company on the right
"C" " on the left

3rd & 4th Lines { "B" Company on the right
"D" " on the left

"A" & "B" Companies are both responsible for keeping touch with the DEVON Regt on the right

Stages of the attack 9. The 1st objective is DANUBE SUPPORT TRENCH.
2nd objective:- SHRINE ALLEY – KIEL LANE
FINAL objective:- APPLE ALLEY. All trenches running forward from here are to be blocked at once on reaching this trench

The assaulting lines will move direct on to their objective. the 1st and 2nd lines not delaying their advance to clear the trenches thoroughly
The Officers Commanding Companies of 3rd & 4th lines are responsible for thoroughly clearing up the trenches and will detail parties for this work previous to the assault
Should any portion of a line be held up the remainder will best assist that portion by pushing on. care being taken to guard the exposed flanks.
Advanced positions of the 1st line will be indicated by flares all along the line on reaching the final objective. and along the line of the most advanced Infantry at:-

9am – 1pm
5pm – 9pm

Boundaries of the area to be cleared by Coys of 2 Border Regt 10. "A" & "B" Companies area:-

Right Boundary:- From our front line at junction of F.11.8 and F.10.1 a straight line to the bifurcation of SWAG LANE – along SWAG LANE (inclusive) – thence a straight line from junction of SWAG LANE & TIRPITZ TRENCH to junction of ORCHARD & APPLE ALLEYS.

Left Boundary:- From our trench to Point "8" in 8345 – thence to junction of MUSHROOM & TIRPITZ TRENCH – thence along the line of trench to the O of 10 South of HIDDEN WOOD – thence to junction of APPLE ALLEY & LUKE TRENCH.

"C" & "D" Companies area:

Right Boundary:- As for the left boundary of "A" & "B" Companies.

Left Boundary:- The German front line trench up to the Junction of APPLE ALLEY & BOIS FRANCAIS TRENCH.

Strong points to be established 11. Right of the 1st Line will establish Strong points at:
I. Junction of MARK & APPLE ALLEY TRENCHES. blocking PEAR TRENCH
II. Junction of LUKE. JOHN & APPLE ALLEY TRENCHES
III. They will also detail a party to block PAPEN TRENCH.
Left of the 1st Line will make strong points at:-
I Junction of BOIS FRANCAIS SUPPORT & APPLE ALLEY
II Junction of BOIS FRANCAIS TRENCH & APPLE ALLEY.
One Lewis Gun is to be included in the garrison of each of the above strong points.
R.E Working parties will be sent forward as early as possible to assist in this work.

Lewis Guns. 12. The Lewis Guns will move in the following positions:-
1 Gun of "A" Compy & 2 of "C" Compy with 2nd Line.
2 Guns "B" " & 1 of D " " 4th Line.
1 Guns "A" " + 1 of D " in reserve.
Each Gun will be preceded by a party of Bombers

Bombers 13. The Bombers will be with their platoons.

Grenadiers 14. Will be distributed under the orders of Lt Kelly Bn Grenade officer.

Equipment ?
15. (a) Greatcoats and Spare Kit will be left in the men's pack which will be clearly marked and stacked in Store at No 7 RUE de CHATEAU. MORLANCOURT under divisional arrangements on the June 1916 at am.
(b) Every man, except Specialists, will be equipped as notified in S.V.1 No 1. dated 17. 6. 16
(c) Equipment of Bombers as notified in SV1 No 1 d/- 17. 6. 16
(d) Carriers will be equipped as in (b) with the exception of the two bandoliers

Special Equipment 16. Coys will draw extra equipment as under from the Qrmr for issue to the men:-
(a)

	Wire Cutters	Shovels	Picks	Hedging Gloves	Bill hooks
A Coy.	30	50	20	25	25
B "	20	75	30	25	25
C "	30	50	20	25	25
D	20	75	30	25	25

(b) For distribution among bombing Sections in addition to hand Grenades

	Rifle Grenades	Smoke Bombs
A Coy	84	30
B "	80	20
C "	120	30
D "	100	16

V.

SAA & Very Light. 17. The Battn Reserve SAA & Very Light Ammunition Store is near the foot of 73 Street. RSM Davenport will take charge of this Store.
Each Company will detail 1 NCO & 8 men to report themselves to the above W.O. to act as ammunition carriers.
The Brigade Store is in LUDGATE CIRCUS.

Water & Rations. 18. Water and rations are stored in the RESERVE TRENCH in 70 Street. Regtl Prov Sgt Park & 4 Reg Police also one private from each Coy will be in charge of the Battn supply and regulate its issue.

Medical 19. Regimental AID POST will be established in the Orderly Room in WELLINGTON REDOUBT.

Communication 20. (a) Lt Warren Bn Signalling Officer will arrange for telephone and visual communication between Coy Commanders & Bn H.Q. also Bn H.Qrs in the captured trenches & those in 71 Street.
(b) Each Coy will detail two good orderlies to report to the Adjutant at Battn H.Q. in the trenches.

Escort to Prisoners 21. Not more than one man for 10 prisoners should be detailed.
(a) Prisoners will be handed over to a collecting depôt at the CITADEL under Capt Newdigate who will give a receipt for them.
(b) Any civilians found anywhere should at once be evacuated under an escort.

Stragglers Post. 22. Each Company will detail a private to work under Sgt as a post to turn back stragglers. This post will be under the orders of Capt Newdigate.

Badges 23. Distinguishing badges to be worn by certain individuals are as stated in S.V.1. No 1 dated 17. 6. 16.

Miscellaneous 24. (a) All papers both official & private are to be destroyed or left behind.
(b) The following maps only will be taken and these are not to be marked in any way except for denoting German trenches MONTAUBAN 1/20.000 - 62D NE — 57D NE. - 57C NW. - 57D SE - 57C S.W. All messages and reports will refer to one or other of these maps.
(c) No public money is to be taken into action.
(d) Attention is drawn to other miscellaneous orders published in S.V.1's

Bde H.Q. 25. Brigade H.Qrs will be in ESSEX AVENUE.

Bn H.Qrs 26 (a) Battn H.Qrs will be in a dugout in 71 Street on the South side in the portion between the SUPPORT & the RESERVE.
(b) After the assault they will move forward to a position in DANUBE SUPPORT near the junction of SHRINE ALLEY & DANUBE SUPPORT TRENCH.

D Strange Lieut
Adjt. 2nd Border Regt.

Instructions regarding War Diaries and Intelligence Summaries are contained in F. S. Regs., Part II. and the Staff Manual respectively. Title pages will be prepared in manuscript.

WAR DIARY
or
~~INTELLIGENCE SUMMARY.~~
(Erase heading not required.)

Army Form C. 2118.

8th Devon Reg.

Vol 12

Place	Date	Hour	Summary of Events and Information	Remarks and references to Appendices
	September	1916	September 1916	
BUIRE-SUR-ANCRE	1/9/16	9am	Battalion training. Musketry. Drill. Bayonet fighting. Trench & strong point digging. Wiring. Classes of instruction in bombing & Lewis Gun. Battalion strength 40 officers 924 O.R.	
(Ref map)	2/9/16	8am	Musketry on range. Practices rapid & (kneeling/application) Shooting good.	
FRANCE 62 D NE.	3/9/16	11am	Divine Service. 5 40 pm. The Brigade given orders to move to MAMETZ in motor lorries	
			Further operations ~~till~~ up to 8-9-16 are given in Appendix I. All orders received in	App I
			Appendix II. Casualties are given in Appendix I.	App II
F.20.a	8/9/16	4am	The battalion arrived from near GINCHY & encamped at F.20.a. The battalion marched off at 2pm	
BUIRE			& arrived at BUIRE at 4 30pm where they were billeted. Capt Pudham from West Indian Reg	
			& 2nd Lt Hay from A.S.C. joined the bat. for duty	
—	9/9/16	7am	The battalion entrained at ALBERT 2 Coys at 9.30am 2 Coys at 10.45 am Arrived at	
ALLERY			~~ALLERY at 2.4P~~ AIRAINES at 3.15 pm & marched to ALLERY where it was billeted at 6 pm.	
	10/9/16		Battalion resting. Divine service at 7pm.	
	11/9/16	9am	Kit inspection. 17 other ranks joined from 3rd Bn. all belonging to the 8th Bn.	
	12/9/16	7am	Physical drill. Bayonet fighting. platoon & Coy drill. 2nd Lt Copner joined from 3rd Bn.	
	13/9/16	7am	Coys. at disposal of Coy. Commanders. Platoon drill, Bayonet Fighting Coy drill	

F H

Army Form C. 2118.

Instructions regarding War Diaries and Intelligence Summaries are contained in F. S. Regs., Part II. and the Staff Manual respectively. Title pages will be prepared in manuscript.

WAR DIARY
or
~~INTELLIGENCE SUMMARY.~~

(Erase heading not required.)

8th Devon Reg.

Place	Date	Hour	Summary of Events and Information	Remarks and references to Appendices
ALLERY	14/9/16	9am	Route march fighting kit. Route ALLERY - METIGNY - ERAUMESNIL - VERGIES back by Northern Road running NE. to ALLERY. 2nd LT. GIRVAN joined from 11th Bn & 4 O.R.	
	15/9/16	7am	Battalion training. Physical Drill, Skirmishing & Musketry, Coy in attack. Judging distances & visual training. Selected officers & N.C.Os under C.S.M. Hooker.	
	16/9/16	7Am	Battalion training Rapid marching & Saluting. Selected officers and N.C.Os under C.S.M. Hooker. Platoon Drill & Rifle exercises. Battalion Drill, Musketry & Judging Distances.	
	17/9/16	11Am	Divine Service 11 Am. Billeting party paraded at 3 PM entrained at ~~Long~~ LONGPRÉ 7.45 P.M.	
ALLERY - LE ROMARIN (PAPOT)	18/9/16		Battalion moves to LE ROMARIN (PAPOT) - 2nd ARMY Area. Marches to LONGPRE entrained by 12 Noon. Battalion moved off 7.30 Am. D Coy (Loading party) & Transport at 5.15 Am. Detrained BAILLEUL 9 P.M. Billeted in Hutment Camp at LE ROMARIN. (Rail route taken ABBEVILLE - RUE - ETAPLES - BOULOGNE - CALAIS - ST. OMAR - HAZEBROUK - BAILLEUL. Returning strength 31 Off. 720 O.R.	

T2134. Wt. W708—776. 500000. 4/15. Sir J. C. & S.

Instructions regarding War Diaries and Intelligence Summaries are contained in F. S. Regs., Part II. and the Staff Manual respectively. Title pages will be prepared in manuscript.

WAR DIARY
or
~~INTELLIGENCE~~ SUMMARY. 8th Devon Regt

(Erase heading not required.)

Army Form C. 2118.

Place	Date	Hour	Summary of Events and Information	Remarks and references to Appendices
PAPOT – LE BIZET	19/9/16	7 AM	Battalion moved up from PAPOT via LE ROMARIN – LEDON – GRAVIER – OOSTHOVE FARM – à la CLEF de la BELGIQUE – CHAPELLE ROMPUE to LE BIZET. relieving 9th Bn WELSH Regt. by Two Coys B & D in Redoubts	
		H.Q. &	Two Coys A & C in Billets at LE BIZET. Battn in Bde support to 9th Bn DEVON Regt. & 2nd Bn BORDER Regt. who are holding Right & Left sectors of Front Line Respectively. 2nd Bn GORDON HIGHLANDERS in Bde Reserve at PONT de NIEPPE. Relief completed by 11.30 P.M	3 O.R. Joined
LE BIZET	20/9/16		Battn in Bde support. Classes for A & C Coy Lewis gunners. Battn holds Redoubts covering sector between C 15 d. 2.5 on Right and C 3 b. 9.4	
	21/9/16		Work being done by B & D Coys in improving redoubts sandbagging & wiring	
	22/9/16		Fatigue party to work under 9th DEVONS 9 AM – 3 PM (A Coy) working party from C Coy repairing HERMAN AVE. (50 men) 8 PM – 2 AM (23.9.16)	
	23/9/16		Working party from A Coy as yesterday. also C Coy 10 men unloading T.M. ammn at MOTOR CAR CORNER 9 P.M. 5 O.R. Joined	
	24/9/16		150 men on Fatigue working on HERMANS AVE. on Right Sector under 9th DEVONS orders and carrying up 2" T.M ammunition.	C Rippon Capt OC 8th Devon Regt

T2134. Wt. W708—776. 500000. 4/15. Sir J. C. & S.

Instructions regarding War Diaries and Intelligence Summaries are contained in F. S. Regs., Part II. and the Staff Manual respectively. Title pages will be prepared in manuscript.

WAR DIARY
or
~~INTELLIGENCE~~ SUMMARY. 8th DEVON REGT.

(*Erase heading not required.*)

Army Form C. 2118.

Place	Date	Hour	Summary of Events and Information	Remarks and references to Appendices
LE BIZET – TRENCHES (LE TOUQUET SECTOR)	25/9/16	7 AM	Battalion relieved 2nd BORDER REGT in Left Subsector. Boundaries being Left GAP F (U.28.a.1.9.) Right Junction of Trenches 98/99 at C.4.a.65.00. Order of Coys B Right A Centre C Left D Support. D Coy have 2 platoons in LANCASHIRE SUPPORT FARM (U.27.b.3.1 to U.27.b.1.3. 1 platoon No 1 TERRACE FUSILIER TRENCH U.27.b.1.3 to U.27.b.1.5. 1 platoon MAISON 1875 U.26.c.7.5. Battn H.Q. at DESPIERRE FARM. (C.3.c.7.7.) Battn Bombers & Lewis Gunners at RESERVE FARM (C.3.b.6.0.) Relief complete 11 A.M. The 22nd Bde hold sector on our left – 2nd GORDONS on our right.	
TRENCHES	26/9/16		Trenches	
	27/9/16		do	
	28/9/16		do No 14 platoon D Coy moved up to FUSILIER TERRACE from MAISON 1875 being relieved by 1 NCO & 3 men 2nd BORDER Regt.	
	29/9/16		Trenches	
	30/9/16		Our Lewis guns by their fire supported a raid by the 9th DEVON Regt on MACHINEGUN HOUSE C.10.b.4.6.5. Fire was kept up for 15 minutes from 10 P.M. to 10.15 P.M. Retaliation was slight except for a few trench mortars all was quiet by 10.45 P.M.	

Army Form C. 2118.

Instructions regarding War Diaries and Intelligence Summaries are contained in F. S. Regs., Part II. and the Staff Manual respectively. Title pages will be prepared in manuscript.

WAR DIARY
or
~~INTELLIGENCE SUMMARY.~~
(Erase heading not required.)

8th Queen Reg

Place	Date	Hour	Summary of Events and Information	Remarks and references to Appendices
PONT NIEPPE	30/9/15		Appendix III	
			(a) Battalion Strength	
			38 Officers 802 other ranks.	
			(b) Casualties during the month. Officers O. Ranks	
			killed — 34	
			wounded 4 76	
			missing 13	
			sick 2 43	
			(c) Drafts	
			Number received 39.	
			Mostly B.E.F. men who were well trained. A few from Devonport well trained.	
			CRP[illegible] Capt	
			Adj 8th Queen Reg	

T2134. Wt. W708—776. 500000. 4/15. Sir J. C. & S.

REPORT ON RECENT OPERATIONS.

APPENDIX 1.

ORDERS RECEIVED.

To O.C.8th DEVONS. 20th Brigade No B.M.O.1.

The Brigade will move up tonight to MAMETZ by lorry as follows:-

9th Devon Regt...............7.p.m.
2nd Border Regt..............7-15 p.m.
2nd Gordon Hrs...............7-30 p.m.
8th Devon Regt...............7-45 p.m.
20th M.G.Coy.................8-0 p.m.
20th T.M.Battery.............8-0 p.m.
Signal Coy...................7-0 p.m.

Transport will follow as soon as possible after battalions have moved, and will proceed to just North of FRICOURT Cemetery.

Packs and Great Coats will be packed separately in the Brigade store.

(Sd) C.C.FOSS. Major.
Brigade Major.
20th Infantry Brigade.

3rd Sept,1916.

To O.C.8th DEVONS. 20th Brigade No B.M.F.26.

Warning Order. Operation to clear Eastern corner of DELVILLE WOOD will be carried out to-day. At 11-0 am Infantry will be withdrawn to distance of 200 yards from enemies position and heavy Artillery will register. Heavy Guns will bombard from noon. At 2-5 pm heavy guns will lift to line of BEER TRENCH. At 2-35 pm heavy guns will search back by lifts of 50 yards to PINT TRENCH. Infantry will advance at 2-5 pm. Field Artillery barrage will lift from edge of WOOD at 2-10 pm and search back at 25 yards per minute arriving on line of BITTER TRENCH at 2-20 pm. Lift from BITTER Trench at 2-35 pm and search back at same pace to line 200 yards East of NEW GERMAN TRENCH and remain during consolidation. Limits of barrage South from point T.13.A.0.0.25. to Southern end of NEW TRENCH T.13.A.95.30.. Northern limit of barrage from point S.18.B.95.80. on a line parallel to and 100 yards Northern side of ALE ALLEY.. 24th Division have given orders to allow right Brigade to give every facility for deployment of troops to carry out attack and to be ready to co-operate inany way desired. 21st Manchesters are placed at disposal of 20th Infantry Brigade for operation. Acknowledge.

(Sd) C.C.FOSS. Major.
Brigade Major.
20th Infantry Brigade.

2-0 p.m. 4th Sept,1916.

O.O.b.

20th Brigade Operation Order No 30.

Map reference GUILLEMONT Sheet 1/20,000. 4th September,1916

1. GUILLEMONT and the line of the road WEDGE WOOD and GINCHY were captured yesterday and some 700 prisoners taken. Some posts are occupied by our men in GINCHY.
2. The Fourth Army is renewing the attack to-day.
3. The 7th Division will reoccupy the whole of GINCHY and capture PINT TRENCH and ALE ALLEY and push forward posts to the high ground further Eastward.
4. The operations will be carried out by the 20th Infantry Brigade to which the 21st Bn Manchester Regiment is attached.
5. OBJECTIVES.
   (a). The operation will be divided into 3 parts. The first will consist of the capture of ALE ALLEY as far East as its junctio with BEER TRENCH and the NEW GERMAN TRENCH T.13.A.58. to T.13. b.0.4. Warning order above holds good for this operation.
   (b).1. The second part fo the operation will consist of the captur of the remainder of ALE ALLEY, of PINT TRENCH from its junction with ALE ALLEY to GINCHY. These two parts will be carried out by 21st Manchester Regt with the 8thnDevon Regt in support.
   (b).2. The capture of the trench East of the village of GINCHY which runs from T.20.A.1.6. to T.14.A.5.2.
   (c). During the third part of the operation, troops will be pushed forward and make good the approximate line T.20.A.7.6. - T.14. D.1.4.(GINCHY TELEGRAPH) - T.14.A.6.4. Touch will be established with the XIV Corps at T.20.A.7.5.
   2nd Border Regt will carry out the parts (b) (2) and (c) with the 2nd Gordon Highlanders in support.
6. ASSAULT.
   The 21st Manchester Regiment will advance at 2-15 pm.
   The barrage will lift from the trench East of GINCHY at 3-15 pm
   The 2nd Border Regiment will move up as close to the barrage as possible.
7. CONSOLIDATION.
   (a) Objective when gained will be consolidated without delay. Strong posts will be established in the vicinity of the following points:-
   (1) T.2.D.A.1.6. (2) T.14.C.5.4. (3) Northern end of trench T.14.A.4.3. (4) In a position outside the North Eastern corner of Orchard T.13.B.9.4. (5) At the junction of PINT TRENCH and LAGER LANE T.7.D.4.0. (6) At the junction of PINT TRENCH and ALE ALLEY T.7.D.3.2. and (such other point as may be deemed necessary.
   The 91st Infantry Brigade will furnish one Infantry battalion to dig back a communication trench from the trench East of GINCHY to GINCHY ALLEY.

(Sd) C.C.FOSS. Major.
Brigade Major.
20th Infantry Brigade.

4-9-1916.

To FACT.   20th Brigade No 39.

FADE will releive 2 Companies of the Brigade on our right which are in position from T.19.B.1.8. to T.13.D.e.e. AAA FILE will releive FAD and FADE less the party of FADE releiving the 2 Companies of Brigade on our right AAA FACT will releive KEEN, completion of reliifs to be reportedAAA Details of other reliefs will be arranged between C.O's concerned AAA In addition to the above reliefs FACT will relieve without fail a party of R.W.Fusiliers and Warwicks which are in a trench approximately due North of the 13 of T.13.AAA Acknowledge.

FACE.   (sd) C.C.FOSS. Major.

20th INFANTRY BRIGADE OPERATION ORDER No 81.   O.O.(81).
September 5th,1916

Ma p reference GUILLEMONT Sheet 1/20,000.

1. Information. The 20th Infantry Brigade will continue the attack on GINCHY to-day 5th September.
2. Our own Forces. The Brigade on our right hold a line just WEST of the road running N and S through GINCHY to a point T.20.a.15. thence to point T.19.b.18.
A party of 2nd Border Regt are relieving two companies of Brigade on our right on a line from T.19.b.18. to T.13.d.e.e.
9th Devons hold PORTER TRENCH and the outskirts of GINCHY.
2nd Border Regt hold STOUT TRENCH.
21st Manchester Regt hold a line running from Zz Trench to S.W. corner of DELVILLE WOOD thence along a trench just inside the WOOD ro a block 50 Yards short of HOP ALLEY. The Brigade on our left hold a line just N of that parallel to the edge of the WOOD from about 50 yards N of ALE ALLEY. There are also isolated parties of the 22nd Brigade in and on the edge of GINCHY. The exact localit is uncertain.
3. The Enemy. The enemy is reported to tbe holding the trench E of GINCHY,ALE TRENCH,HOP ALLEY and E corner of DELVILLE WOOD strongly. He has also strong posts at GINCHY at SQUARE FARM T.13. d.64.,and three - sided Farm T.13.b.60.
4. Operations.
(a) Reliefs. 2nd Border Regt will relieve two companies of the Brigade on our RIGHT under separate orders.
2nd Gordon Highlanders will relieve 2nd Border Regt and 9th Devon Regt (less that portion mentioned above as relieving 2 companies of the Brigade on our right). 8th Devon Regt will relieve 21st Manchester Regt.
(b). 2nd Gordon Highlanders will occupy and consolidate a line from B.M.14.3.7. just E of Ginchy to the NORTHERN end of the ORCHARD T.13.b.84. thence S.W; along the edge of the ORCHARD to the N and S road through GINCHY inclusive,at which point junction will be affected with 8th Devon Regt.
(c) 8th Devon Regt will form a defensive flank from the last mentioned point along VAT ALLEY and thence N.Westwards to include the trenches taken over from 21st Manchester Regt.
5. The Assault,will commence at 3-30 am at which hour troops will leave their assembly trenshes.
6. Artillery.
The following Artillery barrage has been asked for to commence at 3-50 am and continue for 2½hours. Along trench E of GINCHY to road T.14.a.54. thence along a straight line to T.14.a.08.,thence T.13 b. 47.,- N.E. along PINT TRENCH - ALE ALLEY - to corner of DELVILLE WOOD.
7. Reports. Brigade H.Q. will rwmain in present position.

(Sd) C.C.FOSS. Major.
Brigade Major.
20th Infantry Brigade.

Issued at 12-45 am.

To FACE. 20th Brigade.No 49.

Warning Order AAA The operation referred to in para 4 c and d in 20th Infantry Brigade O.O.81 of to-day will take place to-morrow morning 6th September AAA There will be a subsidiary operation to take the corner of DELVILLE WOOD which will be undertaken by KALE AAA Further details will be issued.

FACE.
1-0 p.m. Sept 5th '16.

(Sgd) C.C.Foss, Major,
Brigade Major,
20th Infantry Brigade

FACT. 20th Brigade No B.M.52.

The 2nd Queens will attack and seize the Eastern corner of DELVILLE WOOD this afternoon covered by a bombardment of Stokes Mortars and Medium Mortars AAA The ~~minimum~~ medium mortar bombardment will commence at 3-30 pm and continue till 5-30 pm at which hour the 2nd Queens will advance to the assualt AAA No advance will be made beyond the edge of the WOOD but the line will be strongly consolidated at once and block~~x~~ made up HOP and ALE AILEYS AAA The 8th Devons will be prepared to assist the attack with Bombers AAA

FACE. 3-25.
5-9-1916.

(Sd) C.C.FOSS. Major.

20th INFANTRY BRIGADE OPERATION ORDER NO 82.

Ref: GUILLEMONT Sheet 1/20,000. 5th Sept,1916.

The following amendments and additions will be made in 20th Brigade Operation Order No 81.

1. Information. The attack on GUINCHY detailed in operation order No 81 will take place on 6th September.

2. Our own forces. The French North of the SOMME are advancing with great speed on the line PERONNE - BAPAUME Road along which the enemy is trying to withdraw his guns, and have captured a battery of 420 cm howitzers and a balloon on the ground. The Corps on our right have seized LEUZE WOOD and are advancing towards trench junction T.14.d.85.40. 2nd Border Regt have two companies holding trenches at T.19.a.8.3. running N.W. to T.19.a.6.9. Parts of 22nd Infantry Brigade are holding position approximately

(a) edge of Orchard at S end of GINCHY.
(b) BEER TRENCH.
(c) PILSEN LANE.

Party (a) will be relieved by 2nd Gordon Highlanders. Parties (b) and (c) will be relieved by 8th Devon Regt. O.C.2nd Gordon Highlanders and 8th Devon Regt will detail special parties to relieve these parties of 22nd Infantry Brigade.

3. Objectives. The Brigade objectives will be extended further forward as shown in my B.M.F.2. of to-day, which is attached.

(Sd) C.C.FOSS. Major.
Brigade Major.
20th Infatry Brigade.

5-9-16.

7th Division G.324.

20th Infantry Brigade.

After the capture of GINCHY to-morrow morning, the Divisional Commander wishes you to seize the trench East of the village and to establish a line of posts along the high grounds from GINCHY TELEGRAPH to T.14.a.6.4. and to seize the trench junctions at T.7.d.45.00. and T.7.d.30.20.

Communication will be established with XIVCorps at T.14.d.85.40.

At 6-0 am the Artillery barrage will be advanced to the line T.14.b.5.0. to T.7.d.8.5. and thence Westwards a long a line parallel to ALE ALLEY and 200 yards North of it.

Directly the information is recieved that the high ground has been seizrd and the positions consolidated the barrage will be lifted and to the FLERS line in order to allow patrols to be sent forward.

5-9-16..

(Sd) C.Bonham Carter.Lieut Colonel.
G.S. 7th Division.

O.C.8th Devon Regt.

B.M.F.2.

The dividing line between the 2nd Gordon Hrs and 8th Devon Regt will be the road running North and South through GINCHY, O.C. 2nd Gordon Hrs being responsible for establishing posts and sending forward patrols to the East of the road. O.C.8th Devon Regt will be responsible for gaining ground on the West of this road. Road inclusive to 8th Devon Regimant.
ACKNOWLEDGE by wire.

5-9-16.

(sd) C.C.FOSS.Major.
20th Infantry Brigade.

20th INFANTRY BRIGADE OPERATION ORDER NO 83.

Ref: GUILLEMONT 1/20,000.

6-9-1916.

2nd Gordon Highlanders held a line approxima tely T.13.d.7.0.,T.13.d.0.5.,T.13.d.0'.8. AAA. Four sided farm at T.13.d.6.3. is held by the enemy AAA Snipers have been located in the tree N of this farm AAA 8th Devon Regt are digging a line facing North from DELVILLE WOOD S.18.b.8.2. to S.18.b.9.0. along PILSEN LANE to T.13.a.2.0. and are trying to extend the line towards 13.,in T.13. AAA Hostile Artillery ranging on this new work being assisted by signal lights from ALE ALLEYAAA 2nd Gordon Highlanders will renew the attack at 2- 0 pm assisted by two Companies of 9th Devon Regt who will attack from the S.W. on the line of the GINCHY - GUILLEMONT road AAA O.C. 9th Devon Regt will place at the dispoal of 2nd Gordon Highlanders such men as O.C. 2nd Gordon Highlanders requires as " mopping up" party AAA Ginchy village will be bombarded until 2-0 pm when the barrage will lift on to trench E of GINCHY where it will remain until 3-0 pm AAA Lifts of heavy Artillery will be by 50 yard bounds,and lifts of Divisional Artillery by bounds of 25 yards AAA PINT TRENCH, ALE ALLEY ,LAGER LANE, will be kept under heavy artillery fire until further orders AAA

ACKNOWLEDGE.
Issued at 11-45 am.

(Sd) C.C.FOSS.Major
20th Infantry Brigade.

O.C. 8th Devons. B.M.64.

20th Infantry Brigade Operation Order No 83 beyond continued AAA Troops attacking GINCHY will not advance the East edge of the village until ordered to do so from Brigade Hd Qrs AAA A line will be established and consolidated on the East edge of the village AAA The Artillery barrage will remain on trench East of XXXX village until further orders AAA At 2-0 pm the two rear companies of 9th Devon Regt will move up to STOUT TRENCH in close support of the attack AAA 22nd Manchester Regt will move up so that their leading company is on the line ZZZ TRENCH AAA Acknowledge.

issued at 1-10 pm. 6-9-16.

(Sd) C.C.FOSS. MAjor.
Brigade Major.

O.C.8th Devon Regt. B.M.74.

20th INFANTRY BRIGADE OPERATION ORDER NO '84 AAA The following line will be held by the brigade tonight AAA 2nd Border Regt on the right from T.19.b.3.8. to T.13.d.2.0. aaa 22nd Manchester Regt will relieve the 2nd Gordon Hrs and 9th Devon Regt in PORTER TRENCH and STOUT TRENCH and will get touch with the left of the 2nd Border Regt. 22nd Manchester Regt will also hold ZZ ALLEY and get into close touch with the 8th Devon Regt who will remain intheir present positions AAA 2nd Queens Regt will hold the East corner of DELVILLE WOOD and make a strong post at this point AAA
ACKNOWLEDGE.

(Sd) C.C.FOSS. MAjor.
Brigade Major.
20th Infantry Brigade.

6-9-16.

20th INFANTRY BRIGADE OPERATION ORDER NO 85

Ref : Sheet 1/20,000. 9-1916.

The Brigade will be relieved in the front line tonight 7/8th insts by the 48th and 164th Infantry Brigades. Details of the relief will be arranged between C.O.'s concerned.

Battalions will be relieved as under:-

8th Devon Regt and 2nd Queens Regt by 1/4th North Lancashire Regiment.

The whole of the battalions now under the command of the G.O.C. 20th Infantry Brigade will move back after relief independently to the camp at F.20.a.

Sd. C.C.FOSS. Major.
Brigade Major.
20th Infantry Brigade.

8 Devon Rgt.
Ops at Ginchy
4–7.9.16

Appendix II

Report on Operation from 3-9-16 to 7-9-16

At 5.40 pm on ~~the 3rd~~ 3-9.16 the
OO (a) battalion received orders to move up
to MAMETZ in lorries. At 11.30 pm
the battalion marched from MAMETZ
to MONTAUBAN defences where
it bivouaced.

On the morning of the 4th ~~inst~~
OO (b) orders were received that the
battalion would be in ~~contact~~ support to
an attack made by 22nd Manchesters
on the East of GINCHY. The
battalion was not called on.

At 12 midnight the battalion
OO (c) moved from MONTAUBAN to
carry out ~~OO 81~~ 20th Inf Bde
OO 81, to relieve 21st Manchesters
& to occupy from T 13 b 84
on the right, to a block 50x short of
ALE ALLEY, thus forming

Appendix II

Report on Operations from 3-9-16 to 7-9-16.

At 5.40 pm on ~~[illegible]~~ 3-9-16 the battalion received orders to move to the MAMETZ [illegible]. At 11.[illegible] pm the battalion marched from MAMETZ to [illegible] [illegible] and bivouaced.

On the morning of the 4th [illegible] orders were received that the battalion would be in support ~~[illegible]~~ to an attack made by 22nd Manchesters on the west of GINCHY. The battalion was not called on.

At 12 midnight the battalion moved from [illegible] to [illegible] ~~[illegible]~~ 20th [illegible] [illegible] 31 [illegible] 1st [illegible] [illegible] from T.[illegible].84 [illegible] to a block [illegible] ALE ALLEY. [illegible]

A This Coy[B] went into position as it was getting ~~day~~ light. The remainder of the battalion was then in the following positions. D Coy in DIAGONAL TRENCH C + A Coy ~~in [illegible]~~ ~~AVENUE in~~ GUINCHY ~~AV~~ ALLEY. ready to move up.

About 12 casualties from shell fire occurred ~~on the way up.~~ during the relief.

a defensive flank along VAT ALLEY ~~[illegible]~~ facing N. & making touch with the left of the Gordons objectives. The Gordons were to assault at 3.30 am.

The night was very dark ~~&~~ & the rain very heavy which made progress very slow through very slippery mud. The guides also were not certain of their way. The leading Coy reached the Manchester H.Q. at 3 am. It was not till 2 hours after arriving in GUINCHY ALLEY that a guide for the Coy in ZZ Trench could be found. ~~Then~~ 2 guides from the Warwicks took a party to relieve a detachment at T 13 central. This party returned after dawn, the guides having lost their way. The guides also reported that the detachment had relieved themselves. Orders were given to the guides & to the O.C. relieving party to reconnoit[r]e the ground by day in order to ensure reaching the place

a defensive flank along VAT ALLEY
~~to form~~ & making touch with the left
of the Gordons objective. The Gordons
were to assault at 3.30 a.m.
The night was very dark & the rain
very heavy which made progress very
slow through very slippery mud and the
guides also were not certain of their
way. It was not till 2 hours
after arriving in GUNCHY ALLEY
that a guide for the Coy in 22 Trench
could be found. Then 2 guides
from the Warwicks took a party to
relieve [illegible] at [illegible]
the party [illegible] at dawn, the
guides having lost their way. The
guides also reported that the detachment had relieved themselves [illegible]
[illegible] to the [illegible]
of relieving party & [illegible]
over the ground by day [illegible]
to ensure [illegible] the place.

to keep touch with the right of the Queens
& guard their right flank.

under cover of night.

~~Sept 5th~~ On Owing to the Lateness of ~~During the morn~~ getting into position the attack was postponed.

Sept 5th

During the ~~day~~ morning the 2nd Queens relieved the battalion on the left. ~~them~~ One platoon of A Coy were sent to their assistance in a bombing attack on ALE ALLEY ^ 2 platoons of D Coy were sent to hold the part of DIAGONAL TRENCH in DELVILLE WOOD to get into touch with the right of the QUEENS & render them any support required. Finding the S.E. corner of the wood unoccupied these 2 platoons dug in 10 yards from the S.E. edge of the wood & got into touch with A Coy in Z Z Trench.

Sept 6th

At 3.30 am C Coy were in ~~touch with the Gordons~~ position partly in ZZ trench with their right in touch with the Gordons & partly in an old trench just ~~be~~ in rear of ZZ. The Gordons had to delay their attack owing to having lost connection with part of their men & it was not till 5 am that the advance was made. O.C. C Coy then moved forward on the left of the Gordons & put ~~the~~ his leading platoon in position at T13 c 8.8. facing NE ready to move forward to T13 b 6.4. He then found his remaining platoon had lost connection & did not find them until daylight. Meanwhile ~~[illegible]~~ as no report had been received

~~Sept 6th~~

After dark C Coy & 2 platoons of D were ordered to move up & start digging in on the defensive flank. The 3 remaining platoons of A to move into DIAGONAL TRENCH vacated by D, B Coy to remain in ZZ Trench

Sept 6th

Sept 6th

At 3.30 am C Coy were in ~~touch with the Gordons~~ position partly in ZZ trench with their right in touch with the Gordons & partly in an old trench just to the rear of ZZ. The Gordons had to delay their attack owing to having lost connection with part of their men & it was not till 5 am that the advance was made. O.C. C Coy then moved forward on the left of the Gordons & put ~~the~~ his leading platoon in position ready to move forward to T13 b 6 4. He then found his remaining plats had lost connection & did not find them until daylight.

[illegible] while ~~[illegible]~~ as

[illegible] had been received

^ from just behind ZZ Trench

^ sending bombers on in front. Sniping was very active during these movements & men had to move carefully ~~from~~ by shell holes. & Great care had to be taken moving down the forward slope of the little valley running across PILSEN LANE at T 13 a 7 0.

Lt LOCK was sent up from Bn H.Q. He found the remaining platoons of C Coy ^ & started them digging the defensive flank from S. 18 b. 8.3. At the same time he took B Coy from ZZ TRENCH & the 2 platoons of D & ~~extended~~ pushed them out towards ~~the right~~ GINCHY to continue the same line ^

The line now ran from S 18 b 8 3 to T 13 a 2 1 & thence ~~up from~~ parallel & a few yards N of PILSEN ALLEY to about T 13 central. ~~~~

By this time 9 am Capt Hole had found his remaining platoons & took charge of the PILSEN LANE line. During the early part of this movement the enemy's guns had been unusually inactive, & it was thought that he was moving them back owing to the rapid advance made by the Corps on our right.

A Coy had now been moved up to Z Z Trench in Support

Sketch No 1. is appended giving the ~~present~~ position of the battalion at this time 9 am on Sept 6th.

At about 9 30 am the enemy's guns started to range on the new work & seemed to be directed by Very Lights from ~~[illegible]~~ HOP ALLEY

At 10 am ~~the line~~ PILSEN LANE was heavily bombarded by ~~[illegible]~~ howitzers & field guns

At noon the line was continued a little further towards GINCHY

During the afternoon & ~~[illegible]~~

~~[illegible] the enemy~~

until late in the evening the enemy's shell fire was intense ~~and~~ especially on the edge of DELVILLE WOOD & ZZ TRENCH.

Meanwhile ~~under 2nd Lt F~~ one platoon of C Coy (under 2nd Lt Field & 2nd Lt Jupe) was in an isolated position at T 13. c. 8.8. At about 11 am while the village was being evacuated a strong party of the enemy appeared advancing on their left flank. This advance was successfully checked with rifle fire & a good many casualties inflicted on the enemy.

This party then became subject to heavy shelling & sniping. Knowing both their flanks were not supported & fearing the enemy might work round them in shell holes, they retired by twos to a position at T.13.c.1.5. facing ~~F~~ N.E. ~~the enemy~~

Here they remained till 4.30 pm
Finding themselves out of communication
they then reported to Bn H.Q.
The platoon was kept in battalion
reserve & the officers rejoined the
remainder of the Company & assisted
in extending & consolidating
PILSEN ~~L~~ LANE

Sept 7th.

In the morning, the OC 2nd Queens
relieved the platoon of A Coy which
had been supporting him. This
platoon was put in position in
DIAGONAL TRENCH in reserve.
During the day ~~the position of~~
~~the battalion remained unchanged~~
~~except for extending the PILSEN~~
~~LANE LINE towards GINCHY~~
~~The the~~ PILSEN LANE was
extended towards GINCHY

At the E end of the line a strong post was established & another one 50x behind it to the W.

to a point reached within 50x of the enemy's position in GINCHY. This was done by occupying a line of shell holes. These were not linked up. They proved to be good cover as casualties were light & also had a great advantage in the enemy not being able to locate their position to direct his fire. ~~and~~ ~~During the~~ At intervals during the day this line was shelled by our own heavy ~~ar~~ guns although messages were sent back warning them of it. During the ~~afternoon &~~ day ~~night~~ the enemy's shelling was continuous & at times severe. Snipers also were active. a

A party of the enemy advanced against the E end of the line; but were successfully driven back. About 20 of them were killed.

At about 11 pm the battalion was relieved by the 1/4th Loyal North Lancs Reg; the relief was not an easy matter, but was successfully completed without casualties. The battalion went back to camp near the ~~Citadel~~ CITADEL

The battalion lost 3 officers wounded Capt Moore 2nd Lt [illegible] & 2nd Lt ~~[illegible]~~ Smith, & in other ranks 32 killed, 67 wounded & 15 missing.

10.9.16 Lt Col

Commanding 8th(S) Bn Devon Reg

Ref. GUILLEMONT MAP $\frac{1}{20,000}$

The operation on the right was
not successful in the early morning
~~but as another attack was to be
made~~ The defensive flank was
found not to be ~~extended [illegible]~~
continued far enough to G18C114
One platoon of C Coy had become
detached & had got into position
at T 13 c 7.8. B Coy was
then ordered to move from Z.Z.
Trench to C Coys position &

The operation on the right was
not successful in the early morning
~~but as another attack was to be
made~~ The defensive flank was
found not to be ~~extended [illegible]~~
continued far enough to G18C114
One platoon of C Coy had become
detached & had got into position
at T 13 c 7.8. B Coy was
then ordered to move from Z.Z.
Trench to C Coys position &

Prefix..........Code..........m.	Words	Charge	This message is on a/c of:	Recd. at..........
Office of Origin and Service Instructions.	Sent		..............Service.	Date..........
	At..........m.			From..........
	To..........			
	By..........		(Signature of "Franking Officer.")	By..........

TO { OC all Coys

Sender's Number	Day of Month	In reply to Number	
*	6 9 16		AAA

Information Orders

The French are advancing with great speed on the line PERRONE – BAPAUME RD along which the enemy is trying to withdraw his guns. French have captured 1 battery of 42 cm Howitzers & a balloon.

The Corps on our right have seized LEUZE WOOD & are advancing towards trench junction T 14 d 85 60

BORDER REG have 2 Coys holding T 19 a 3.6 & T 19 a 6.9.

9th Devons in reserve at FOLLY TRENCH

Objectives are 1st points to be established from high ground GINCHY TELEGRAPH to T 14 a 6.4. 5th stage trench positions at T 7 d 4.5 to T 7 d 3.2

At 6am barrage will be on line T 14 c 5.0 to T 7 d 3.5 thence W. along a line parallel & 200x N of ALE ALLEY.

From

Place

Time

The above may be forwarded as now corrected. (Z)

.... Censor. .... Signature of Addressor or person authorised to telegraph in his name.

* This line should be erased if not required.

T. & W. & J. M. Ltd., London. W 14042/M44. 75,000 12/15. Forms C 2121/10.

Prefix.......... Code..........

Office of Origin and Service Instructions.

Sent
At..................m.
To....................
By....................

This message is on a/c of:

..............................Service.

(Signature of "Franking Officer.")

Date....................

From....................

By....................

TO

Sender's Number	Day of Month	In reply to Number	AAA
*			

Directly the high ground has been captured & information reaches that it has been the barrage will lift on to the FLERS LINE in order to allow patrols to go forward. Dividing line between GORDONS & DEVONS is road running N & S through GINCHY. B Coy are going forward to capture the ground on the W. of road, including the road. It is reported that GORDON Have occupied GINCHY & the QUEENS have occupied the E end of DELVILLE WOOD.

POSITION 1 BATT.

A Coy in 22 TR. B Coy [illegible] [illegible] [illegible] with Defensive Flank 2 platoons of D the same. 2 platoons of D & of A in support to the QUEENS [illegible] of DELVILLE [illegible]

Every opportunity of pushing forward patrols should be taken.

From

Place

Time 7.7 am

The above may be forwarded as now corrected.

(Z) [illegible]

.... Censor.

.... Signature of Addressor or person authorised to telegraph in his name.

* This line should be erased if not required.

T. & W. & J. M. Ltd., London. W 14042/M44. 75,000 12/15. Forms C 2121/10.

APPENDIX 11.

Report on Operations from 3-9-16 tp 7-9-16.

0.0. (a). At 5-40 pm on 3-9-16 the battalion recieved orders to move up to MAMETZ in lorries. At 11-30 pm the battalion marched fro m MAMETZ to MONTAUBAN defences where it bivouaced.

0.0. (b). On the morning of the 4th orders were received that the battali would be in support to an attack made by 22nd Manchesters on the West of GINCHY. The battalion was not called on.

0.0. (c). At 12 midnight the battalion moved from MONTAUBAN to carry out 20th Infantry Brigade Operation Order 81, to relieve 21st Manchesters and to occupy from T.13 b. 84. on the right, to a block 50 yards short of AIE ALLEY, this forming a defensive flank along VAT ALLEY facing North, and making touch with the left of the Gordons objective. The Gordons were to assualt at 3-30 am.

The night was very dark and the rain very heavy which made progress very slow through very slippery mud. The guides also were not certain of their way. The leading company reached the Manchesters Head Quarters at 3-0 am. It was not till 2 hours after arriving in GINCHY ALLEY that a guide for the company in ZZ Trench could be found. Thid Company "B" went into position as it was getting light. The remainder of the battalion was then in the follo-wing position. "D" Company in DIAGONAL Trench "C" and "A" Companies in GINCHY ALLEY ready to move up. About 12 casualties from shell fire occurred during the relief. Two guides from the Warwicks took a party to rellieve a detachment at T.13.Central. This party returned after dawn, the guides having lost their way. The guides also reported that the detachment had relieved themselves. Orders were given to the guides and to the O.C. relieving party to recon neitre the ground by day in order to ensure reaching the place under cover of night. Owing to the lateness of getting into position the attack was postponed.

September 5th.

During the morning the 2nd Queens relieved the battalion on the left. One platoon of "A" Company was sent to their assistance in a Bombing attack on AIE ALLEY to keep touch with the right of the Queens and guard their right flank. Two platoons of "D" Company was sent to hold the part of DIAGONAL Trench in DELVILLE WOOD to get into touch with the right of the Queens and render them any support required. Finding the S.E. corner of the WOOD unoccupied these two platoons dug in 10 yards from S.E. edge of the WOOD and got into touch with "A" Company in ZZ Trench. After dark "C" Company and two platoons of "D" Company were ordered to move up and start digging in on the defensive flank. The three remaining platoons of "A" Company to move into DIAGONAL TRENCH vacated by "D" Company, "B" Coy to remain in ZZ Trench.

September 6th.

At 3-30 am "C" Company were in position partly in Z.Z.Trench with their right in touch with the Gordons, and partly in an whole trench just in rear of ZZ. The Gordons had to delay their attack owing to having lost connection with part of their men and it was not until 5-0 am that the advance was made. O.C."C" Company then moved forward on the left of the Gordons and put his leading platoon in position at T.13 c. 8.8. facing North East, ready to move forward to T.13.b.6.4.. He then found his remaining plateon had lost connection and did not find them until day light. Meanwhile, as no reoprt had been received, Lieut LOCK was sent up from battalion Head Quarters. He found the remaining platoons of "C" Company from just behind ZZ TRENCH and started th m digging the defensive flank from S.18.b.8.3. At the same time he took "B" Company from ZZ TRENCH and the two Platoons of "D" Company and pushed them out towards GINCHY to continue the same line, sending bombers in front. Sniping was very active during these movements and men had to move carefully by shell holes. Great care had to be taken movinh down the forward slope of the little valley running across PILSEN LANE at T.13.a.7.0. The line now ran from S.18.b.8.3. to T.13. a.2.1. and thence parallel to a few yards North of PILSEN ALLEY to about T.13.central. By this time 9-0am Capt Hole had found his remaining platoons and took charge of the PILSEN LANE line. During the early part of this movement the enemies guns had been unusually inactive, and it was thought that he was moving them back owing to the rapid advance made by the Corps on our right. "A" Coy had now been moved up to ZZ Trench in support. Sketch No 1 is appended giving position of the battalion at this time, 9-0am on September 6th. At about 9-30 am the enemies guns started to range on the new work and seemed to be directed by Very Lights from HOP ALLEY. At 10-0 am PILSEN LANE was heavily bombarded by Howitzers and Field Guns. At noon the line was continued a little further towards GINCHY. during the afternoon until late in the evening the enemy's shell fire was intense especially on the edge of DELVILLE WOOD and ZZ Trench. Meanwhile one platoon of "C" Company under 2/Lieut FIELD and 2/Lieut JUPE was in an isolated position at T.13.c.8.8.. At about 11-0 am while the village was being evacuated a strong party of the enemy appeared advancing on their left flank. This advance was successfully checked with rifle fire and a good many casualties inflicted on the enemy. This party then became subject to heavy shelling and sniping. Knowing both their flanks were not supported and fearing the enemy might work round them in shell holes, they retired by twos to a position at T.13.c.1.5, facing N.E. Here they remained till 4-30 pm. Finding themselves out of communication they then reported to battalion head quarters. The platoon was kept in battalion reserve and the officers rejoined the remainder of the company and assisted in extending and consolidating PILSEN LANE.

September 7th.

In the morning the 2nd Queens relieved the platoon of "A" Company which had been supporting them. This platoon was put in position in DIAGONAL TRENCH in reserve. During the day PILSEN LANE was extended towards GINCHY and a point reached within 50 yards ~~within~~ of the enemy's position in GINCHY. This was done by occupying a line of shell holes. These were not linked up. They proved to be good cover as casualties were light, and also had a great advantage in the enemy not being able to locate their position to direct his fire. At the E. end of the line a strong post was established and another one 50 yards behind it to the West. At intervals during the day this line was shelled by our own heavy guns although messages were sent back warning them of it. During the day the enemies shelling was continuous and at times severe, Snipers were active. A party of the enemy advanced against the East end of the line but were successfully driven back. About 20 of them were killed. At about 11-0 pm the battalion was relieved by the 1/4th Royal North Lancashire Regiment. Relief was not an easy matter, but was successfully completed without casualties. The battalion went back to camp near the CITADEL.

The Battalion Lost 3 Officers wounded, Capt MOORE, 2/Lieut Old and 2/Lieut SMITH, and in other ranks 32 killed, 87 wounded and 15 missing.

B. C. James. Lieut Colonel.

10-9-1916. Commanding, 8th (Ser) Bn Devon Regiment.

Reference GUILLEMONT Map 1/20000.

Appendix 1 attached, showing orders received.

Report on the work of A. Company, 8th Devon. Regt. during the operations before Guinchy.

The company moved from Montauban ~~south~~ at midnight on Monday the 4th. – & took up a position in Longueval Alley, moving on to Old German Alley at midnight on Tuesday the 5th. During the ~~4th~~ 5th Longueval Alley was occasionally heavily bombarded by the enemy, but the fire was inaccurate & no casualties were incurred. At 8. p.m on the ~~4th~~ 5th No. 1 Platoon joined the Queen's in Delville Wood, & stayed there ~~for~~ until Thursday evening, but suffered no casualties, although often under heavy fire.

2, 3 & 4 Platoons moved forward to Z. Z. Avenue at 6 a.m on the morning of Wednesday, the 6th, & remained there until relieved by A Coy, 1/4th Loyal North Lancashire Regt. – ~~on~~ at 10 p.m on Thursday, the 7th. During all this time the trench was subjected to a very heavy bombardment, which at times became violent – especially during the attack on Guinchy on Wednesday afternoon. The casualties were extremely slight, however, and, although four enemy kite balloons were observing, the fire of the heavy guns, which came mostly from the direction of Martinpuich, was ineffective.

The fire from a whizz-bang battery was far more dangerous & several men were buried as the result of direct hits ~~off~~ on the parados.

There was also steady fire from snipers in the portion of Delville Wood held by the Germans.

The casualties were so ~~light~~ few, in my opinion, because the men dug in thoroughly, and kept still. I think that the lack of movement may have misled the enemy observers, for they did not seem certain as to which portions of the trenches were being held & which not. ~~the poor~~ They often concentrated a very heavy fire for some time on the unoccupied portion of ZZ avenue — between the right ~~flank~~ of the Company & the left flank of A Coy ~~that held by the~~ 22nd Manchesters, — when it was perfectly empty.

R.L. Machin 2Lt
10. 9. 1916.

—

Sir,

I have the honour to report that the company under my command left Montauban at 12-15 a.m. on Sept 4th and proceeded to Battalion Head Quarters in Longueval Alley which was reached at 3 a.m. No guides were available to guide the company to the position to be occupied. Half a platoon together with a bombing section and Lewis Gun Section under 2/Lieut Drake were sent to relieve a strong point [illegible] in the outskirts of Ginchy. A guide from the Welsh Fusiliers accompanied this party which however returned at Daybreak the guide having been unable to locate the strong point.

Shortly after 5 a.m. a guide was obtained who guided the company to [illegible] trench and from there another guide was obtained for ZZ Alley. The company was obliged to proceed to this trench.

T.

over the open as the communication trench
had been obliterated in places by shell
fire. As we were under enemy observation
the enemy placed an artillery barrage
on the company as a result of which
5 ~~of~~ casualties were sustained. Z Z.
ALLEY was reached at 6 a.m. and D
company of the [illegible] Manchesters was
relieved. The company set to
work cleaning and improving the trench
which was in a bad condition.
Intermittent artillery fire all day and
a heavy barrage from 5.30 p.m.
which loosened about 6.30 p.m. altho'
heavy artillery fire was kept up intermittently
all night. About 6 a.m. this fire
died away and a quiet period ensued
for a couple of hours.
About 6 p.m. the company moved
to S.E corner of DELVILLE WOOD and
commenced to dig Trench in a [illegible]
easterly direction in front of PILSEN
LANE. From 8 AM onwards

2

There was intermittent heavy artillery fire on this part of the line. About [illegible] the Company was moved further to the right to continue the trench [illegible] from the right of C Company and the trench was dug as far as T 13 a 6.1. On Septr 7 about 70 men from C Company together with men of B Company were moved further to the right to continue the trench from this point and dig to about T 13 central. The remainder of the company strengthening the trench already dug. At midnight the company was relieved by the Loyal North LANCS Regt.
During the 6th [illegible] heavy artillery fire continued all day.

[illegible] Capt
Comndg B Coy

10/9/16.

To O.C. F.A.C.T.

7.15. a.m.

Have moved along ZZ trench to junction with DELVILLE WOOD & started along PILSEN AVENUE. At present have seen no sign of Capt Hole & that part of his Company not with me.

Have come back to DIAGONAL TRENCH & find D. Coy have not moved up so, except for Capt Hole's small party which no one knows of there can be no digging party out.

Am I to move on along Pilsen Av under these conditions.

To C.O. FACT 9.55 a.m.

C & B Coys are digging in from DELVILLE WOOD roughly at Pt S18 b 8.2 to S18 b 9.0 and from thence along PILSEN LANE to T13 a 2.0. I am sending for D Coy to work further along PILSEN LANE to the EAST & will send bombers ahead. There is considerable sniping & the guns are trying to range on our work, being assisted by Huns firing lights probably from HOP ALLEY.

Capt HOLE is there & from what I can make out Field & Pipe are down towards GINCHY with the Gordons. OLD is wounded

G. Steel
Lieut

To ~~[illegible]~~ C.O. F.A.C.T

I find the majority of C. Coy with 2/Lt Old did not get further than the right of B. Coy in 2 2 trench.
I am now just going to lead B Coy up & have directed Old to follow & keep in touch with me.
As far as I can make out the Gordons have not yet been successful in the village.

G D Lost

6.50 a.m

Capt H.L.

1/ The C.O. wishes you to improve the trench as far as you have gone and make a good strong point at the end but not to dig out any further.
The 22 Manchesters are holding the front line now & are in Strut and Porter trench their original line so you are in front of them. I have warned them of your position.

2/ I am sending you up 30 boxes of bombs to dump at the MOUND. [illegible] and [illegible] are joining you this morning.

3/ We have sent for flares & will send them to you and will get up more water for you as soon as possible.

4/ If when you have completed the digging you find the line too crowded will you send back a proportion to rest at Headquarters.

5 Would you inform the C.O. at once of any enemy movement observed.

"A" Form. Army Form C. 2121.

MESSAGES AND SIGNALS.

No. of Message

Prefix ... Code ... m.	Words	Charge	This message is on a/c of:	Recd. at ... m.
Office of Origin and Service Instructions.	Sent		... Service.	Date
	At ... m.			From
	To			
	By		(Signature of "Franking Officer.")	By

TO: FACT ~~FAD~~ ~~FADE~~ ~~FILE~~
FALL ~~FAIR~~ ~~SIGNALS~~ ~~BOMB~~

Sender's Number.	Day of Month	In reply to Number	AAA
* BMA 13	Sept 5		

Following from French Army through Corps begins French have taken enemys front line system between BARLEUX and CHILLY on a front of 14 kilometres aaa CHILLY and SOYECOURT captured aaa Prisoners taken during day 1400

Alan Nock 2nd Lieut For OC A Co.

From FACE

Place

Time

R. M. Burrows Capt for Brigade Major

The above may be forwarded as now corrected. (Z)

Censor. Signature of Addressor or person authorised to telegraph in his name.

* This line should be erased if not required.

(4198) Wt. W14042—M44. 300000 Pads. 12/15. Sir J. C. & S.

"C" Form (Duplicate).
MESSAGES AND SIGNALS.

Army Form C. 2123.
(In books of 50's in duplicate.)
No. of Message ....

9M 36

Charges to Pay.	Office Stamp.
£ s. d. Army B	9pm

Service Instructions.

Handed in at DH Office ......m. Received ......m.

TO All Battns

Sender's Number	Day of Month	In reply to Number	AAA
G 325	5th		

Following from ACORN begins
In view of successes further south patrolling is to be very active on your front in order to ascertain if enemy is withdrawing his troops

FROM DAB
PLACE & TIME 8 20 pm

Wt. 432—M437 500,000 Pads. H W V 5/16 Forms C.2123.

Army Form C. 2123.
(In books of 50's in duplicate.)

"C" Form (Duplicate).

MESSAGES AND SIGNALS.

No. of Message ....

8 pm

Service Instructions.

Charges to Pay. £ s. d.

Army 6

Office Stamp.

FP 5/9/16

Handed in at .... Office .... m. Received .... m.

TO All Battns

Sender's Number	Day of Month	In reply to Number	AAA
Q 11284	5th		

Following message received from ACORN AAA French are advancing with great speed north of SOMME on the line PERONNE–BAPAUME road along which the enemy are trying to withdraw his guns AAA Battery of 420 cm hows and sausage on ground captured AAA 14th Corps have seized LEUZE WOOD and are advancing now on the trench junction T 14 D 8 2 4

FROM DAB

PLACE & TIME 6.50 pm

Wt. 432—M437 500,000 Pads. H W V 5/16 Forms C.2123.

Army Form C. 2123.
(In books of 50's in duplicate.)

"C" Form (Original).

MESSAGES AND SIGNALS. No. of Message..................

Prefix............Code............Words............
£ s. d.
Charges to collect

Received
From FACK
By Bricol

Sent, or sent out
At.......m.
To.......
By.......

Office Stamp.
FA
6/9/16

Service Instructions.

Handed in at.......Office.......m. Received.......m.

TO FACT FAD FILE FALL

*Sender's Number	Day of Month	In reply to Number	AAA
SC 9A	6TH		

Ration	Parties	will	be	sent
to	NW	Corner	of	BERNAFAY
WOOD	at	5PM	or	as soon
after	as	Possible	AAA	They
should	bring	empty	petrol	tins
with	them	to	be	refilled
at	watercarts			

FROM FACE
PLACE & TIME

* This line should be erased if not required.

Wt. 432—M437 500,000 Pads. H W V 5 16 Forms C.2123.

The Adjutant 8th Devons Regt

Our own artillery are shelling our trenches also our own men are being knocked out by our own rifle fire

2/Lt [illegible]

D Coy

Please send stretcher bearers

P.T.O.

and are sleeping | [illegible]
at your mercy. | [illegible]
Think it is our own
rifle fire, tho' our
artillery is dropping
just short of the
trenches. The Turks
on the right have
all retired

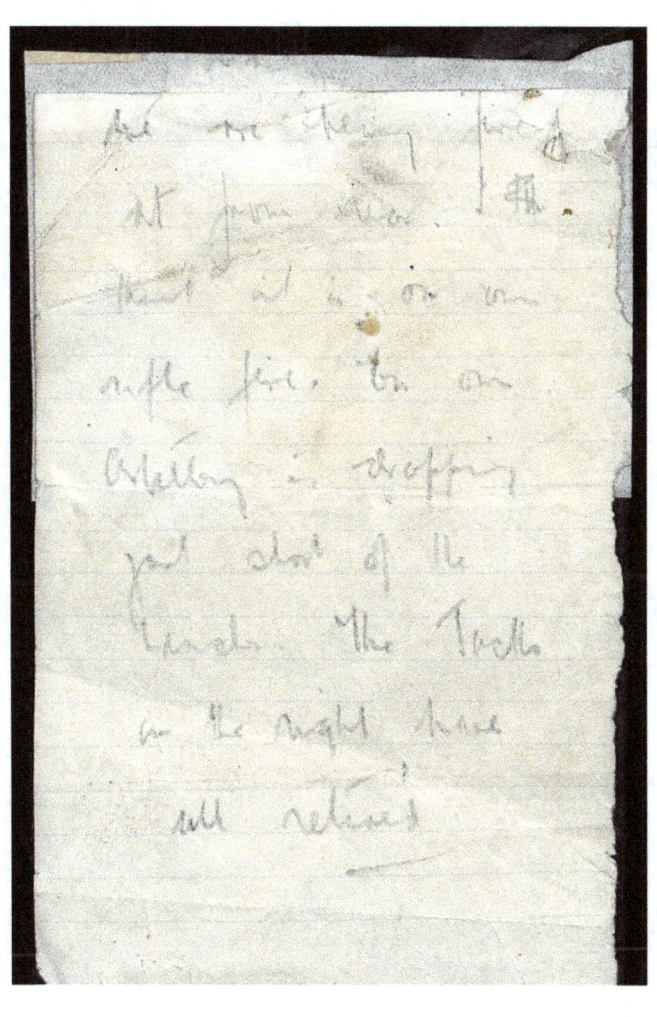

"C" Form (Original).

Army Form C. 2123.
(In books of 50's in duplicate.)

MESSAGES AND SIGNALS. No. of Message..................

Prefix.......... Code.......... Words..........	Received	Sent, or sent out	Office Stamp.
£ s. d. Charges to collect	From.......... By..........	At FA m. To Army By.......... 6/9/16	8.45 pm
Service Instructions.			

Handed in at...Office..............m. Received..............m.

TO: KEEP FACT FAD FADE FILE

*Sender's Number	Day of Month	In reply to Number	AAA
BM72	6		

you will send up 2 platoons to occupy ZZ ALLEY at once AAA Report when they are in position AAA FAD and FILE are holding STOUT trench AAA Acknowledge addressed KEEP repeated FACT FAD FADE FILE

FROM
PLACE & TIME: FACE 7.5 pm

* This line should be erased if not required.

Wt. 432—M437 500,000 Pads. H W V 5 16 Forms C.2123.

"A" Form.

MESSAGES AND SIGNALS. No. of Message........

Prefix........ Code........m.	Words	Charge		Recd. at..........m.
Office of Origin and Service Instructions.	Sent		This message is on a/c of: ....Service.	Date..........
	At..........m.			From..........
	To..........			By..........
	By..........		(Signature of "Franking Officer.")	

TO { Adjutant | Fact

Sender's Number	Day of Month	In reply to Number	AAA
*			

My	ration	party	has	lost
itself	as	there	are	no
more	of	it.	I	have
only	34	men	left	&
will	not	be	able	to
cover	any	frontage	at	all.
Might	if	necessary	this	A
Boys	3	platoons	take	on
my	job	&	I.	remain
in	Dugout	Trench	in	consequence
of	my	lack	of	men

From O.C. D Coy

Place

Time

The above may be forwarded as now corrected. (Z)

..................Censor. ....Signature of Addressor or person authorised to telegraph in his name.

* This line should be erased if not required.

T. & W. & J. M. Ltd., London. W 14042/M44. 75,000 12/15. Forms C 2121/10.

"A" Form. Army B[illegible]

MESSAGES AND SIGNALS. No. of Message

Prefix..........Code..........m. Office of Origin and Service Instructions.	Words	Charge	This message is on a/c of: ....Service. (Signature of "Franking Officer.")	Recd. at..........m.
	Sent			Date..........
	At..........m.			From..........
	To..........			
	By..........			By..........

TO { Adjutant | Tact

Sender's Number	Day of Month	In reply to Number	AAA
*			

Diagonal	Trench	&	part	of
a	trench	U	take	&
be	Trinity	Alley		
U	am	practically	in	touch
with	Tay	on	my	left
on	Cork	with	nobody	on
right.				
State	of	trenches	extremely	bad

From J.C.D

Place

Time

The above may be forwarded as now corrected. (Z)

.... Censor. | Signature of Addressor or person authorised to telegraph in his name.

* This line should be erased if not required.

T. & W. & J. M. Ltd., London. W 14042/M44. 75,000 12/15. Forms C 2121/10.

"A" Form. Army Form C. 2121.

MESSAGES AND SIGNALS.

No. of Message

Prefix....Code....m.	Words	Charge		Recd. at....m.
Office of Origin and Service Instructions.	Sent		This message is on a/c of: ....Service.	Date
	At....m.			From
	To			
	By		(Signature of "Franking Officer.")	By

TO Adjutant FACT

Sender's Number	Day of Month	In reply to Number	AAA

Sr	ROCK	has	sent	for
one	platoon	this	has	gone
to	reinforce	him		

From O.C. D. Coy

Place

Time 9.45 am

The above may be forwarded as now corrected. (Z)

Censor. Signature of Addressor or person authorised to telegraph in his name.

* This line should be erased if not required.

T. & W. & J. M. Ltd., London. W 14042/M44. 75,000 12/15. Forms C 2121/10.

Adjt.
8 Devons.

The line is now extended down Pilson Lane. I am not exactly sure how far down it goes but am going to see and with cover as much of the Road to Guichy as possible.

I enclose a note from Fenwick. Please notify our artillery of our exact positions. On the left we run forward up the wood.

If you can send me up another man Stretcher bearer.

C B Hole Capt.
C Coy.

6.15 pm.

35

C.O. 8th Devons.

Sir. Beg to acknowledge yr minute which [illegible] has answered for me. The ground is so shell starred that operations would be difficult to notice.

We have had a few more casualties but slight usually.

I would suggest 12 stretchers being sent up in order that the wounded may be collected at once.

We shall all be glad of a change.

C. B. Hole. Capt
Comdr. C. Coy.

stretchers of [illegible]

7.55 pm

40

OC. B Coy.

Please state as nearly as you can what your position is, ~~who are on~~ & if you are in touch with your flanks, if so who are on your flanks. Also state state of Ammn

5-9-16
7 am

Cdg
C R Page Capt

Office of Origin and Service Instructions.	Charge	This message is on a/c of:	Recd. at.............m.
	Sent At.........m. To....... By.......	...............Service. (Signature of "Franking Officer.")	Date....... From....... By.......

TO O.C. A Coy

Sender's Number	Day of Month	In reply to Number	
* FA 22	5.9.16		AAA

Please send one platoon up to DIAGONAL TR. to report to Capt Moore to go out & dig themselves in on the defensive flank. Please get this done immediately & report to me when they have joined Capt Moore.

Have C Coy moved yet?

From Coy

Place

Time 11.20 pm

The above may be forwarded as now corrected.

(Z) .... Censor. Signature of Addressor or person authorised to telegraph in his name. C... Capt

* This line should be erased if not required.

T. & W. & J. M. Ltd., London. W 14042/M44. 75,000 12/15. Forms C 2121/10.

"A" Form. Army Form C. 2121.

MESSAGES AND SIGNALS.

No. of Message

Prefix ... Code ... m.	Words	Charge	This message is on a/c of:	Recd. at ... m.
Office of Origin and Service Instructions.	Sent At ... m. To ... By ...		... Service. (Signature of "Franking Officer.")	Date ... From ... By ...

TO			
all units	FACE	15th MMG	Battery
KALE	KEEP	Z 4 TMB	EAGER
DAB			

Sender's Number.	Day of Month	In reply to Number	AAA
* BM 49	Sept 5		

Warning	order	AAA	The	operation
referred	to	in	para	4
c and	d in	20th Inf	Bde OO	81 of
today	will	take	place	tomorrow
morning	6th	Sept	AAA	There
will	be	a	subsidiary	operation
to	take	the	corner	of
DELVILLE	WOOD	which	will	be
undertaken	by	KALE	AAA	Further
details	will	be	issued	

From FACE

Place

Time 1 PM

C O [illegible] Major Brigade Major

The above may be forwarded as now corrected. (Z)

Censor. Signature of Addressor or person authorised to telegraph in his name.

* This line should be erased if not required.

(4198) Wt. W14042—M44. 300000 Pads. 12/15. Sir J. C. & S.

"A" Form. Army Form C. 21..

MESSAGES AND SIGNALS. No. of Message

Prefix...........Code..........m. | Words | Charge | This message is on a/c of: ....Service. (Signature of "Franking Officer.") | Recd. at..........m.

Office of Origin and Service Instructions.

Sent At..........m. To.......... By..........

Date.......... From.......... By..........

TO O.C. All Coys

Sender's Number | Day of Month | In reply to Number | AAA

Batt. will parade at 12 midnight.
Move off by Coys under guides.
Batt will relieve KEEN (2nd Mans)
Objectives & to hold ZZ ALLEY &
T 13 a 0.4. to T.13.6.6 4 to
form a defensive flank facing North.
Gordons are holding position from T.14.
c. 3.0. to T 14 a. 0.5. Strong Pt at T
14 a. 0.5. be formed by Gordons.
2 Coys Borders will occupy position
from 19.b.3. 6 to 13. d 0.0.
B. Coy. & half Coy D Coy will dig trench
to form defensive flank & gain
touch with Gordons N. of GINCHY at
Strong Pt. On completion of work
D Coy will occupy whole of
Z.Z ALLEY.

From

Place

Time

The above may be forwarded as now corrected. (Z)

Censor. Signature of Addressor or person authorised to telegraph in his name.

* This line should be erased if not required.

W. & W. & J. M. Ltd., London. W 14042/M44. 75,000 12/15. Forms C 2121/10.

"A" Form. Army Form C. 2121.

MESSAGES AND SIGNALS.

No. of Message

Prefix............Code............m. | Words | Charge

Office of Origin and Service Instructions.

Sent
At..................m.
To..................
By..................

This message is on a/c of:

....................Service.

(Signature of "Franking Officer.")

Recd. at..............m.
Date..................
From..................
By....................

TO: Adjutant [illegible]

Sender's Number	Day of Month	In reply to Number	
* B 2	5/9/16		AAA

My	company	occupies	Z Z	Trench
from	near	Western	Bome.	of
Delville	Wood	to	Corps	Boundary
AAA	I	am	not	yet
in	Touch	with	Troops	on
either	flank.	AAA		
Trenches	in	poor	condition	but
am	working	on	repair	of
them.				

From: O.C. B Coy.

Place

Time: 9 25 am.

The above may be forwarded as now corrected.

.... Censor.

(Z) [illegible]

Signature of Addressor or person authorised to telegraph in his name.

* This line should be erased if not required.

T. & W. & J. M. Ltd., London. W 14042/M44. 75,000 12/15. Forms C 2121/10.

From 2/Lt M E G Fenwick
No 6 Platoon -

To Capt G-B- Holt
C Coy -

We have had many Casualties
from our own shell fire
please send a message back to
this effect to head quarters -
Please send up stretcher bearers
as soon as possible -
I am in the centre of the line
please let me have a message
at once if you have any further
instructions

M E G Fenwick

6-10 pm by Pte Swain -

54

O.C. Batt^n on our right.

Will you kindly inform me what your dispositions are on S E edge of DELVILLE WOOD ?

Do you hold HOP ALLEY ?

" " BITTER TR ?

What about edge of Wood ?

We hold EDGE TR from S.12.D 60.00. to S.18 b.9.7, with advanced posts about S.18 b.8½.9., T.7.C.20.00., T.7.C.10.1½.

L.G & M.G. trained along North of ALE ALLEY.

5/9/16

[illegible] Major
Cmd. [illegible]

It was reported your Div held ALE ALLEY – BEER junction. Is that so?

Prefix.........Code.........m.	Words	Charge	This message is on a/c of:	Recd. at.........
Office of Origin and Service Instructions.	Sent		..........Service.	Date.........
	At..........m.			From.........
	To..........			
	By..........		(Signature of "Franking Officer.")	By.........

TO { O.C. all Coys

Sender's Number	Day of Month	In reply to Number	
* FA 23	6-9-16		AAA

Operation Orders

The French are advancing with great speed on the line PERRONE–BAPAUME RD along which the enemy is trying to withdraw his guns. French have captured 1 battery of 420 cm Howitzers & a baloon.

The Corps on our right have seized LEUZE WOOD & are advancing towards trench junction T 14 d 85 40

BORDER REG have 2 Coys holding T 19 a 8.6 & T 19 a 6.9.

9th Devons in reserve at FOLLY TRENCH

Objectives are line of posts to be established from high ground GINCHY TELEGRAPH to T 14 a 6.4. & to seize trench junctions at T 7 d 40.50 & T 7 d 3.2. At 6 am barrage will be on line T 14 b 5.0 to T 7 d 8.5 & move N. along a line parallel & 200x N of ALE ALLEY.

From

Place

Time

The above may be forwarded as now corrected. (Z)

.... Censor. Signature of Addressor or person authorised to telegraph in his name.

* This line should be erased if not required.

T. & W. & J. M. Ltd., London. W 14042/M44. 75,000 12/15. Forms C 2121/10.

Office of Origin and Service Instructions.	Sent	Service.	Date.
	At.....m.		From
	To		By
	By	(Signature of "Franking Officer.")	

TO

Sender's Number	Day of Month	In reply to Number	AAA
*			

Directly this high ground has been captured & information received that it has been the barrage will lift on to the FLERS LINE in order to allow patrols to go forward.
Dividing line between GORDONS & DEVONS is road running N & S through GINCHY.
B Coy are going forward to capture the ground on the W of road, including the road. It is reported that GORDONS have occupied GINCHY & QUEENS have occupied the E end of DELVILLE WOOD.
POSITION of BATT.
A Coy in ZZ TR. B Coy as ordered. C Coy in [illegible] [illegible] flank 2 platoons of the same. 2 platoons of D [illegible] in support to the QUEENS N.E. of DELVILLE WOOD.
Every opportunity of pushing forward patrols should be taken!

From
Place
Time 7.7 am

The above may be forwarded as now corrected. (Z)

Censor. [illegible] Capt [illegible]
Signature of Addressor or person authorised to telegraph in his name.

* This line should be erased if not required.

T. & W. & J. M. Ltd., London. W 14042/M44. 75,000 12/15. Forms C 2121/10.

MESSAGES AND SIGNALS. No. ...

Prefix............Code............m. | Words | Charge

Office of Origin and Service Instructions.

Sent
At..............m.
To..............
By..............

This message is on a/c of:
.......................Service.
(Signature of "Franking Officer.")

Recd. at..............m.
Date..............
From..............
By..............

TO O.C. Cantonment [?]

Sender's Number | Day of Month | In reply to Number | AAA

C Coy will occupy ~~Diagonal~~
DIAGONAL TR.
A Coy in reserve will occupy
LONGUVAL ALLEY
Battalion H.Q. will be in LONGUVAL
ALLEY at S 24 a 2.9.

From
Place
Time

The above may be forwarded as now corrected. (Z)

.......................Censor.
Signature of Addressor or person authorised to telegraph in his name.

* This line should be erased if not required.

T. & W. & J. M. Ltd., London. W 14042/M44. 75,000 12/15. Forms C 2121/10.

To Adjutant
8th Devons

Casualty report as far as known.

No 11825 Pte Cleave. F. Killed 6-9-16

10755 " Gale. W. Gloucester att: Killed 6-9-16

24796 - Jones. A. Wounded 6 9-16 D.C.L.I.

26754 " Jewell. F. wound. 5th 9-16 D.C.L.I

26989 " Overton. G. wound. 5th 9-16 D.C.L.I

(Buried + dug out, still at duty 5 men)

27004 Pte Wilsted. W. Acc: bayonet, slight foot: duty; Report sick at first opportunity.

Lieut

7/9/16

Cmdg A. Coy
8th Devon Regt

Capt HOE of C Coy

~~[illegible]~~ock

The brigadier has asked that we are to withdraw from the extreme ~~[illegible]~~ right of our line, where it runs down the slope at about T.13.a. 4.1., & that we are only to hold as far as the ~~[illegible]~~ big mound at T.13.a.2.0. ~~[illegible]~~ that is to still hold on to high ground. ~~[illegible]~~ Those troops that are withdrawn are to report to Bn. H.Q. where they will put in to position again.

C.E. Pepys Capt

7.9.16
8¼ am

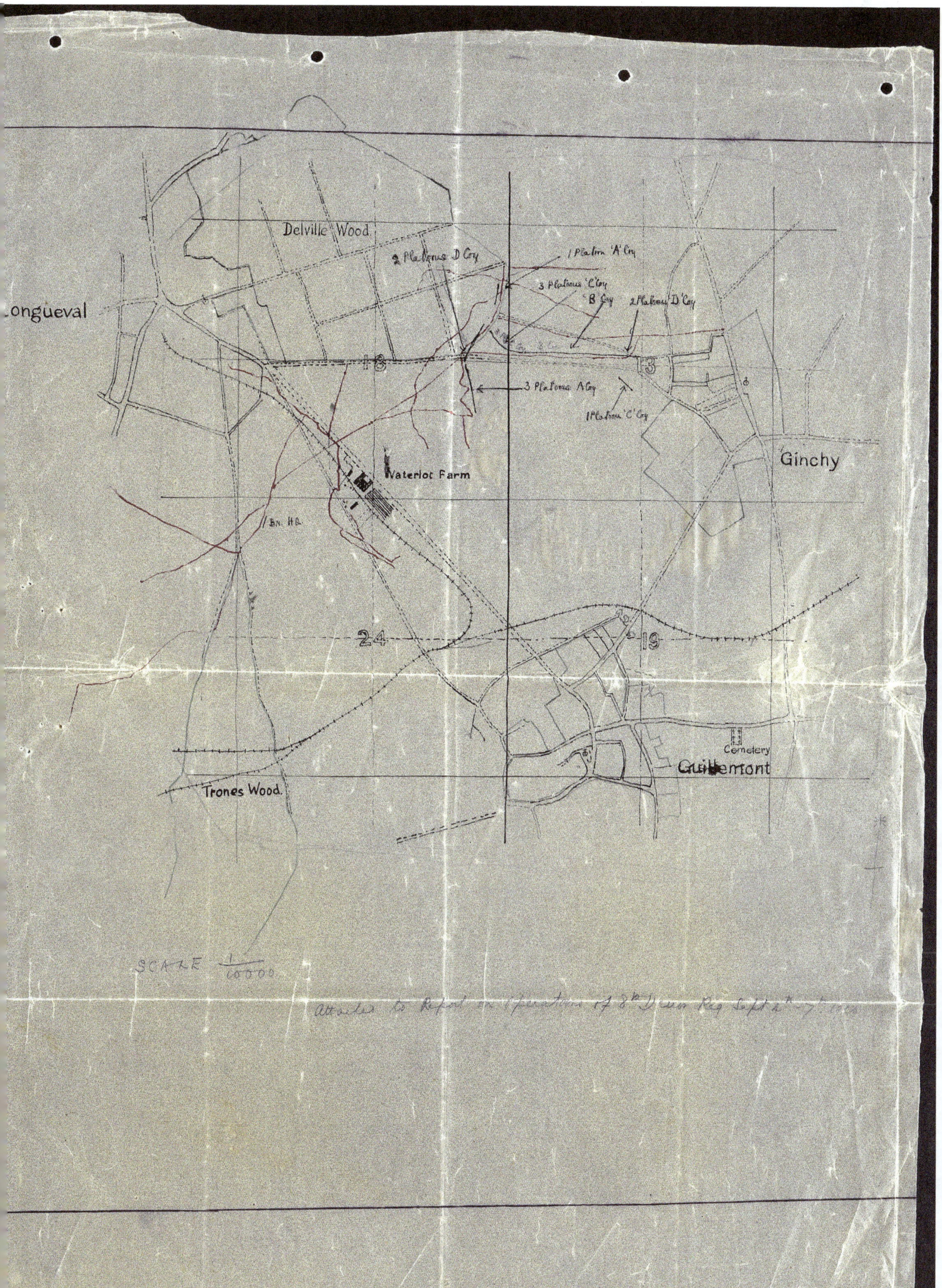

Delville Wood
Longueval
2 Platoons D Coy
1 Platoon 'A' Coy
3 Platoons 'C' Coy
'B' Coy
2 Platoons 'D' Coy
18
13
3 Platoons A Coy
1 Platoon 'C' Coy
Ginchy
Waterlot Farm
Bn. HQ.
24
19
Cemetery
Guillemont
Trones Wood.
SCALE 1/10000

Instructions regarding War Diaries and Intelligence Summaries are contained in F. S. Regs., Part II. and the Staff Manual respectively. Title pages will be prepared in manuscript.

WAR DIARY
or
~~INTELLIGENCE SUMMARY.~~
(*Erase heading not required.*)

Army Form C. 2118.

8th DEVON Regt

Vol 13

Place	Date	Hour	Summary of Events and Information	Remarks and references to Appendices
	October		October 1916	
TRENCHES – PONT DE NIEPPE	1/10/16		The Batt was relieved by 2nd BORDER REGT. and moved into ~~support~~ Bde Reserve at PONT DE NIEPPE. Relief of AB & C Coys (front line) complete by 10.15 AM. D Coy at LANCASTER SUPPORT FARM was relieved separately by ... P.M. Coys. billets in huts on road to LES TROIS TILLEULS (C 23d) H.Q. at C 23b 3.2.	
PONT DE NIEPPE	2-10-16		Battalion bathing. Kit inspections & gas drill. Strength of battalion 38 Officers & 802 other ranks.	
– –	3-10-16	9 am	Platoon & Coy drill Bayonet fighting.	
– –	4-10-16	9 am	Drill Improving billets & laying floor boards. C Coy move from huts to billets.	
– –	5-10-16	9 am	Drill & work on billets.	
– –	6/10/16	8 am	Bathing. Every available man of working party in the evening. Men returned to billets in LE BIZET.	
TRENCHES TOUQUET SECTOR	7/10/16	7.30 am	Battalion relieved the 2nd Border Regt in Brigade Left subsector LE TOUQUET SECTOR. Relief complete at 12.5 pm. 2nd Gordons on ~~left~~ right ... on Left. Trench strength 27 off 597 ORs	
	8/10/16		Very quiet during day. We made a gas attack at 9 pm. See Appendix I	App I
	9/10/16		Very quiet all day. Casualties nil.	

Instructions regarding War Diaries and Intelligence Summaries are contained in F. S. Regs., Part II. and the Staff Manual respectively. Title Pages will be prepared in manuscript.

WAR DIARY
or
~~INTELLIGENCE SUMMARY~~

(Erase heading not required.)

Army Form C. 2118.

8th Devon Reg

Place	Date	Hour	Summary of Events and Information	Remarks and references to Appendices
TRENCHES (LE TOUQUET SECTOR)	October 10/10/16		Very quiet all day. Work carried on as usual in all parts of line.	
—	11/10/16		Very quiet. Capt S. S. Barber ~~wounded~~ wounded.	
—	12/10/16		Our artillery & trench mortars active in preparation of a raid made by the 2nd Border Reg from our line at 7.40 pm. The raiders entered the enemy's trenches & killed 2, but obtained no identities. They suffered in casualties 1 off 3 men killed 6 wounded. The enemy's artillery retaliation was weak, but his trench mortars were very active. A certain amount of damage done to our trenches. One man wounded.	
LE BIZET	13/10/16		Relieved by 2nd Border Reg. Relief complete at 12.50 pm. A & C Coys to garrison the redoubts in the subsidiary line LYS FARM., STATION REDOUBT. SEVEN TREES. RESERVE FARM. GUNNERS FARM. CHESHIRE AV. H.Q. & B & D Coys to LE BIZET in billets. One man killed. 2nd Lt A C CAMERON rejoined the battalion.	
—	14/10/16		All available men on working parties	
—	15/10/16		All available men on working parties.	
—	16/10/16		All available men on working parties.	
—	17/10/16		All available men on working parties	
—	18/10/16		All available men on fatigue parties in the day.	
TRENCHES. (LE TOUQUET SECTOR.)	19/10/16	8am	Relieved the 2nd Border Reg in trenches. Relief complete 8.40 pm. 2nd Gordons on right 2nd Warwicks on left. Owing to ~~heavy~~ rain trenches getting full & falling in in places.	

Army Form C. 2118.

Instructions regarding War Diaries and Intelligence Summaries are contained in F. S. Regs., Part II. and the Staff Manual respectively. Title Pages will be prepared in manuscript.

WAR DIARY
or
~~INTELLIGENCE SUMMARY~~
(Erase heading not required.)

8th Devon Reg.

Place	Date	Hour	Summary of Events and Information	Remarks and references to Appendices
TRENCHES. (LES TOUQUET SECTOR.)	20/10/16		A good deal of rain. Worked at clearing & pumping trenches & rebuilding where fallen in. Enemy trench mortared the centre Company for an hour, damaging the trench, but no casualties.	
— —	21/10/16		Very quiet. Repairing & clearing trenches.	
— —	22/10/16		Very quiet. Work carried on.	
— —	23/10/16		Very quiet.	
— —	24/10/16		Very quiet.	
— — —	25/10/16	2.45pm	Relieved by 2nd Bat. Border Reg. Battalion marched back to billets & huts at PONT NIEPPE.	
PONT NIEPPE				
— —	26/10/16		2 Companies bathing & inspections. 2 Companies on fatigue.	
— —	27/10/16		2 Companies bathing & inspections. 2 Companies on fatigue.	
— —	28/10/16		Every available man on fatigue.	
— —	29/10/16		Fatigues. Divine service at 6 pm.	
— —	30/10/16		144 men on fatigue.	
— —	31/10/16		Billets & men being thoroughly cleaned.	
			Strength of the battalion 35 officers 784 O'Ranks. Casualties during the month. Killed 3 ORs. Wounded 1 off. 13 ORs. Sick 3 off 28 ORs. 8 men struck off strength to the M.G. Corps.	

[illegible] Capt
Adj 8th Bn Devon Reg.

2449 Wt. W14957/M90 750,000 1/16 J.B.C. & A. Forms/C.2118/12.

REPORT ON GAS ATTACK.

Primary precautions.	By 8-45 p.m., all men had been moved from Front Line, except the Sentries and Lewis Gunners, who wore their Box Respirators during the attack.
Discharge.	Gas was discharged from 9-0 p.m., to 9-20 p.m., along all our front and smoke candles from T.100. The wind was S.S.W., at five miles per hour. No gas blew back. The front line was reported all clear of gas at 10-15 p.m.
Enemy Signals.	No audible gas alarm was heard; at 9-1 p.m., one red rocket bursting into three parts was fired; at 9-5 p.m., three of the same were fired; at 9-10 p.m., four red rockets bursting into green.
Behavioue of the enemy.	From 8-45 p.m., to Zero, sniping was more considerable than usual. At 9-0 p.m., the Enemy immediately opened considerable rifle and machine gun fire. This continued with Trench Mortar fire till 9-20 p.m.. About twenty 77mm. shells pitched near our Support line in the centre and on the right. At 9-20 p.m., their was a burst of fire from heavy and medium Trench Mortars for a few minutes. On the right, they were falling mostly on the Support, on the left on the Front Line. At 9-20 p.m., the rifle and machine gun fire slackened and at 9-30 p.m., night firing was normal.
Patrols.	Between 11-0 p.m., and midnight two Patrols went out. They were unable to get near the enemy trenches as he was very much on the alert. They reported that they could hear the enemy working on his lines.

Instructions regarding War Diaries and Intelligence Summaries are contained in F. S. Regs., Part II. and the Staff Manual respectively. Title pages will be prepared in manuscript.

WAR DIARY
or
~~INTELLIGENCE~~ SUMMARY.
(Erase heading not required.)

8th Devon Reg. 20/7

NOVEMBER 1916 Vol 14

Army Form C. 2118.

Place	Date	Hour	Summary of Events and Information	Remarks and references to Appendices
	November 1916			
PONT NIEPPE	1/11/16	8-30 am.	The Battalion relieved by 1st Wilts Reg. marched to billets & huts at LA CRÈCHE Arrived 11.30 am	
(Ref map. Sheet 36 1/40,000)			Strength of battalion 35 Officers 784 O'Ranks	
LA CRÈCHE	2/11/16	8-30 am	Battalion moved to billets at THIEUSHAUK. Arrived 12 noon. Good billets.	
THIEUSHAUK	3/11/16	9 am	Platoon & Company drill.	
(Ref HAZEBROUCK Map 1/40,000.)	4/11/16	7 am.	Battalion training. Short march Bayonet Fighting. Rifle exercises. Extended order Drill	
	5/11/16	10 am	Divine Service. Inspection of billets. 2nd Lt YAXLEY joined the battalion	
—	6/11/16	9 am	Route march THIEUSHAUK – EECKE – ST SYLVESTRE – CAESTRE – THIEUSHAUK. 7 miles.	
			G.O.C. 20th Inf Bde inspected billets in the afternoon.	
— —	7/11/16	9 am.	Lectures & Physical exercises in billets. (Wet all day.)	
—	8/11/16	7 am	Short march Bayonet fighting. Visual training. Coy Drill.	
LYNDE	9/11/16	7.15 am	Battalion moved to billets at LYNDE. Arrived 1.15 pm Route CAESTRE – HAZEBROUK.	
SERQUES	10/11/16	7.15 am	Battalion moved to billets at SERQUES. Arrived 6 pm Route RENESCURE – ST OMER – TILQUES.	
NORTLEULINGHEM	11/11/16	8 30 am.	Battalion moved to billets at NORTLEULINGHEM. Arrived 12 noon. Route MOULLE.	
— —	12/11/16	11 am	Divine Service.	
— —	13/11/16	9 am.	Battalion training. Attack on a trench position. Musketry & Lewis Guns on range in afternoon.	
— —	14/11/16	8 am	Inter Brigade Field day. Battalion formed the advance guard & led an attack on a position.	

T2134. Wt. W708—776. 500000. 4/15. Sir J. C. & S.

167

WAR DIARY
or
~~INTELLIGENCE SUMMARY~~
(Erase heading not required.)

8th Devon Reg

Army Form C. 2118.

Instructions regarding War Diaries and Intelligence Summaries are contained in F. S. Regs., Part II. and the Staff Manual respectively. Title Pages will be prepared in manuscript.

Place	Date	Hour	Summary of Events and Information	Remarks and references to Appendices
Ref HAZEBROUK MAP 1/100,000. SETQUE	November 15/11/16	9.15 a.m.	Battalion left NORTLIEULINGHEM & marched to billets at SETQUES. Arrived 2.20 pm. Route MENTQUE-BOISDINGHEM – ACQUIN – LUMBRES.	
RADINGHEM	16/11/16	8.30 am	Battalion left SETQUE & marched to billets at RADINGHEM Chateau. Route LUMBRES – WAYRANS – CLÉTY – AVROULT – AUDINCTHUN-WANDONNE. Distance 17 miles. No one fell out.	
— —	17/11/16		Battalion resting.	
VERCHIN (LENS MAP)	18/11/16	10.15 am	Battalion marched to billets in VERCHIN ROUTE MONTEVILLE – FRUGES.	
[struck-through] OEUF	19/11/16	9.45 am	Battalion marched to billet at OEUF Route CRETY – ERIN – BERMICOURT – BEAUVOIS. 75 O.Rs reinforcements arrived from 11th Devon Reg.	
BUIRE AU BOIS	20/11/16	10.10 am	Battalion marched to billets at BOIRE-AU-BOIS. Route FILLIEVRES – MONT HOBERT.	
DOULLENS	21/11/16	7.45 am	Battalion marched to DOULLENS Route WAVANS.	
BERTANCOURT	22/11/16	8.15 am.	Battalion moved to BERTANCOURT. Route AUTHIEULLE – VAUCHELLES – BUS.	
MAILLY MALLET	23/11/16	8 am.	Battalion moved to MAILLY MALLET. At 9 pm Battalion moved to trenches at BEAUMONT HAMEL. Relief was a difficult matter owing to mud & bad guides. On the right the South Staffs. On the left The 2nd Gordon Highlanders.	
TRENCHES) BEAUMONT HAMEL	24/11/16		The line consists of a certain amount of very bad & sticky trenches, some funk holes, & some good German dug outs in the reserve line. Difficulty in communication owing to the mud. Hostile artillery surprisingly quiet. The enemy seems vague about our line.	
— —	25/11/16		Situation quiet. 90 of the enemy were seen moving towards our left front. The Reg. on right also reported a great deal of enemy movement. Battalion stood-to but nothing more occurred.	
— —	26/11/16		Situation quiet. No change.	
	27/11/16	5.30 am	Battalion relieved by 9th Devon Reg. marched to billets at MAILLY-MAILLET. The men very done & a good deal of bad feet.	

Army Form C. 2118.

Instructions regarding War Diaries and Intelligence Summaries are contained in F. S. Regs., Part II. and the Staff Manual respectively. Title Pages will be prepared in manuscript.

WAR DIARY
or
~~INTELLIGENCE SUMMARY~~

(Erase heading not required.)

8th Devon Reg.

Place	Date	Hour	Summary of Events and Information	Remarks and references to Appendices
MAILLY MAILLET.	28/11/16		Battalion resting & drying & cleaning. Bathing. A few men on town fatigues	
—	29/11/16		Battalion still resting. Transport moved back to BERTRANCOURT. 50 men went to ACHEUX on fatigue unloading at Railhead, 50 men to ACHEUX guarding prisoners of war. 80 men on RE trench fatigue.	
—	30/11/16		Bathing. 80 men on RE trench fatigue. Village lightly shelled during the day. No casualties. Strength of Battalion 32 Officers 828 Other Ranks — Officers joined battalion 2, wounded 1, sick in hospital 5. Other Ranks wounded 5 missing 2, in hospital (not evacuated) 120.	

A C Cameron, 2Lt.
A/Adjt 8th Devons
for. Capt. Comdt.

2449 Wt. W14957/M90 750,000 1/16 J.B.C. & A. Forms/C.2118/12.

20th Brigade.

7th Division.

8th BATTALION

DEVONSHIRE REGIMENT

DECEMBER 1 9 1 6

Army Form C. 2118.

Vol 15

Instructions regarding War Diaries and Intelligence Summaries are contained in F. S. Regs., Part II. and the Staff Manual respectively. Title pages will be prepared in manuscript.

WAR DIARY
or
~~INTELLIGENCE~~ SUMMARY.
(Erase heading not required.)

8th Devon Regt.
December, 1916

Place	Date	Hour	Summary of Events and Information	Remarks and references to Appendices
MAILLY MAILLET.	1-12-16		Battn relieved the 9th Devons in the line in BEAUMONT HAMEL sector - Relief complete by 7.30 AM no casualties - working hard all day - Trenches much improved with the drier weather - 2nd Gordons on left. 1st S. Staffs on right.	
Trenches BEAUMONT HAMEL Sector	2-12-16		Weather fine - Low visibility & slight frost. Able to start wiring front line at 3 PM. Wiring in progress all along the front.	
"	3-12-16		Weather as before. 24 hours in the company reliefs started. This is working excellently & avoiding sickness & trench feet. Draft of 85 OR. joined battalion.	
"	4-12-16		Weather as before. Some accurate shelling by the enemy in the morning on Cross road near Bn HQ. No casualties to our men. Continuation of NEW MUNICH TRENCH to our left occupied by us, joining up our left with right of 2nd GORDONS - with good results. Wiring in progress all night.	
"	5-12-16		Relieved at dusk by 20th MANCHESTERS. Relief complete by 7.30 Pm. Battalion moved back to huts at BERTRANCOURT in divisional reserve. ~~Relief complete at~~ Three slight casualties.	
BERTRAN-COURT	6-12-16		Battalion resting. Feet & kit inspection. Very little sickness owing to dry conditions in trenches. Huts cold & wet, camp very muddy.	
"	7-12-16		Major Whitsman 4th Bn. Middlesex Regt assumed temporary command of battalion. Battn found 270 men for road mending fatigues. Lewis Gun & Bombing classes for remainder. Inspection of draft of 3.12.16. mostly new recruits from Training Reserve but good material on the whole.	
"	8-12-16		Baths for whole battalion. Classes continued in morning.	
"	9-12-16		Battn found fatigues as on 7th inst. 2Lts G. CUMMINGS. H. DREW & A. EVANS joined battalion. One officer & 26 OR went on fatigue to ACHEUX guarding prisoners.	

Instructions regarding War Diaries and Intelligence Summaries are contained in F. S. Regs., Part II. and the Staff Manual respectively. Title Pages will be prepared in manuscript.

WAR DIARY
or
~~INTELLIGENCE~~ SUMMARY

(Erase heading not required.)

Army Form C. 2118.

8th Devon Regt.

Place	Date	Hour	Summary of Events and Information	Remarks and references to Appendices
BERTRANCOURT	10.12.16		CAPT. G.B. HOLE to hospital. MAJOR WHITEMAN called away to command another battalion. CAPT. S.H. DUFF took temporary command of Battalion.	
TRENCHES BEAUMONT-HAMEL Section	11.12.16		The Battn relieved 2nd H.A.C. in Brigade reserve. The whole battalion in very comfortable German dug outs close together. Ground muddy and very cut up. Trench strength [illegible] offs. [illegible] OR. Relief complete at 4. P.m.	
"	12.12.16		Very quiet, rain and mist. Everybody working to keep the dug outs from being flooded. Successful in most cases. Major P.V. DAVIDSON 2nd Warwicks assumed command of Btn.	
"	13.12.16		Relieved the 2nd Gordons in the line at dusk. Two casualties (wounded) during the relief. Relief complete by 8. P.m. 2nd Border Regt on our left. 11th Division on our right.	
"	14.12.16		C & D coy relieved A & B coy in front line. This was necessitated by bad condition of outpost line of shell holes. Work was in progress during the night on these posts. Enemy very quiet except for intermittent shelling in and behind reserve positions. No casualties.	
"	15.12.16		Battalion relieved by 2nd Gordons. Relief complete by 6.45 P.m, no casualties. Returned to former position in Brigade Reserve at Q 17.a. 8.8.	
"	16.12.16		C & D coys on fatigue A & B coys improving dug outs.	
"	17.12.16		20th Inf Bde relieved by 22nd Inf Bde. Battn remained in same position as close support Battn of Brigade in divisional support, and came in case of attack under orders of G.O.C. 22nd. Inf: Bde. All available men on fatigue.	
	18.12.16		Every available man on RE fatigues.	
	19.12.16		Every available man on RE fatigues. 2LT. RENTON & 50 OR returned from ACHEUX.	
	20.12.16		Every available man on RE fatigues. 2LT. MITCHEL & 8 OR's joined the Battn from the base.	

Army Form C. 2118.

Instructions regarding War Diaries and Intelligence Summaries are contained in F. S. Regs., Part II. and the Staff Manual respectively. Title Pages will be prepared in manuscript.

WAR DIARY
or
~~INTELLIGENCE~~ SUMMARY

(Erase heading not required.)

8th Devon Regt

Place	Date	Hour	Summary of Events and Information	Remarks and references to Appendices
BEAUMONT-HAMEL Sector	21-12-16.		All available men on RE fatigues.	
"	22-12-16.		Relieved by 9th Devons in the early morning. Relief complete by 6.30 AM. Moved back to billets at MAILLY MAILLET in Brigade reserve. On return to billets all available men on RE fatigues.	
MAILLY MAILLET	23-12-16.		All available men on RE fatigues. Baths in evening for A & B coys.	
"	24-12-16		All available men on RE fatigues. Baths in evening for C & D coys & HQ.	
"	25.12.16.		No fatigues. Xmas dinners at 1.30 PM. As much preparation as possible had been made under the circumstances. Dinners were by companies. Every man had beer and puddings and presents from Mayoress of Exeter, socks chocolate etc.	
Trenches BEAUMONT HAMEL sector.	26.12.16.		Battalion relieved 1st R.W. Fusiliers in the line. Relief complete at 8.30 PM. No casualties. 9th Devons on our left 11th Division on our right. Trench strength. 17 off: 397 OR.	
"	27.12.16		Enemy fairly quiet. Ground very heavy but improving under slight frost. Bombardment of enemy's front line opened by our Corps artillery. Very good shooting. Enemy retaliation mainly on & behind support line. No casualties. 7 prisoners taken.	
"	28.12.16		Bombardment continued but less intense. Little enemy retaliation. 2LT C.D.L. CALEB & 2LT R GIBBONS joined the battalion with draft of 32 OR. All returned wounded men from 1st 2nd 8th 9th Bns. 3 prisoners taken.	
"	29.12.16.		A & B coys relieved C & D coys before dawn. No casualties. Thaw set in making ground very heavy in places. Bombardment continued. Some of our heavy artillery dropping very short. A good deal of enemy retaliation on front line. One man wounded. 4 prisoners taken.	

Instructions regarding War Diaries and Intelligence Summaries are contained in F. S. Regs., Part II. and the Staff Manual respectively. Title Pages will be prepared in manuscript.

WAR DIARY
or
~~INTELLIGENCE SUMMARY~~
(Erase heading not required.)

8th Durh Regt.

Army Form C. 2118.

Place	Date	Hour	Summary of Events and Information	Remarks and references to Appendices
Trenches BEAUMONT HAMEL Sectn	30.12.16		Heavy rain in the early morning. Great discomfort according by in front line, but very little sickness. Artillery of both sides much quieter. C & D coys relieved A & B late in the evening. No casualties. 8 prisoners taken making 22 in all.	
"	31.12.16		Quiet all day. Battalion relieved by 2nd GORDON HGRS in the evening. Relief complete by 8. PM. No casualties. Battalion moved back into immediate support in & near BEAUMONT-HAMEL in dug outs and shelters.	
			Strength of the Battalion. 34. officers 769. OR.	
			Total casualties for the month.	
			Killed 3 OR. Wounded 23 OR. Sick. 2 off. 52 OR.	
			Struck off strength 3 off. 70 OR.	

A C Cameron Lt.
A/Adjt. 8th Durh

2449 Wt. W14957/M90 750,000 1/16 J.B.C. & A. Forms/C.2118/12.

7th DIVISION.

20th INF. BDE.

8th DEVONSHIRE REGIMENT.

JANUARY 1917.

Army Form C. 2118.

Instructions regarding War Diaries and Intelligence Summaries are contained in F. S. Regs., Part II. and the Staff Manual respectively. Title Pages will be prepared in manuscript.

WAR DIARY
or
~~INTELLIGENCE SUMMARY~~
(Erase heading not required.)

8th Devon Reg

JANUARY 1917

Vol 16

Place	Date	Hour	Summary of Events and Information	Remarks and references to Appendices
Trenches BEAUMONT-HAMEL Sector	1-1-17		Batt. resting, except 50 men on Salvage & other working parties. 2LT. J.F.C. MARSHALL joined batt.	
	2.1.17		50 men on working parties, remainder improving dug outs. Garrison of GREEN line working on shelters in the LINE and improving trench.	
"	3.1-17.		120 men on working parties. Improvements as before. Capt. C. FROOD. 2LTS K.B. ARMSTRONG.	
"	4.1-17.		All available men on working parties. [K.C.W. LACEY & N.M. PIZEY. from 1st R. Dvn. Yeo. joined the batt.	
"	5.1-17		Batt. relieved by 2nd Bn. R. Warwickshire Regt in the morning. Relief complete 2.15 P.M. no casualties. Batt. moved back to billets in barns at LOUVENCOURT. All settled in by 7 P.M.	
LOUVENCOURT	6.1.17.		Batt. resting & cleaning up. Foot, kit inspection &c.	
"	7.1-17.		Church Service in Church army hut at 6 P.M. Lecture to all NCO's in the morning. 34 OR's joined batt. from the base (mainly men from training reserve batts. of Oxon & Bucks L.I. & R. Warwickshire Regt.)	
"	8.1-17.		A Coy. on the range in the morning. B Coy in afternoon. Grouping & application lying at 50x. Later repeated in the helmets. NCO's class in the morning under R.S.M. for young LCpls & NCOs of draft. Remainder of batt. on training, physical drill arms drill bayonet exercises. Baths for B C D Coys & HQ. 40 men on road cleaning & other fatigues.	
"	9.1-17.		Training for all coys & NCOs class continued. Baths for A Coy. 2LT. L.C.W. HARDING joined batt. with draft of 25 OR from base (men from 3rd Devons, some recruits & some ex-expeditionary men).	

2449 Wt. W14957/M90 750,000 1/16 J.B.C. & A. Forms/C.2118/12.

Instructions regarding War Diaries and Intelligence Summaries are contained in F. S. Regs., Part II. and the Staff Manual respectively. Title Pages will be prepared in manuscript.

WAR DIARY
or
~~INTELLIGENCE SUMMARY~~

(Erase heading not required.)

8th Devon Reg

Army Form C. 2118.

Place	Date	Hour	Summary of Events and Information	Remarks and references to Appendices
LOUVENCOURT	10.1.17		Battalion went a march in fighting order as strong as possible about 7 miles – Fatigues as before. Regimental Concert in evening. C & D Coys on range –	
	11.1.17		Training continued. Musketry, Squad drill, physical drill. Classes as before.	
	12.1.17		Training continued. Bayonet fighting, close order drill. Physical drill. All Coys on range. Classes as before. 100 men on fatigue –	
	13.1.17		Billets inspection by C.O. kit & other inspections. Classes concluded. 100 men on fatigue – 2Lt FENWICK rejoined Bn from hospital.	
	14.1.17		Church service 11 AM. 150 men on fatigue. Cleaning up of billets & surroundings.	
TRENCHES BEAUMONT HAMEL sector	15.1.17		The Battn. moved from LOUVENCOURT to trenches near BEAUMONT HAMEL. relieving 2/1st HAC. relief complete 7.30 pm. no casualties. Trench strength 23 off. 411 O.R. 9th Devon Regt on left. 11th Division on Right –	
"	16.1.17		Enemy fairly quiet. Considerable improvement effected in advanced posts, and new posts now held. thoroughly reconnoitred.	
"	17.1.17		Enemy's artillery active most of the day. 1 man killed and 2 wounded. C & D coys relieved A & B coys in the line at dusk without casualties. Five patrols were sent out in the early part of the night to discover if possible position of line held by enemy. Two went a considerable distance, under intermittent enemy shell fire and reconnoitred their objectives without discovering enemy. One patrol encountered strong enemy post, and after careful examination returned. Camouflage suits were worn owing to the snow on the ground.	

Instructions regarding War Diaries and Intelligence Summaries are contained in F. S. Regs., Part II. and the Staff Manual respectively. Title Pages will be prepared in manuscript.

WAR DIARY
or
~~INTELLIGENCE SUMMARY~~
(Erase heading not required.)

Army Form C. 2118.

8th Devon Reg.

Place	Date	Hour	Summary of Events and Information	Remarks and references to Appendices
Trenches	17-1-17	(Contd).	Draft of 27 OR joined Battn. 2LT. K. DUNCAN joined Bn.	
BEAUMONT HAMEL	18-1-17		Enemy artillery activity continued. 2 men killed & one wounded. Battn was relieved by 2nd GORDON HIGHRS. at dusk. Relief complete 7.45 pm. No casualties. One coy was left in STATION RD at disposal of OC. 2nd Gordons as a reserve for a minor enterprise which was contemplated. Remainder of Battn in immediate support in dugouts in & around BEAUMONT HAMEL.	
	19-1-17		Battn resting. Carrying party of 200 OR in the evening for RE.	
BUS	20-1-17		Battn relieved by 16th HLI at midday. Relief complete 12.45 pm. No casualties. Marched back to huts at BUS-les-ARTOIS. 2LT E.H. LITTLEWOOD joined Battn. Draft of 44 OR (from 1/7th Devon Cyclist Bn) joined Bn.	
—	21-1-17		Battn resting. Voluntary church service in afternoon.	
—	22-1-17		Battalion resting.	
BEAUVAL	23-1-17	8.35am	Battalion marched to billets at BEAUVAL. ROUTE ARQUEVES - RAINCHEVAL - BEAUQUESNE.	
—	24-1-17		Battalion rest reorganizing.	
—	25-1-17		Battalion reorganizing. 2nd LTS PUDDICOMBE, JOHNSON & SMITH joined the battalion	
—	26-1-17	7am	Battalion training. Draft of 124 OR joined the battalion from 2nd Line Devon Yeomanry	
—	27-1-17	—	Battalion training.	
—	28-1-17	10.30am	Divine service.	
—	29-1-17	7am	Battalion training. Battalion visited by the Corps Commander, Lt Gen Congreve V.C. etc.	
—	30-1-17	7am	Battalion training. Battalion visited by the Army Commander.	
BERNOIS	31-1-17	8.35am	Battalion moved to billets & huts at BERNOIS. Route MONTRELET - CANAPLES - HALLOY.	
			Casualties during the month. Killed O. Ranks 6. Wounded O. Ranks 9. Sick Officers 7. O. Ranks 370.	
			Strength of the battalion. Officers 44 O. Ranks 897.	[illegible] Capt 8th Devon Reg.

7th Division.
20th Inf. Bde.

8th Devonshire Regiment.

February, 1917

Vol 17

War Diary

8th Bn The Devonshire Regt

February 1917

197

Instructions regarding War Diaries and Intelligence Summaries are contained in F. S. Regs., Part II. and the Staff Manual respectively. Title Pages will be prepared in manuscript.

WAR DIARY
or
~~INTELLIGENCE SUMMARY~~
(Erase heading not required.)

Army Form C. 2118.

8th Devon Reg.
FEBRUARY 1917

Place	Date Feb 1917	Hour	Summary of Events and Information	Remarks and references to Appendices
PERNOIS	1·2·17	9 am	Battalion training	
—	2·2·17	9 am	Battalion training	
—	3·2·17	9 am	Battalion training. 2nd Lt Cornelius joined the battalion.	
—	4·2·17		Divine Service	
—	5·2·17	8 am	Battalion training & bathing.	
—	6·2·17	9 am	Battalion training	
—	7·2·17	9 am	Battalion training. Draft of 35 O.Rs joined the battalion; all have previously served with the battalion, with the exception of 4.	
—	8·2·17	9 am	Battalion training	
—	9·2·17	9 am	Brigade training.	
—	10·2·17	9 am	Battalion training	
—	11·2·17		Divine Service 11 am & 12 noon	
—	12·2·17	9 am	Battalion training. 2nd Lt R M. Thomson joined the battalion.	
—	13·2·17	9 am	Battalion training	
—	14·2·17	9 am	Battalion training	
—	15·2·17	9 am	Brigade parade. Battalion bathing. 2nd Lt PRICHARD joined the battalion.	
BEAUVAL	16·2·17	9.50 am	Battalion moved to billets in BEAUVAL. Route CANDAS-MONTRELET-BONNEVILLE.	
—	17·2·17	7.10 am	Battalion, with the 7th Division, inspected near PUCHEVILLERS at 11 am by Gen. Nivelle C-I-C the French Armies. The Division advanced in review order. One batt. (2nd Gordon Highlanders) marched past in column. The battalion held the position on the right of the line of the infantry of the Division. Field Marshall Sir Douglas Haig C-I-C & Gen. Gough Commanding V Army were present.	
BEAUQUESNE	18·2·17	9.55 am	Battalion moved to billets at BEAUQUESNE.	
—	19·2·17	9 am	Battalion training.	
—	20·2·17	9 am	Battalion training.	
BERTRANCOURT	21·2·17	11 am	Battalion moved to huts at BERTRANCOURT. Route RAINCHEVAL-ARQUEVES-LOUVENCOURT-BUS.	
—	22·2·17		3 Coys on fatigue. Classes of instruction.	
	23·2·17		Cleaning camp. Classes of instruction.	

2449 Wt. W14957/M90 750,000 1/16 J.B.C. & A. Forms/C.2118/12.

WAR DIARY
or
INTELLIGENCE SUMMARY.
(Erase heading not required.)

Army Form C. 2118.

Instructions regarding War Diaries and Intelligence Summaries are contained in F. S. Regs., Part II. and the Staff Manual respectively. Title pages will be prepared in manuscript.

Place	Date	Hour	Summary of Events and Information	Remarks and references to Appendices
	February			
BERTRANCOURT	24-2-17		400 men on a working party.	
— —	25-2-17	5 am	Battalion temporarily attached to the 91st Bde & standing by ready to reinforce them. Situation is that the enemy has retired all along this front to the ACHIET LE PETIT line leaving covering parties behind at various places to delay our advance. 8 am Battalion transferred to 22nd Brigade. 3 pm Battalion transferred back to 20th Bde. Standing by ready to move all day.	
MAILLY MALLET.	26-2-17	2.15 pm	Battalion marched to billets at MAILLY MAILLET. Route FORCEVILLE. Our patrols report they hold part of PUISIEUX where they are meeting with resistance from the enemy's covering troops.	
— —	27-2-17		Two Companies on tramway fatigues. Our line has advanced on the whole of the Army's front. 7th Division reported to be holding a line N. of PUISIEUX.	
— —	28-2-17		Small fatigue parties.	
			Strength of battalion. Officers 46. O. Ranks. 910.	
			Casualties during the month. Officers: NIL. O Ranks NIL. Sick 149.	
			C R [illegible] Capt. Adjutant 8th Devon Reg.	

7th Division

20th Inf Bde.

8th Devonshire Regiment.

March 1917.

Instructions regarding War Diaries and Intelligence Summaries are contained in F. S. Regs., Part II. and the Staff Manual respectively. Title pages will be prepared in manuscript.

20/7

WAR DIARY
or
~~INTELLIGENCE SUMMARY.~~
(Erase heading not required.)

8th Devon Reg

Army Form C. 2118.

Place	Date	Hour	Summary of Events and Information	Remarks and references to Appendices
March	1917			
TAILLY MALLET	1.3.17		500 men on road work.	
PUISIEUX-AU-MONT	2.3.17		Battalion moved at 4.15 pm & relieved the 2nd Royal Warwickshire R. in PUISIEUX & the posts North of PUISIEUX, the left sector of the Divisional front. The 2nd Gordons on our right, 8th Wilts (19th Div.) on our left. Position of posts taken over L 14 d. 7.8. on a line running round the N. edge of the village to the N.W. corner of the village at L.14.a 3.1. A defensive left flank was formed with posts holding the W. edge of the village from L.14.a 2.1 to L.14.c.1.2. The supporting Coy occupied a trench on the S. edge of the village, the Reserve Coy a trench running E & W 200x S. of the village. The centre & N. part of the village was not occupied owing to heavy shelling.	Ref HEBUTERNE Map 1/10 000
—	—			
—	3.2.17		At day break in a heavy mist posts were pushed forward to a line running from L 15 a 0.2 to L 14 b 2.9. Supporting posts along the sunken road ~~at~~ from L. 14.d. 3.9 to L. 14 a 6.1. & at L.14.a. 7.3. An officer's patrols went out towards L.10.c. They pursued 2 unarmed Germans who retired on to a strong post L 10.c 15.70. where rifle fire was encountered. 2nd Lt BECKETT was wounded & 2nd Lt Jope hit but all returned to our line. During the day the enemy shelled the village & roads heavily, but caused no casualties. In the evening an officers patrol went out towards L.9 a & found the enemy at L.9.c 3.8. Other patrols nothing to report, except enemy posts N. of the dried up stream.	
	4.2.17		Day very bright & clear & little movement possible. Enemy shelled the village heavily. Three officers patrols went out at about 9 pm with orders to reach if possible the ACHIET – BUCQUOY line	

208

T2134. Wt. W708—776. 500000. 4/15. Sir J. C. & S.

Army Form C. 2118.

Instructions regarding War Diaries and Intelligence Summaries are contained in F. S. Regs., Part II. and the Staff Manual respectively. Title pages will be prepared in manuscript.

WAR DIARY
or
~~INTELLIGENCE SUMMARY.~~
(Erase heading not required.)

8th Devon Reg.

Place	Date	Hour	Summary of Events and Information	Remarks and references to Appendices
	March 1917			
PUISIEUX	4.3.17		& to reach BUCQUOY. Our patrol 2nd Lt YARLEY'S reached within 30x of the line & then encountered bombs & rifle fire. The other two, 2nd Lt SCOTT & 2nd Lt EVANS, met opposition from advanced posts.	
— —	5.3.17		In the early morning, the posts were advanced to (1) L 15. b. 3 4 (2) L.9. c. 8 3. (3) L 9. c. 5. 8. (4) L. 8. d. 95. 90. 3 ins of snow fell during the night making movements very plain. 2nd Lt PREADY was wounded putting out one post. Artillery fire very much less. At about 9pm the battalion was relieved by 14th Y & Ls. & marched to billets in MAILLY.	
MAILLY MAILLET	6.3.17		Battalion resting	
— — —	7.3.17		Battalion training & bathing	
— — —	8.3.17		Battalion training. Musketry on the range.	
— — —	9.3.17		Battalion training in the attack	
— — —	10.3.17		Battalion training in the attack.	
— — —	11.3.17		Divine Service. Inspection of billets & kit.	
— — —	12.3.17		Battalion training in the attack	
— —	13.3.17		Battalion training in the attack in conjunction with the 2nd Gordons.	
— —	14.3.17		Battalion standing by ready to move	
— —	15.3.17		Battalion training in the attack with the 2nd Gordons	
—	16.3.17		Battalion standing by & practicing the attack	

T2134. Wt. W708—776. 500000. 4/15. Sir J. C. & S.

Instructions regarding War Diaries and Intelligence Summaries are contained in F. S. Regs., Part II. and the Staff Manual respectively. Title pages will be prepared in manuscript.

WAR DIARY
or
INTELLIGENCE SUMMARY.
(Erase heading not required.)

Army Form C. 2118.

Vol 18

Place	Date	Hour	Summary of Events and Information	Remarks and references to Appendices
March			8th Devon Regiment March, 1917	
MAILLY	18th	10am	Battalion moved to day into bivouac in PUISIEUX.	
PUISIEUX	19th		Battalion on road work	
St LEGER	20th		Battalion moved to St LEGER & took over an outpost line from the 6th [illegible] running from B 4 b. 9.2. – T 28 c 4 6. – T. 27. b 3.7. The enemy holding the S. edge of CROISILLES in a strongly wired position. The 2nd [illegible] on our right holding a line from St LEGER WOOD to E of MORY. [illegible] on our left. During the night our patrols gained touch with the enemy.	Ref Maps 57 B. [illegible] 51 B. S.W.
ERVILLERS	21st		Battalion relieved in the evening by the 2nd [illegible] Reg. & marched to billets in ERVILLERS	
—	22nd		Battalion collecting R.E. material	
—	23rd		Battalion on road work.	
—	24th		Battalion on road work.	
—	25th		Battalion on road work.	
MORY	26th		Battalion relieved the 9th Devons in the MORY sector holding a line of posts S.W. of ECOUST. Anzacs on the right, [illegible] on the left. During the night fighting patrols tried to advance our line. They were held up by heavy M.G. & rifle fire & were not successful in the centre, where [illegible] advanced 300 yds. [illegible] 9 casualties.	

207

T2134. Wt. W708—776. 500000. 4/15. Sir J. C. & S.

Instructions regarding War Diaries and Intelligence Summaries are contained in F. S. Regs., Part II. and the Staff Manual respectively. Title Pages will be prepared in manuscript.

WAR DIARY
or
~~INTELLIGENCE SUMMARY~~

(Erase heading not required.)

Army Form C. 2118.

8th Devon Reg

Place	Date	Hour	Summary of Events and Information	Remarks and references to Appendices
	March 1917			
MORY	27.3.17		Our posts & trench of the sector were continually shelled. In the evening the right half sector was handed over to the 2nd Gordons, from C.8.c.7.2 – C.7.a.8.2. The Company relieved went into support of the Gordons who attacked the enemy posts, but were not successful.	
—	28.3.17		At dawn A Coy on the left advanced their posts in the direction of the windmill at T.24.d.1.5 in support of an attack on CROISILLES. The advance was quite successful, but the post at the windmill had to withdraw again to T.24.c.9.1 owing to heavy fire & the failure of the attack on the left. A Coy lost 9 killed and 7 wounded in this operation. During the day posts & lines of approach to MORY were shelled fairly continually. In the evening the battalion was relieved by the 2nd Border Reg, leaving 1 Company C Coy in support of the Gordons. The battalion marched to billets at ERVILLERS.	
ERVILLERS	29.3.17		Battalion moved to billets and shelters at COURCELLES	
COURCELLES	30.3.17		Battalion resting & working on roads	
—	31.3.17		Battalion resting.	
			Strength of Battalion Officers ORs	
			Casualties during march Killed Officers NIL. ORs 12. O'R. MISSING 3. Wounded do 2. do 22. Sick do 6. do 131.	

C R[illegible] Capt &
Adj 8th Devon Reg.

Instructions regarding War Diaries and Intelligence Summaries are contained in F. S. Regs., Part II. and the Staff Manual respectively. Title pages will be prepared in manuscript.

WAR DIARY
or
INTELLIGENCE SUMMARY.
(Erase heading not required.)

Army Form C. 2118.

8th Devon Regt
APRIL - 1917
Vol 17

Place	Date	Hour	Summary of Events and Information	Remarks and references to Appendices
	April			
COURCELLES LE-COMTE.	1.4.17		Battalion resting and was doing various repairs to billets. At 10 pm the Battalion moved off to their assembly position in front of ECOUST.	
ECOUST	2.4.17		The battalion captured the village of ECOUST-ST MEIN. Account of operations is in Appendix I	App I
COURCELLES LE-COMTE	3.4.17		Battalion relieved in the line at 3.30 am & marched to billets & tents in COURCELLES	
ABLAINZEVELLE	4.4.17		Battalion marched to billets & tents at ABLAINZEVELLE.	
— —	5.4.17		Battalion marched to PUISIEUX to bathe. Baths found to be out of order.	
— —	6.4.17		Battalion training & working parties.	
— —	7.4.17		Battalion training	
— —	8.4.17		Training & working parties.	
— —	9.4.17		Training & working parties. Draft of 1 officer 2nd Lt Rodwell & 79 other ranks joined the	
— —	10.4.17		Training & working parties. battalion from 3rd Reserve Bn Devon R. Some well trained N.C.Os but the men do not look promising & lack smartness	
—	11.4.17	7.15 am	Bathing. Battalion moved to billets in COURCELLES at 2.45 pm.	
COURCELLES.	12.4.17	9.30 am	Battalion moved to billets in ABLAINZEVELLE. All battalion on fatigues	
ABLAINZEVELLE	13.4.17		Training and fatigues.	
— —	14.4.17		—	
— —	14.4.17		Divine Service at 8.30 am and 6.30 pm. Parade service cancelled owing to rain.	
— —	15.4.17		Battalion training. Draft of 117 other ranks and Lt Ephraums joined the Battalion men come from Devon, Hants and Wilts training Reserves. They have the appearance of being a fairly good draft.	
—	16.4.17		Training. Two companies doing musketry on the range. RAMC sick to hospital	
—	17.4.17		Fatigues. four companies. LT. CARR-HARRIS RAMC sick to hospital. Capt. YOUNG RAMC assumed duties of medical officer i/c battalion	
	18.4.17		Battalion training.	
	19.4.17		Battalion moved from billets to camp near GOMIECOURT preparatory to going in to line.	

21
—
H

1577 Wt. W10791/1773 500,000 1/15 D. D & L. A.D.S.S./Forms/C. 2118.

Army Form C. 2118.

Instructions regarding War Diaries and Intelligence Summaries are contained in F. S. Regs., Part II. and the Staff Manual respectively. Title Pages will be prepared in manuscript.

WAR DIARY
or
INTELLIGENCE SUMMARY
(Erase heading not required.)

Place	Date	Hour	Summary of Events and Information	Remarks and references to Appendices
ECOUST ST-MEIN	20.4.17		Battalion moved from camp at 6.30 pm and moved to the line relieving after dusk the 2nd Bn QUEENS in section between ECOUST ST MEIN & BULLECOURT. 2nd GORDONS on left. ANZAC corps on right. Relief complete by 1 AM. 1 OR killed 2 wounded. Scattered enemy shelling. Trench strength	
	21-4-17		Dry and warm. Reciprocal artillery activity. 2Lt CW VAKLEY wounded, 1 OR wounded	
	22-4-17		Dry and warm. Aeroplanes, machine gun anti-aircraft fire very active. two other ranks wounded. Two new posts pushed forward some 150 X without resistance.	
	23-4-17		Dry but cooler. Considerable artillery fire on both sides. 2 OR killed & 5 wounded. 2Lt CORNELIUS to hospital. Capt GD LOCK to hospital.	
	24-4-17		Dry and warm. 1 O.R killed 5 wounded. 2 more new posts successfully pushed forward without resistance	
	25.4.17		Dry but cooler, cloudy. 2 OR killed 3 wounded. Considerable artillery fire on both sides. Patrols report enemy wire badly damaged. Line held by posts & MGs. Plenty of very lights. 3 officer patrols sent out. no casualties	
	26.4.17		Dry, cloudy. 2Lt BOND to hospital. 5 OR wounded. Reinforcements 2Lts HOLDSWORTH & COPNER (both reported in England). Bn relieved in evening by 2nd BORDER R. Relief complete by 1.45 AM. HQ & B.D coy to shelters near VAULX VRAUCOURT. C & A coys in cellars in ECOUST ST MIEN. Coys in position by 3. AM. 27th. Battalion in brigade support.	
	27.4.17		Battalion resting & cleaning.	
	28-4-17		Battalion resting & cleaning. working on shelters & trenches. Wounded 1 OR in ECOUST.	

2449 Wt. W14957/M90 750,000 1/16 J.B.C. & A. Forms/C.2118/12.

Instructions regarding War Diaries and Intelligence Summaries are contained in F. S. Regs., Part II. and the Staff Manual respectively. Title Pages will be prepared in manuscript.

WAR DIARY
or
INTELLIGENCE SUMMARY
(Erase heading not required.)

8th Devon Regt.

Army Form C. 2118.

Place	Date	Hour	Summary of Events and Information	Remarks and references to Appendices
~~[illegible]~~ ECOUST-ST-MEIN	29-4-17		Battalion relieved in Brigade support by 2nd Bn QUEENS REGT. Returned to billets at ABLAINZEVELLE. No casualties. Billeted by 3 am 30-4-17.	
	30-4-17		Battalion resting & refitting.	
			Total casualties for April.	
			Killed officers 4 O Ranks 34	
			Wounded officers 4 O Ranks 104	
			Missing officers nil. O Ranks 1	
			Sick officers 6. O Ranks 81.	
			Strength of Battalion.	
			Officers 39. O Ranks 924	
			[illegible] Lt Col. Cmdg.	

2449 Wt. W14957/M90 750,000 1/16 J.B.C. & A. Forms/C.2118/12.

8TH SER BATTALION THE DEVONSHIRE REGT.

-:- REPORT ON OPERATIONS -:-
at
E C O U S T
on
2nd APRIL 17.

Ref:- Maps, FRANCE
57.c.N.W. & 51.b.S.W.
Scale:- 1/20,000.

1. INFORMATION ABOUT THE ENEMY.

The enemy were holding the line running through NOREUIL - ECOUST - CROISILLES. This line was a strongly fortified and defended line of outposts covering his main line of defence known as the HINDENBURG LINE, which runs about North of the line of these Villages.
Previous to the attack on the 2nd, the enemy's intention to hold these Villages was clear. He had put up a strong resistance to our attempts to capture his advance posts in front of his wire. It afterwards transpired that he held troops in readiness in dugouts in ECOUST ready to counter attack if any part of this line of outposts was broken. This was to ensure the completion of defences of the HINDENBURG LINE.

2. ORDERS AND DISPOSITIONS.

The 20TH INFANTRY BRIGADE were ordered to capture ECOUST - LONGATTE and the ground on the South West and North East of it. The 8th DEVON REGIMENT were ordered to attack ECOUST with the 2nd GORDON HIGHLANDERS on their right, the 9th DEVON REGIMENT on the left.
The dividing lines between the Battalion and the GORDONS was from the road at C.8.a.21 to the road junction at C.2.d.6.6., and between the 9th DEVON REGT; was from C.1.d.0.2. - C.2.a.44. - U.2.6.c.7.1. - U.27.a.0.4.
Two objectives were given, the first being:-
C.3.c.1.2. - C.2.b.26. - C.2.b.2.8. - U.25.b.4.3. which was to be dug in on and consolidated at once. The second, to establish a line of posts on the front ~~C.3.b.5.0~~ C.3.b.03. - the Station at U.27.c.04. - U.20.c.5.4
Several changes in the orders for the formation and assembly position for the attack had to be made owing to the changing hands of the post at C.8.c.1.8. which was held finally by the enemy with two machine guns on the night of the 1/2nd and were a source of great danger to the success of the attack.
The attack was to be carried out by two Companies in two waves, one Company in Support which took over the Advanced posts on the night of the 1st/2nd and one Company in Reserve at BATTALION HEADQUARTERS at B.18.a.5.5.
The leading Companies to form up on a tape from C.7.d.82. - C.7.a.5.5. At Zero minus 20 to advance to a line running through C.8.d.2.7. - C.7.b.4.6. - C.1.a.0.2.
At Zero to advance under a creeping barrgge, starting 200 yards in front of this line, and moving forward at 100 yards in three minutes. A pause of 30 minutes to be made on the first objective, while the barrage remained 200 yards in front of it. To advance again under the creeping barrage to the second objective.

3. ASSEMBLY MARCH.

The weather was most favouable for the march. It was a beautiful still moonlight night. A long halt was made at ERVILLERS when the men had a meal and hot tea. Owing to the brightness of the moon, the assaulting Companies could not get into their position as early as ordered, but this was done with no hitches when the moon set down.

4. <u>THE ATTACK.</u>

(a). The right Company ("B" Coy: under Captain DUFF) at 0.15, the Company advanced within 100 yards of the enemy's wire, where the men lay down under a slight rise. At 5.15 a.m. the line went forward under the barrage. Machine Gun fire was opened from behind the enemy's wire, which caused a few casualties. The wire was found to be uncut, except in the road at C.8.a.19., where there was a gap on the road. The platoon opposite this gap was immediately rushed through, and its Lewis Gun team engaged and knocked out a machine gun which emerged from a house at C.2.c.3.4. The remainder of the Company was hustled through the gap and split up to work through the village, one platoon working in rear, as moppers up. The actual movements of the Company from this point, xxxxxxxxx are obscure, as all the Officers became casualties. A great deal of hand to hand took place. Lewis guns were used to great advantage aginst machine guns, and bombs and rifle grenades against rifle men in windows and strong positions. In particular, a Lewis gun was rought into action from a mound near the CHURCH at C.2.a.6.1. on to a machine gun holding up our left Compa-ny and the Battalion on our left.

The leading platoon were the first through the village and pushed on under the barrage beyond the first objective, and attempted to establish posts at the Station and at C.2.b.5.4. These posts came under very machine gun and rifle fire causing many casualties and killing the officer while trying to dig in, and they eventually had to retire.

The remainder of the Company formed a line of posts at C.2.b.82. - C.2.b.6.5. - C.2.b.2.8.38.

The Company wa s very much reduced by this time owing to heavy fighting and casualties. The mopping up platoon found a great deal to do, as many of the enemy reappeared from cellars and hiding places.

This Company reported reaching the first objective at 6.0 a.m. afterwards no reports were received, the Officers all having become casualties.

No touch wa-s kept with the GORDONS on the right xxxxx during the advance, owing to the Company going through the gap on the left and the GORDONS getting held up.

(b). The left Company ("D" Company under Lieut PERKINS) at 0.15 the C ompany moved forward to the line of outposts. At Zero, it advanced to the attack. The two right p latoons penetrated the wire from C.2.c.11.0 to C.1.d.33. The left platoon found itself held up by uncut wire and Machine gun fire. Considerable casualties were suffered penetrating the trenches and outskirts of the village. The O.C. Company, Lieut PERKINS, wa-s killed here. The right platoons worked along the main street running North East, the outer platoon along the trenches and the GORDONS on the West of the road. A good deal of fighting took place during this advance. On reaching the CROISILLES - ECOUST Road, a party of the enemy consisting of two Officers, 22 men and two machine guns were found in action at C.2.a.4.5. This party was captured, so enabling the left platoon to advance.

(c). Support Company. ("A" Coy under Captain PRIDHAM).
The support Company followed the attacking Companies at about 200 yards distance. Their action was chiefly to 'mop up' the village. In doing so, they took prisoner an Officer and about 20 prisoners and knocked out 2 Machine Guns with Lewis Gun fire, which had re-appeared after the leading Companies advanced. The Officer Commanding Company was wounded at the beginning of the advance. The Company advanced on to the final objective where posts were formed.

(d). Reserve Company. The Reserve Company, ("C" Company under 2nd Lieutenant COOPER) were not called on du ing the attack.

5. CONSOLIDATION.

Consolidation was immediately begun after gaining the objectives. Posts were establishd at :-
C.2.b.8.3. - C.2.b.5.4. - Th station at U.27.c.0.4. - U.27.c.8.7. - U.27.c.4.7. - U.26.d.9.1. - U.26.d.6.4. - U.26.d.45. - U.26.c.8.5. The Railway Embankment from C.2.b.5.8. - U.26.c.6.2. - was strongly held and consolidated. This was completed by 7.45.a.m. The right was not in touch with the GORDONS till some time later. The left was well in touch with the 9th DEVON REGT; who had come across too much to their right in front of the embankment. The majority of these men withdrew later.
On the left, the position was very strong owing to the embankment. On the right, the post at the station and C.2.b.5.4. came under heavy fire. After sustaining heavy casualties, including their officer killed, they were withdrawn to a less exposed position by the O.C.Company, he was wounded in doing so. As the position was not strong and the right Company had lost heavily, one platoon of the Reserve Company was sent up to establish themselves at C.2.d.5.9. in support of the posts and to keep touch with the GORDONS and our line at C.2.b.4.6. Later another platoon of the Reserve Company was sent to consolidate at C.2.b.4.3.
At 10.45 a.m. the Advance posts on the right were counter-attacked by 60 of the enemy from a S.E. direction. This attack was completely broken up by Lewis Gun fire. The Post at later came under very heavy machine gun and field gun fire and lost 75% casualties and had to withdraw. It was too light when they were established for them to dig in properly. At 11.0 a.m. the remaining two platoons of the Reserve Company moved by Sections to C.7.b.1.5. where they dug in. BATTALION H.Q. moved at 4.0 p.m. to the same spot.

6. GENERAL.

On the right flank, touch was not maintained at first with the GORDONS, but later this was established after consolidating the objectives.
On the left touch was maintained throughout the action with the 9th DEVON REGT; except when they were held up in the Cemetery.
The result of the action was entirely successful. A very strong position, strongly held, was captured from a picked body of ~~xxxxxx~~ troops of the enemy and was held.

At nightfall, some of the posts were pushed further forward to straighten the line and all posts were strengthened. Patrols were sent out towards BULLECOURT. At 3.30 a.m. 3rd instant, th position was handed over to the 20th MANCHESTER REGIMENT. 22 prisoners were taken including 2 Officers (or under- Officers). Two Machine guns were brought back and five others were put out of action. A large quantity of Lewis gun ammunition was expended.
All ranks agree that this weapon was invaluable.
In spite of heavy casualties among the teams, the 16 guns were brought out, and in addition, another one found in the possession of the enemy. Bombs and rifle grenades were freely used in the Village, the latter on occasions were very useful.

Our casualties were:-
6 Officers and 112 Other Ranks.
<u>KILLED:-</u> 2nd Lieut PERKINS, 2/lieuts FENWICK & CALEB.
<u>WOUNDED:-</u> Captain DUFF, Captain PRIDHAM & 2 /lt MITCHELL.
<u>OTHER RANKS</u>. 25 KILLED 89 WOUNDED and 2 MISSING.

7th DIVISION.

20th INF BDE.

8th DEVONSHIRE REGIMENT.

May 1917.

...ions regarding War Diaries and Intelligence Summaries are contained in F. S. Regs., Part II. and the Staff Manual respectively. Title pages will be prepared in manuscript.

WAR DIARY
or
INTELLIGENCE SUMMARY.
(*Erase heading not required.*)

Army Form C. 2118.

8th Devon Regt.
8 Devon Rgt
Vol 20

Place	Date	Hour	Summary of Events and Information	Remarks and references to Appendices
			MAY 1917	
ABLAINSEVELLE	1.5.17		Battalion training.	
	2.5.17		Battalion training - fatigues.	
	3.5.17		Battalion moved at 9 AM. to a position of readiness near [illegible] in support to operations carried out by 62nd Division. In position by 11 am. Moved to Camp at MORY by 8 PM. Trench strength 39 officers 740 O Ranks	
Trenches near BULLECOURT	4.5.17 to 9.5.17		[Report on operations which took place between these dates will be found attached in form of an appendix. Draft of 15 O.R. & 3 off: 2Lts A W WALL, L S [illegible], W G REED joined Bn 7.5.17. Daily casualties attached to report on operations]	
Mory	10.5.17		Batn returned to camp at MORY. All in by 7 AM. In the evening moved to billets in COURCELLES all in by 8 PM.	
COURCELLES	11.5.17		Batn resting. baths for all.	
	12.5.17		Batn resting. refitting. reorganising.	
	13.5.17		Church Parade in the morning. Resting.	

22

T2134. Wt. W708—776. 500000. 4/15. Sir J. C. & S.

Instructions regarding War Diaries and Intelligence Summaries are contained in F. S. Regs., Part II. and the Staff Manual respectively. Title pages will be prepared in manuscript.

WAR DIARY
or
~~INTELLIGENCE SUMMARY.~~
(Erase heading not required.)

Army Form C. 2118.

8th Devon Regt.

Place	Date	Hour	Summary of Events and Information	Remarks and references to Appendices
COURCELLES	4.5-17.		Fatigues for 200 men. Battn moved in morning to their old billets at ABLAINSEVILLE. Move complete by 12 noon.	
ABLAINSEVILLE	15-5-17.		Battn. reorganising. Baths. Fatigues. 2Lt F W PINKARD rejoined Battn.	
″	16-5.17.		Battn reorganising. Light training.	
″	17.5.17.		Light training and fatigues. Range practices.	
″	18-5-17.		Light training. Range Practice. 2Lt. L.J. Rolf joined Bn.	
″	19-5-17.		Light training & fatigues. Range practice.	
″	20.5.17		Church parade in the morning. 50 men on fatigue.	
″	21-5-17.		Progressive training commenced. Range practice. 2Lt Copner transferred R.F.C.	
″	22-5.17.		Bn. training. fatigues. 2Lt CORNELIUS rejoined Battn.	
″	23-5-17.		Bn training. Draft of 2Lt. E.J. BAKER & 21 O.Ranks (returned sick & wounded) joined Battn. Baths for all.	
″	24.5.17		Bn training. fatigues.	
″	25.5.17		Bn training. Range practice.	
″	26.5.17		Bn training. Fatigues. 2Lt Rodwell transferred R.F.C.	
″	27.5.17.		Divine service. Army Commander attended parade.	

Instructions regarding War Diaries and Intelligence Summaries are contained in F. S. Regs., Part II. and the Staff Manual respectively. Title pages will be prepared in manuscript.

WAR DIARY

or

INTELLIGENCE SUMMARY.

(*Erase heading not required.*)

Army Form C. 2118.

Place	Date	Hour	Summary of Events and Information	Remarks and references to Appendices
HBLAINSEVILLE	28.5.17		Battn training. Range practise.	
	29.5.17		Battn training. Fatigues. Draft of 5 ORanks (returned wounded) 2LTS TQ. LeDenne & Ff. Tall joined battn. LT + QM ECOME to hospital.	
	30.5.17		Battn field day - attack on wood. Gas demonstration in the evening, gas cloud passing over the whole brigade.	
	31.5.17		Battn training - fatigues.	
			Total casualties for the month.	
			Officers. Killed 5. Wounded 6 Missing Nil Sick 3.	
			ORanks. Killed 50 Wounded 182 Missing 7 Sick 67.	
			Total effective strength 31.5.17. - 34 off. - 718 ORanks.	
			ACameron Lt.	
			A/Adj. 8th Devon Regt.	

T2134. Wt. W708—776. 500000. 4/15. Sir J. C. & S.

8th (Service) Battalion The Devonshire Regiment.

Ref: Sheet:- 51.b.S.W.
Special ECOUST-ST
MEIN 1/10,000.

REPORT ON OPERATIONS
in and around
BULLECOURT between
the dates of
4th May to 10th MAY 17.

GENERAL SITUATION.

At dawn on May 3rd, the 5th Corps attacked sections of the HINDENBURG LINE. The area immediately round BULLECOURT was allotted to the 62nd Division. The 7th Division was in Corps reserve. The 62nd Division attack met with very partial success and on the day of the assault, the 22nd Infantry Brigade (7th Division) was ordered up to support the 62nd Division. The 20th Infantry Brigade were in readiness to support the 22nd Infantry Brigade.

Early in the morning of May 4th, the 20th Infantry Brigade began to take an active share in the operations, the 8th DEVON REGIMENT being put at the disposal of G.O.C., 22nd Infantry Brigade.

The report of ensuing operations is in the form of a diary, each day's opera-tions being treated separately.

4th MAY.1917. At 5 a.m. the 20th Infantry Brigade moved forward to a position near MORY in immediate readiness, the 8th DEVON REGIMENT being at L'HOMME MORT.

At 6 p.m. orders were received that the 8th DEVON REGIMENT was to move forward in support to operations to be carried out by 22nd Infantry Brigade, and was to be under orders of G.O.C., 22nd Infantry Brigade.

Accordingly at dusk the BATTALION moved forward and took up positions as follows:-

1 Company holding Embankment in U.27 c & d.
Remainder in assembly positions rea-dy to move forward and take over a line running through centre of BULLECOURT, which was to be attacked at 10.30 p.m. by 2nd ROYAL WARWICK REGIMENT and 1st ROYAL WELSH FUSILIERS.

This attack proved unsuccessful, and before da-wn the BATTALION relieved these Units of 22nd Infantry Brigade, and elements of 62nd Division. Dispositions, 1 Company in very advanced Posts in U.27.a & b, 1 Company on Railway Embankment as above, 1 Company in Quarry at C.3.c.0.0 and 1 Company in Cellars in ECOUST, BATTALION H.Q. C.2.d. 9.9.,

5th MAY 1917. The BATTALION remained in positions as above.

At 12 noon orders were received to push daylight patrols into the HINDENBURG FRONT LINE in U.27.b., as it was thought that this line was lightly held by day. This operation was entrusted to the Company holding Advanced Posts ("C" Company, Captain S.RENTON,MC), so as to give the patrols as little open ground to cover as possible.

Captain RENTON set out from his Company Headquarters at U.27.c.1.5., but before he ha-d gone 100 yards he came under heavy Machine Gun and rifle fire and was killed, his 2 Orderlies being wounded. The operation was then abandoned, as the enemy garrisons were shown to be too alert. Throughout the day, there was considerable shell fire by the enemy.

6th MAY 1917. On this day the BATTALION was not engaged in active operations. In the evening the 20th Infantry Brigade relieved the 22nd Infantry Brigade, 8th DEVON REGIMENT remained in their previous positions, the 2nd BORDER REGIMENT moved in support in ECOUST, the 2nd GORDON HIGHLANDERS and 9th DEVON REGIMENT going into assembly positions in U.28.c. for an attack on South East corner of BULLECOURT

6th MAY 1917. Contd. To facilitate Artillery preparations, the Company of the 8th DEVON REGIMENT holding Advanced Posts in U.27.a. & b. was withdrawn to a position in Reserve on the Embankment in C.2.a.& b. Great difficulty was experienced in this withdrawal, owing to the number of men occupying these Posts, the brightness of the moon, and the alertness of enemy Machine Guns. One Platoon was unable to withdraw till the following night.

7th MAY 1917. The Battalion took no part in the operations of the 2nd GORDON HIGHLANDERS and 9th DEVON REGIMENT referred to above. These were entirely successful and a line was ~~found~~ formed running from U.27.b.9.2. to U.28.a.0.6, and thence along German second line to U.28.a.8.8, with a support line running round S.E. edge of Village between these two points. These two lines will be referred to here after as the GREEN and the BLUE lines respectively. While these operations were in progress and throughout the day a very heavy barrage, mainly of H.E. was put down in the subsector held by 8th DEVON REGIMENT. This was particularly intense along Railway Embankment from C.2.a.9.9. to U.28.c.1.4. Although the men were really well dug in, fairly heavy casualties were sustained.

In the evening, orders were received for operations which will be described under the following day :-

8th MAY 1917. (a). MOVES. During the night 7/8th, 2 Companies of 8th DEVON REGIMENT moved to positions in BLUE LINE as follows:-

"C" Company, (2nd Lieut C.J.HOLDSWORTH) between U.27.b.9.2. and U.28.a.4.3.

"D" Company, (2/Lieut F.W.GIRVAN) between U.28.a.4.3. and U.25.a .5.7.

Remaining two Companies continued in position on Railway Embankment, U.27.c.& d, and in Quarry at C.3.c.0.9.

BATTALION H.Q. moved to U.28.c.8.2.

2nd BORDER REGT relieved 2nd GORDON HIGHLANDERS and held the GREEN LINE.

One Company 9th DEVON REGIMENT remained in BLUE LINE on right of 8th DEVON REGIMENT, three Companies on the Embankment in U.28.c. and C.4.b.

2nd GORDON HIGHLANDERS in support positions in vicinity of ECOUST.

These moves were accomplished with few casualties.

(b). OBJECTIVES. The two Companies of 8th DEVON REGIMENT holding the BLUE LINE were ordered to attack a section of BULLECOURT Village bounded as follows:- U.27.b.8.2. direct to U.27.b.9.4 thence on the North by Road running North West to Cross Roads U.27.b.15.85. On the South by the HINDENBURG Front Line to junction with Road in U.27.b.17. This will hereafter be referred to as the RED RECTANGLE.

(c). INSTRUCTIONS.

(1). The assault was to be made by the two Companies holding BLUE LINE by means of a bombing attack up front HINDENBURG LINE the greatest care being taken to put sentries on all dugouts and cellars and to block up all communication trenches. Strong Points to be established at U.27.b.2.8 at U.27.b.1.7 and any other suitable points. R.E. parties were placed at the disposal of O.C. 8th DEVON REGIMENT for consolidation. On arriving at the Road in U.27.b.1.7. the intention was to bomb inwards and so secure Road on North boundary of objectives.

8th MAY 1917. Continued.

INSTRUCTIONS.

(2). "C" Company was ordered to make the attack, whilst "D" Company extended to the left alongxx the BLUE LINE to keep in touch with "C" Coy; and form a support in case of emergency.

(3). The attack was to be made under an artillery creeping barrage which traversed the RED RECTANGLE both latterally and vertically.

(4). Companies of 9th DEVON REGIMENT on Railway Embankment w ere at disposal of 8thDEVON REGT for c-arrying parties.

(d). ATTACK.

At 11 a.m., (Zero hour) "C" Company (2/lieut C.J. HOLDSWORTH) advanced down BLUE LINE for about 150 yards in a formation of alternate Bombing Sections, rifle Sections and Lewis Gun Sections meeting little resistance and capturing 4 enemy dugouts. When the leading bombers came to within 50 yards of the ECOUST - BULLECOURT Road, they found it strongly held and were met with showers of egg bombs and Machine Gun fire. There was clearly an entrenched enemy strong point on the West bank of the road extending North and South from U.27.b.6.3. This was a very commanding position as xxxxxxx our men had to advance up hill against a strong ~~position~~ Entrenched work. The enemy were holding this position in force, and as we advanced, strong supports were seen coming up. It is estimated that the garrison and supports to this post must ha-ve been at least 150 men.

2nd Lieutenant HOLDSWORTH was killed early in the attack and his Company forced to retire out of bombing range.

2nd Lieutenant DREW then assumed command and organised a second advance, whichmet with the same result, and after some confused fighting he established himself in a strong point at about U.27.b.7.5.2.5. All was quiet by 1.30 pm.

(e). SUPPORTS.

"D" Company (2/Lieutenant GIRVAN F.W). extended along BLUE LINE as ordered, but as this Company xxxx had already suffered severely from shell fire, it was considered inadviseable to push a third attack that day.

30 men of 9th DEVON REGIMENT were used to carry up reserve bombs.

(f). ENEMY METHODS.

The enemy for his defence relied on egg bombs thrown from his strong point, and Machine gun fire. He also harrassed our advance considerably by sniping from houses in rear. He put down an indiscriminate barrage over the whole of our front positions in BULLECOURT mainly of H.E. coming from approximately due West. "D" Company suffered particularlyheavily over this.

From 8.30 to 10 p.m. a heavy barrage of H.E. was put down on Railway Embankment in U.28.c.

(d). GENERAL.
Our attack was handicapped by the weather conditions. Throughout the morning there was a steady drizzle which made the trenches ~~mady~~ muddy and made it very difficult to keep Lewis Guns in action.
Difficulty was experienced over our artillery whichshowed a tendancy to shoot to the right ontour front and support positions in GREEN and BLUE LINES.

9th MAY 1917. On the evening of May 8th, orderesd were received to repeat the attack of the previous day, with certain modifications.

(a). MOVES. The two remaining Companies 8th DEVON REGIMENT ("A" & "B" Companies) relieved respectively one Company 9th DEVON REGIMENT on right of BLUE LINE and one Company 9th DEVON REGIMENT on Railway Embankment in C.4.b.
The 2 Companies 9th DEVON REGIMENT moved to positions previously held by "A" & "B" Companies 8th DEVON REGIMENT.

(b). OBJECTIVES. The objectives were the same as on the previously day. One additional Strong Point was arranged for to be placed at Road ~~xxxx~~ and trench junction at about U.27.b.50.65.
One subsections of 20th MACHINE GUN CORPS was put at the disposal of O.C. 8th DEVON REGIMENT for garrison of strong point.

(c). INSTRUCTIONS.
(1). "C" Company to proceed as before.
"D" Company to remain in their defensive positions in BLUE LINE.
"B" Company to move up in support of "C" Company as required.
"A" Company to send forward a patrol of one platoon to proceed down road running North West through BULLECOURT from GREEN LINE and if possible to establish Strong Point referred to above, at U.27.b.50.65.
(2). The artillery barrage to be as before.
2 Guns of 20th Trench Mortar Battery were in addition placed at disposal of O.C. 8th DEVON REGIMENT. These under the personal supervision of O.C. 20 th TRENCH MORTAR BATTERY, were placed in position near Point 31, (U.28.a.3.1.) at about 9 a.m. on 9th instant.
O.C. 20th TRENCH MORTAR BATTERY then reconnoitred out own and enemy positions, and co-operated with the artillery in a most accurate barrage on enemy Strong Points along West side of ECOUST BULLECOURT Road. He got his guns into position in daylight and fired a 100 rounds under very trying conditions.

(d). ATTACK.
(1). "C" Company (2/Lieut DREW) moved off ~~xxxx~~ for the assault at 12 noon (Zero hour). Owing to the losses sustained by this Company, one Platoon of "B" Company under 2/Lieutenant MARSHALL was placed at their disposal.
Owing to known strength of enemy Strong Point, O.C. Company adopted this formation.- All Bombing Sections in front followed by Lewis Guns; ~~with~~ riflemen behind, with orders in event of the Strong Point being taken to push through, and, while the StrongPoint was being assaulted, to engage enemy snipers with heavy rifle fire.

(d). **ATTACK.**

(2). The enemy clearly expected our attack.
As soon as the barrage lifted, the Strong Point was strongly manned with bombers, and support were seen moving up in three distinct bombing parties which worked up the trench and on the left and right.
Simultaneously a most effective shrapnel barrage was put down in the valley immediately East of the ECOUST - BULLECOURT Road.
The assaulting troops were compelled to retire some hundred yards and the only two Officers remaining in the Company became casualties.
The Acting Company Sergeant Major then took charge and organised ~~the~~ a second attack at about 12.30 p.m. which was again driven back by enemy bombers, and the enemy counter-attacked, adavanced up BLUE LINE, The remains of "C" Company being either passed over or driven back in some confusion.

(3). 2nd Lieutenant MARSHALL who was holding the Company reserves at about U.28.a.2.2. then took charge.
He organised his reserves ~~xxxxxxxxxxx~~ into a defensive line on either side of the trench at U.28.a.2.2. and was given a-ble suppo-rt by a Vickers Machine Gun firing at about that point. He joined up with 2nd BORDER REGIMENT on his right who converged on enemy's left flank.
All Lewis Guns in "C" Company were now out of action and rifle grenades expended or unserviceable, owing to lack of cartridges, so he had to content himself with rifle fire, which was very efficacious for defence thoughnot sufficiently preponderant for offence.

(4). As soon as the position became known (about 1.15 p.m.) the remaining three Platoon of "D" Company were sent up in support under Lieutenant DRAKE carrying bombs and rifle grenades followed by one Company (50 men) of 9th DEVON REGIMENT to act a s carrying party and to come under orders of Lieutenant DRAKE for any offensive action. At the same time "D" Company were ~~making~~ ordered to pass all available bombs and rifle grenades along the line to 2nd Lieutenant MARSHALL. Lieutenant DRAKE moved up over the open to U.28. Central, thence to the left up Sunken Road. This was at the time subject to an heavy artillery barrage, and the old German front line wire to rifle and machine gun fire.
Lieutenant DRAKE accordingly sent his men forward by twos and threes.

(5). As soon as the leading Platoon of these supports reached 2nd Lieutenant MARSHALL with rifle grenades, he counter attacked, bombing down the BLUE LINE until he reached eventually the ECOUST - BULLECOURT Road, where he lined the bank from about U.27.b.70.05 to U.27.b.8.3. with Lewis Guns and Bombers covering his flanks.
The enemy were caught between our barrage (re-opened on enemy Strong Point) and his attack, and were driven out towards ECOUST, where they were met by Lewis Gun fire from U.27.c.

(6). By this time Lieutenant DRAKE had come up withremainder of "B" Company and found a support line in Valley East of the road withcovering party on his flanks. This position was maintained~~xxx~~ despite a counter attack at 4 p which failed completely. The carrying parties of 9th DEVON REGIMENT rendered most loyal and valuable assistance. At least 250 enemy were engaged of which ~~xxx~~ half must have become casualties.

(7). **GENERAL.**
The fine weather made movement far easier. The enemy sniping, as on previous day, was very heavy and accurate. Our artillery rendered every support, but the tendancy to shoot to the right was again noticed.

(7). GENERAL.
(Continued). The enemy attacked in three columns of bombers converging on one position with plentiful supplies of bomb carriers in rear. They wore no equipment and had their pockets full of bombs.

(8). In the evening position was taken over by 2nd GORDON HIGHLANDERS without difficulty and BATTALION moved to Camp near MORY.

(9). The "A" Company patrol went some 200 yards into Village and suffered severely. The remainder retired on 2nd BORDER REGIMENT Strong Point, about U.27.b.8.5.

-:- GENERAL OBSERVATIONS ON OPERATIONS -:-

The following points came out as result of operations:-

(1). Very Advanced Posts especially if strongly held are a source of danger. Advanced Posts should be a reasonable distance away from enemy line and be only about one Section strong.

(2). The egg bomb is an invaluable asset to the enemy as he can out-range us with it. Till we are supplied with them, rifle grenades are essential.
On the last day's operations, the turning point all the time was the supply or lack of rifle grenades.
The issue of our new egg bomb will be a great asset, as it is handier to manipulate then the rifle grenade.

(3). The enemy engaged were some of the GRENADIER REGT DES KONIG of the GUARDS DIVISION and fought exceedingly well and cleanly.
They gave the impression that the Village was tenaciously and efficiently held.
The formation they adopted has been referred to above.

(4). The success of Stokes Mortars and Vickers Gun was most marked. There was little use of Lewis guns.
A considerable number of the guns engaged were destroyed by direct hits from H.E. shells and many of the remainder became out of action owing to the mud.
Had better fortune been experienced with Lewis guns, there was every opportunity for their use.

(5). The value of the rifle as a weapon was once more clearly demonstrated in the last day's operations at the point where the enemy counter-attacks had penetrated to its furtherest point. Our Lewis guns were out of action, and Rifle grenades expended and Mills bombs comparatively useless against the egg bombs. The attack was held up purely by rifle fire for some ¾ of an hour pending arrival of rifle grenades when we were able to push forward again.

MAJOR,

12th MAY 17. COMMANDING 8TH (S) BN THE DEVONSHIRE REGT.

8th S. BN THE DEVONSHIRE REGIMENT.

CASUALTIES FOR PERIOD
5th May 1917 -:- 9th May 1917.

	OFFICERS.	OTHER RANKS.
Killed i/a	5.	49.
Wounded i/a	6.	164.
Missing	-	9.

OFFICER CASUALTIES.

Captain	RENTON	S.	(MC).	Killed i/a	6/5/1917.
2nd Lt;	HOLDSWORTH	CJ.		do	8/5/1917.
2nd Lt;	DUNCAN	K.		do	9/5/1917.
2nd Lt;	SMITH	GH.		do	9/5/1917.
2nd Lt;	CUMMING	LG.		do	9/5/1917.
Captain	LITTLEWOOD	EH.		Wounded i/a	6/5/1917.
2nd Lt;	ARMSTRONG	VB.		do	8/5/1917.
2nd Lt;	ARMSTRONG	FC.		do	5/5/1917.
2nd Lt;	GREGORY	ED.		do	9/5/1917.
2nd Lt;	DREW	GA.		do	9/5/1917.
2nd Lt;	PINKARD	FW.		Wounded (Shell) (Shock)	6/5/1917.

7th DIVISION.

20th INF BDE.

8th DEVONSHIRE REGIMENT.

JUNE 1917.

Army Form C. 2118.

Instructions regarding War Diaries and Intelligence Summaries are contained in F. S. Regs., Part II. and the Staff Manual respectively. Title Pages will be prepared in manuscript.

WAR DIARY
or
~~INTELLIGENCE SUMMARY~~

(Erase heading not required.)

8th Devon Regt
June 1917

Vol 21

Place	Date	Hour	Summary of Events and Information	Remarks and references to Appendices
ABLAINSEVELLE	1-6-17		Training & fatigues.	
"	2-6-17		Training Range practice Baths.	
"	3-6-17		Divine service.	
"	4-6-17		Route march – about 9 miles	
"	5-6-17		Training, fatigues, range practice.	
"	6-6-17		Training, fatigues.	
"	7-6-17		Bn day with Brigade manoeuvres, with 2nd Border Regt. Open order attack.	
"	8-6-17		Training, fatigues – Baths.	
"	9-6-17		Training Range practice	
"	10-6-17		Divine service. Regimental sports in afternoon, draft of 26 o.Ranks (returned wounded & sick) joined Batn.	
"	11-6-17		Fatigues. Batn in billets till the evening train.	
"	12-6-17		Field firing in the morning. Bombing demonstration in afternoon. Examination of section commanders by Divnl bombing officer.	22
"	13-6-17		Bn moved to camp (huts & tent shelters) in vicinity of Mory.	30
MORY	14-6-17		Bn moved into Bde support. 1 Coy at L'Homme Mort, 3 coys & Bn HQ in E Coast Trench. Strength 20 officers 461 other ranks. 2 killed one wounded during relief. Relief completed 1am. 2nd Border R. in support on Right. 58 Div on left. Very hot and brilliant sunlight.	

2449 Wt. W14957/M90 750,000 1/16 J.B.C. & A. Forms/C.2118/12.

Instructions regarding War Diaries and Intelligence Summaries are contained in F. S. Regs., Part II. and the Staff Manual respectively. Title Pages will be prepared in manuscript.

WAR DIARY
or
INTELLIGENCE SUMMARY
(Erase heading not required.)

8th Devon Regt.

Army Form C. 2118.

Place	Date	Hour	Summary of Events and Information	Remarks and references to Appendices
ECOUST.	15.6.17		RE fatigues in the line. 2LT JOHNSON killed - 2 other ranks killed five wounded. Intermittent shelling. Very hot and sunny.	
"	16.6.17		RE fatigues in the line. 3 OR killed. 9 other ranks wounded. Very hot & sunny. 14 OR (returned wounded) joined Bn.	
Trenches Bullecourt	17.6.17		Very hot & sunny. 1 other rank killed 2 wounded in morning. In the evening Bn relieved 2nd Gordon H. Relief complete 1am. Bn in front line at BULLECOURT. 9th Devon R on right. 58th Division on left. No casualties	
"	18.6.17		Very hot & sunny. Quiet day. Some shelling in early morning - Patrols out at night & work on trenches. Killed 1 other rank	
"	19.6.17		Very hot & sunny. Quiet day. Some shelling early morning & in evening. Patrols at night work on trenches. 3 OR wounded	
"	20.6.17		Weather changing some heavy showers. Which impeded work. Quiet day with usual shelling. Gas discharged by Bde on our right at 2am. Our section not affected by enemy retaliation. 2 OR wounded	
"	21.6.17		Weather unsettled. Patrols & work as before. Quiet. 2LT W J WYATT joined Bn.	
Ecoust	22.6.17		Weather unsettled. Rather increased shelling. Bn relieved in evening by 2nd GORDON H. Relief complete 1am. No casualties. Bn returned to Bde support in cellars &c. at ECOUST	
	23.6.17		Bn. resting.	
	24.6.17		Heavy shelling of Church at ECOUST from 7.30am to 9.30am. All calibres up to 150 cm. No casualties. 3 Coys on W. Parties,	

Army Form C. 2118.

Instructions regarding War Diaries and Intelligence Summaries are contained in F. S. Regs., Part II. and the Staff Manual respectively. Title Pages will be prepared in manuscript.

WAR DIARY
or
INTELLIGENCE SUMMARY
(Erase heading not required.)

Place	Date	Hour	Summary of Events and Information	Remarks and references to Appendices
ECOUST	25/6/17		In the evening Bn relieved by 20th Manchester R. & returned to camp (tents & tent shelters) in vicinity of MORY. Relief complete by 12 MN. No casualties. 2LT SW TUCKER & 2LT J W CUNNINGHAM joined Battn.	
MORY.	26/6/17		Resting & cleaning up.	
ERVILLERS.	27/6/17		In the morning camp moved to spot ½ mile S of ERVILLERS. Tents & tent shelters. Settling in generally. D Coy to support line ST LEGER – VAULX VRAUCOURT.	
	28/6/17		Bn training. Baths. D Coy returned.	
	29/6/17		Bn training. Range practice.	
	30/6/17		Bn training.	
			Total casualties.	
			Officers. Killed 1 – Wounded Nil – Missing Nil – Sick 4.	
			O Ranks. Killed 6 – Wounded 14 – Missing Nil – Sick 39.	
			Effective strength of Bn. 35 – officers. 687 – O Ranks.	
			R C Cameron Lt. Adjt. 9th Devon Regt.	

2449 Wt. W14957/M90 750,000 1/16 J.B.C. & A. Forms/C.2118/12.

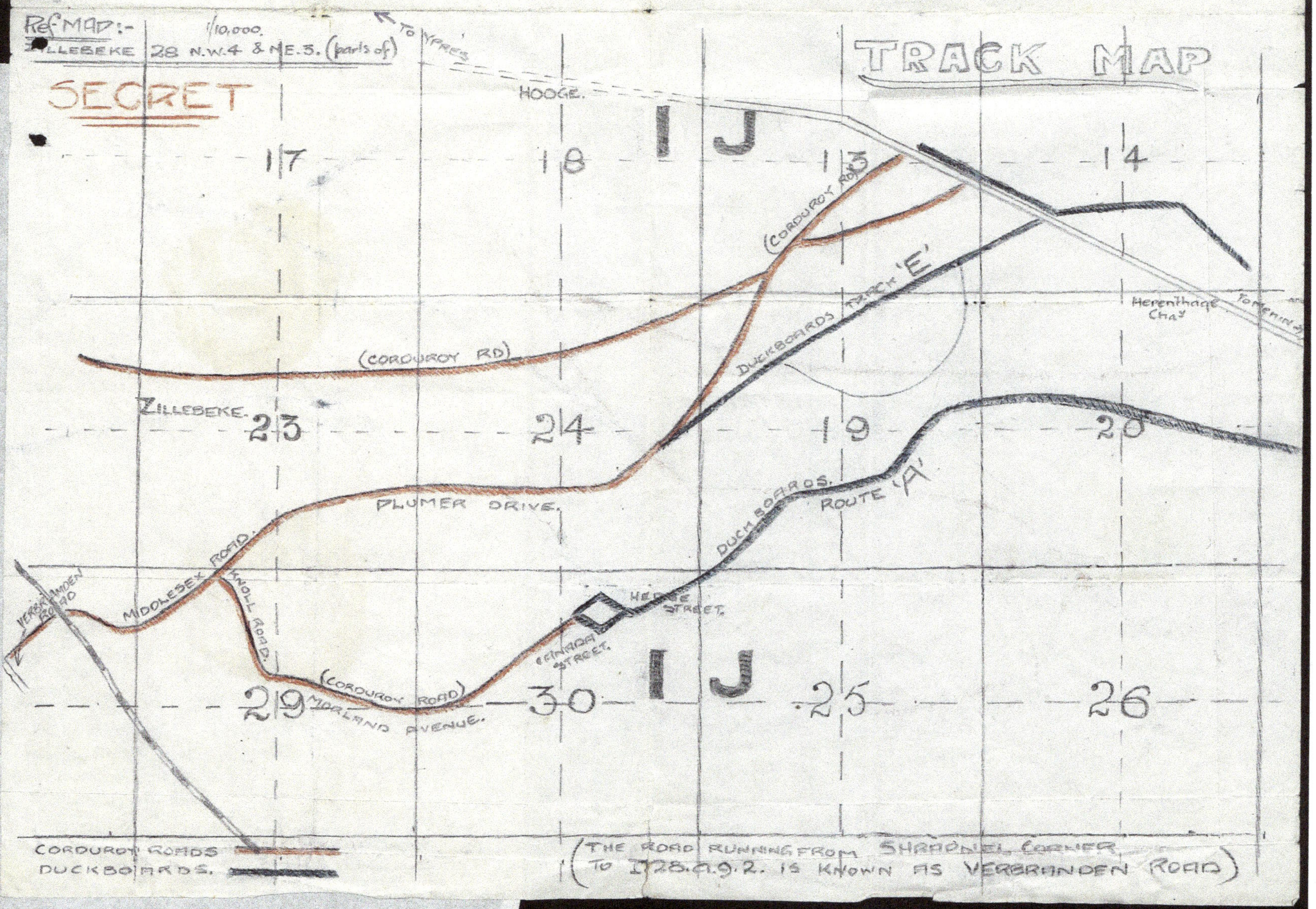

Ref MAP:- 1/10,000.
ZILLEBEKE 28 N.W.4 & N.E.3. (parts of)
TO YPRES
SECRET
TRACK MAP
HOOGE.
I J
17
18
13
14
(CORDUROY RD)
(CORDUROY RD.)
DUCKBOARDS TRACK 'E'
Herenthage Chat
ZILLEBEKE.
23
24
19
20
PLUMER DRIVE.
DUCKBOARDS. ROUTE 'A'
MIDDLESEX ROAD.
KNOLL ROAD.
VERBRANDEN ROAD
STREET.
STREET.
(CORDUROY ROAD)
MORLAND AVENUE.
29
30
25
26
CORDUROY ROADS
DUCKBOARDS.
(THE ROAD RUNNING FROM SHRAPNEL CORNER TO I.28.a.9.2. IS KNOWN AS VERBRANDEN ROAD)

7th DIVISION.

20th INF BDE.

8th DEVONSHIRE REGIMENT.

JULY 1917.

Instructions regarding War Diaries and Intelligence Summaries are contained in F. S. Regs., Part II. and the Staff Manual respectively. Title Pages will be prepared in manuscript.

WAR DIARY
or
~~INTELLIGENCE SUMMARY~~
(Erase heading not required.)

Army Form C. 2118.

8th Devon Regt.

Vol 22

Place	Date	Hour	Summary of Events and Information	Remarks and references to Appendices
FRVILLERS	1-7-17		Battalion ~~training~~ at diving [illegible] in morning. Very heavy thunderstorm in evening two or three tents blown down. One company to support line.	
"	2-7-17		Battalion training. Coy returned from support line, no casualties.	
"	3-7-17		Route march about 10 miles. Very hot. Bn snipers to 3 days field firing near PUSIEUX.	
"	4-7-17		Battalion training baths.	
"	5-7-17		Battalion training. 2Lt PENNINGTON joined battalion. Draft of 27 ORs (returned wounded)	
ECOUST	6-7-17		Bn relieved 1 R.W.F. in left support. 3 coys in cellars & dugouts at ECOUST. 1 coy in bivouacs at L'HOMME MORT. Relief complete at 1 am no casualties. 9th Devon R on right 91st Bde on left.	
	7-7-17		RE working parties. Lewis gun classes. Fine. E.A. active.	
	8-7-17		RE working parties. Lewis Gun classes. ~~[illegible]~~. ~~[illegible]~~. Very heavy rain	
~~[illegible]~~	9-7-17		Bn relieved 2nd Gordon H in the left subsector. Relief complete 1.15 am no casualties. 2nd Border R on Right 91st Bde on left. Draft of 86 O.Ranks joined Bn. mainly old Ex [illegible] men and returned wounded. Fine. E.A. active.	2 E 76
Trenches [illegible]	10-7-17		Fine. Quiet except for E.A. 1 O.Rank wounded. Work on trenches.	
"	11-7-17		Rain. E A again active. Considerable miscellaneous shelling with H.E. All men working on trenches & wire.	

Army Form C. 2118.

Instructions regarding War Diaries and Intelligence Summaries are contained in F. S. Regs., Part II. and the Staff Manual respectively. Title Pages will be prepared in manuscript.

WAR DIARY
or
INTELLIGENCE SUMMARY

(Erase heading not required.)

8th Devon Regt

Place	Date	Hour	Summary of Events and Information	Remarks and references to Appendices
Trenches BULLECOURT	12-7-17		Fine. E A fairly active. Considerable shelling & trench mortar activity in early morning 4 O Ranks wounded. In evening Bn relieved by 2nd GORDON H. Relief completed 1.30 am. Bn returned to support in ECOUST. No casualties in relief.	
"	13-7-17		Fine. RE working parties. E.A. very active. 2LT. V. TARBET [illegible] joined battalion.	
"	14-7-17		Dull & colder. RE working parties. Work on dugouts etc.	
Ecoust.	15-7-17		Dull but fine. In the evening Bn relieved 2nd Gordon H in the line. Relief complete 1.30 am no casualties. 91st Bde on left. 2nd Border R on right.	
"	16-7-17		Dull slight rain. Work on trenches and wire. Quiet.	
"	17-7-17		Clear & fine. Considerable E A activity & shelling with H.E. on front line & Bn HQ – 1 O rank killed & 1 wounded.	
Camp near Ervillers	18-7-17		Dull all day. Heavy rain in evening. Trench fever. Relieved in evening by 22nd Inf Bde (1st R.W.F.) and returned to old camp, huts tents & bivouacs, near Ervillers – Relief complete 2 am. 1 O Rank killed. 2LT A W Wall & 10 other ranks wounded	
"	19-7-17		Resting & cleaning.	
"	20-7-17		Resting. Cleaning.	

2449 Wt. W14957/M90 750,000 1/16 J.B.C. & A. Forms/C.2118/12.

Army Form C. 2118.

WAR DIARY
or
~~INTELLIGENCE SUMMARY~~
(Erase heading not required.)

8th Devon Regt.

Instructions regarding War Diaries and Intelligence Summaries are contained in F. S. Regs., Part II. and the Staff Manual respectively. Title Pages will be prepared in manuscript.

Place	Date	Hour	Summary of Events and Information	Remarks and references to Appendices
[illegible] Camp near ERVILLERS	21.7.17.		Training and baths.	
	22.7.17.		Whole battalion on R.E. working parties.	
"	23.7.17.		Training. Coys in rotation on Div! range. Classification practices started.	
"	24.7.17.		Training. Classification on 30x range. Lt N. BUCKINGHAM. 2Lts S. SILLEY. W.B. ASHPLANT. N.E. FASKEN. C. NAPER. and 7 O Ranks (returned sick) rejoined Batt.	
"	25.7.17.		Training & Baths.	
"	26.7.17		Whole Batt. on RE working parties.	
"	27.7.17		Training. Rain & thunder.	
"	28.7.17		Bullet & bayonet range. Training.	
"	29.7.17		Divine Service. Thunder & rain.	
ECOUST	30.7.17.		Whole Batt. on RE working parties. In evening relieved 1st R.W.F. in Bde Reserve. 2 Coys in ECOUST & Bn HQ. 2 at L'HOMME MORT. Relief complete 12 m.n. No casualties. 9th Bde on left 2nd Border R on right. 2Lt Marshall 16 OR joined Bn.	
"	31.7.17		In evening 1 coy moved back from ECOUST (& Bn HQ) to camp near Mory. Still remaining in Brigade Reserve. 2 coys occupying [illegible].	
			Total casualties for month. Officers: Killed Nil, wounded 1, missing Nil, Sick 3. O Ranks: Killed 4, wounded 11, missing Nil, Sick 83. Strength 8th: Officers 39, O Ranks 771.	

R Chambers [illegible]
8th Devon Regt

2449 Wt. W14957/M90 750,000 1/16 J.B.C. & A. Forms/C.2118/12.

7th DIVISION.

20th INF BDE.

8th DEVONSHIRE REGIMENT.

AUGUST 1917.

Instructions regarding War Diaries and Intelligence Summaries are contained in F. S. Regs., Part II. and the Staff Manual respectively. Title pages will be prepared in manuscript.

WAR DIARY
or
~~INTELLIGENCE SUMMARY.~~
(*Erase heading not required.*)

Army Form C. 2118.

8th Devon Regt
Vol 23

24a

August 1917

Place	Date	Hour	Summary of Events and Information	Remarks and references to Appendices
Mory	1-8-17		Wiring parties in the line & RE working parties. Very wet.	
Trenches Bullecourt	2-8-17		Still wet. Bn relieved 2nd Gordon Highlanders in the line in the evening. Relief complete 1 am. No casualties. 9th Devon Regt on right, 2nd Borders on left. Trench strength 17 officers 445 O.Ranks. 2nd Lt R MARSHALL joined Bn.	
	3-8-17		Work concentrated on wiring and front line. Fine. One other rank wounded.	
	4-8-17		Enemy active on left with HE & light T.Ms. and some Gas shells. 4 O.Ranks wounded (gas) 1 O.Rank wounded.	
	5-8-17		Quiet. Work on wire and front line & fire stepping. On right B/C relieved A & D in line. No casualties.	
	6-8-17		Quiet. Colder & windy. 1 other rank wounded. Work on same lines. Enemy rather more active.	
	7-8-17		Warm & fine. Considerable aerial activity throughout the day on both sides. One hostile machine brought down.	
Ervillers	8-8-17		Quiet all day. Very heavy rain in evening. 1 O.Rank killed one wounded. In the evening Bn relieved by 2nd/5th W Yorks. Relief complete 3 am no casualties on relief. Bn moved back to huts at ERVILLERS.	

Instructions regarding War Diaries and Intelligence Summaries are contained in F. S. Regs., Part II. and the Staff Manual respectively. Title Pages will be prepared in manuscript.

WAR DIARY
or
~~INTELLIGENCE SUMMARY~~
(Erase heading not required.)

8th Devon Regt

Army Form C. 2118.

Place	Date	Hour	Summary of Events and Information	Remarks and references to Appendices
ERVILLERS.	9/8/17		Battalion in rest at Hutment Camp ERVILLERS.	
BAILLEULVAL	10/8/17		Battalion moved to BILLETS in BAILLEULVAL. Showery day.	
— " —	11/8/17		Companies at disposal of Coy Commdrs for cleaning up	
— " —	12/8/17		Bn Parade for Divine Service at 11.45am (Rect E.C. Crosse) Commdg Officer Conference of all Officers ~~[illegible]~~ & senior N.C.Os. (Subject Discipline)	
— " —	13/8/17		B & D Coys on Baths & range A & C Range in the morning & Night Operations in the evening (Forming up)	
— " —	14/8/17		B & D Coys ~~take dinners out~~, Coy Training & firing dummy rifle grenades. A & C Coys Baths & range. Stretcher Bearer Classes of six men per Coy started. (Bn paraded at 7am under R.S.M for Bn Drill & at 2pm under C.O for Bn drill).	
— " —	15/8/17	7am	Bn under RSM for Bn Drill & to practise for Inspection as under.	
		9.30	Coys at disposal of Coy Commdrs for cleaning up	
		11.am	Bn Parade with 9th Devon R under Lt Col Morris DSO (9th Devon R)	
— " —		3pm.	Bn & 9th Devon R inspected by Lt Genl Sir G.M. Bullock K.C.B. Commdg The Devonshire Regiment. Heavy Storm previous to Inspection	
— " —	16/8/17	9am	Bn at Field Operations under C.O.	
		9pm	Bn practise Forming up on a tape under C.O	
— " —	17/8/17		A & C take dinners out for Coy Training	
			B & D alternately on range & Coy Training near Billets	

Instructions regarding War Diaries and Intelligence Summaries are contained in F. S. Regs., Part II. and the Staff Manual respectively. Title pages will be prepared in manuscript.

WAR DIARY
or
~~INTELLIGENCE~~ SUMMARY.
(Erase heading not required.)

9th Bn ... [illegible]

Army Form C. 2118.

Place	Date	Hour	Summary of Events and Information	Remarks and references to Appendices
BAILLEULVAL	18/8/17		Bn Field Operations under C.O. Half holiday. Last 2 drafts Anti-Gas Appliances inspected by Divl Gas Officer.	
"	19/8/17		Bn attends at Baths. Church Parade at 11.45 am. (Cath EC [illegible])	2pm 9th Divn Sports
"	20/8/17		Bn Field Operations under C.O. Drummers out. Divnl Genl's Conference of all C.O.s 2nd commands Adjutants & Coy Commanders in Division at the Theatre GROSVILLE at 5.30 pm. (Subject main points "New German Pepper Pot Defence" & the necessity for using Guide lines over the open instead of Communication Trenches) attended.	
"	21/8/17	-	B & D take dinners out for Coy Training. A & C Rifle ~~Long~~ Range & ~~training near Billets~~. Bullet & Bayonet Range under CSM. [illegible] near billets. ~~All~~ C.O. 2nd Command, Adjutant & Coy Commanders attend ½ day Gas Course at Gas School RANSART.	
"	22/8/17	-	A & C Coy Training & Night Operations. B & D Range & Coy Training near Billets. L.G. Classes started.	
"	23/8/17		~~Bn~~ A & C & B & D alternately on Field Firing Range & Coy Training. B & D Night Operations. 2Lt Perkins, 2Lt Traylen, 2nd Lt Piddlecombe, 2Lt Golding & 37 ORs. Off. joined the Bn	
"	24/8/17		Preliminary Heats run off for Divnl Fair at HENDECOURT-LEZ-RANSART. Bn Parade at 9am & march to ~~HENDECOURT~~ FICHEUX to watch Demonstration by 23rd Bde of a 3rd Bn "mopping up" for another Bn	

A7092). Wt. W12839/M1297 750,000. 1/17. D. D & L., Ltd. Forms/C2118/14.

Instructions regarding War Diaries and Intelligence Summaries are contained in F. S. Regs., Part II. and the Staff Manual respectively. Title Pages will be prepared in manuscript.

WAR DIARY
or
~~INTELLIGENCE SUMMARY~~
(Erase heading not required.)

8th Bn R.M.F.

Army Form C. 2118.

Place	Date	Hour	Summary of Events and Information	Remarks and references to Appendices
BAILLEULVAL	25.8.17	-	Divisional fair at HENDECOURT. No training. Fine day.	
"	26.8.17		Fine. Divine service in the morning	
"	27.8.17		Training near billets. Co's kit inspection. Wet	
"	28.8.17		Two hours training in morning – Rest of time given up to cleaning for move. Co's conference.	
BUSSEBOOM	29.8.17		Battalion entrained at railway at SAULTY and proceeded to PROVEN. Detrained there at about 11 pm and marched 8 miles to hutment camp near BUSSEBOOM. D Coy found unloading party for the Brigade.	
	30.8.17		Resting in camp.	
STEENVOORDE	31.8.17		Bn moved back to billets in and near STEENVOORDE. Arrived at billets 8 pm. Very crowded. No men fell out on line of march.	
			Total casualties for month	
			Officers. Sick 1; Wounded, Killed, Missing } Nil. Ranks: Sick 37, Wounded 8, Killed 2, Missing Nil.	
			Effective strength. 44 officers 957 Ranks.	
			A Chandler Capt Adjt. 8th Bn RMF	

7th DIVISION.

20th INF BDE.

8th DEVONSHIRE REGIMENT.

SEPTEMBER 1917.

Instructions regarding War Diaries and Intelligence Summaries are contained in F. S. Regs., Part II. and the Staff Manual respectively. Title Pages will be prepared in manuscript.

Army Form C. 2118.

WAR DIARY
or
INTELLIGENCE SUMMARY
(Erase heading not required.)

8th Devon Regt.

Vol 24

Place	Date	Hour	Summary of Events and Information	Remarks and references to Appendices
BUSSBOOM	1-9-17		Battalion drill in the morning. In the afternoon Bn moved suddenly to billets in and near Steenvoorde. Bn correctly billeted by 10 pm. Good billets but scattered. No men fell out on march.	
STEENVOORDE	2-9-17		Bn resting cleaning billets foot inspection &c.	
"	3-9-17		Bn drill in morning and coy: parades.	
"	4-9-17		Bn moved in afternoon to billets just north of Hazebrouck at La Breard[illegible]. Very comfortable but very scattered. Correctly billeted by 6 pm. 2Lt S.D. Gregory, 2Lt R.W. Evans rejoined battn. Draft of 29 O.R. joined battn.	
HAZEBROUCK	5-9-17		Foot inspections cleaning up & light work.	
"	6-9-17		Coy training. 2Lt J.S. Farleigh joined Bn.	
"	7-9-17		Coy training. 40 men on fatigue. Platoon football league started.	
"	8-9-17		Coy training 40 men on fatigue. Draft of 12 OR joined Bn	
"	9-9-17		Divine service. 40 men on fatigue.	
"	10-9-17		Coy training in morning. Gas demonstration in afternoon	
"	11-9-17		Baths for whole Bn. Coy training.	
"	12-9-17		Training in attack formation by ½ battalion.	

2449 Wt. W14957/M90 750,000 1/16 J.B.C. & A. Forms/C.2118/12.

Instructions regarding War Diaries and Intelligence Summaries are contained in F. S. Regs., Part II. and the Staff Manual respectively. Title Pages will be prepared in manuscript.

WAR DIARY
or
INTELLIGENCE SUMMARY
(Erase heading not required.)

8th Dun Rif.

Army Form C. 2118.

Place	Date	Hour	Summary of Events and Information	Remarks and references to Appendices
Renescure	13.9.17		Bn moved in morning to billets in Aire–Cassel road near Renescure at La Crosse. Correctly billeted by 2 pm. Good billets but scattered. No one fell out on the march.	
"	14.9.17		Bn resting & cleaning up.	
Tatinghem	15.9.17		Bn moved in morning to billets in Tatinghem. Correctly billeted by 2 pm. No one fell out on march. Comfortable billets.	
"	16.9.17		Divine service resting & cleaning up	
"	17.9.17		Coy training. B Coy on 600x range.	
"	18.9.17		Bn day. Attack formation.	
"	19.9.17		Bde day attack formation. A & C on bullet & bayonet range in afternoon.	
"	20.9.17		Dawn attack practice in morning. C.O's inspection of billets. Lt H Roper rejoined Battalion.	
"	21.9.17		Baths for whole Bn in the morning. 600x range in afternoon	
"	22.9.17		All coys on 600x range all day. Dinners on the range.	
"	23.9.17		Divine service.	

2449 Wt. W14957/M90 750,000 1/16 J.B.C. & A. Forms/C.2118/12.

Army Form C. 2118.

Instructions regarding War Diaries and Intelligence Summaries are contained in F. S. Regs., Part II. and the Staff Manual respectively. Title Pages will be prepared in manuscript.

WAR DIARY
or
INTELLIGENCE SUMMARY 8th Devon Regt.

(Erase heading not required.)

Place	Date	Hour	Summary of Events and Information	Remarks and references to Appendices
TATINGHEM	24-9-17		Bn took part in Divisional practice attack scheme in conjunction with the QIIIrd Inf Bde in the neighbourhood of LEULINGHEM. Operations from 9 am to 4 pm. Object of practice to emphasize new formation for attack & Bn. "leap frogging".	
"	25-9-17		Bn took part in same scheme as on 24th in conjunction with 22nd Inf Bde. 2Lt G.A. Drew rejoined the Battn. Draft of 92 O Ranks joined Bn. All old Expeditionary Force men, mostly from Devons here rejoining.	
"	26-9-17		Bn formed skeleton enemy for scheme on 24th & 25th. Draft on 400x range in afternoon.	
"	27-9-17		Bn scheme in normal attack formation.	
BAYENGHEM	28-9-17		Bn moved in the morning to billets at BAYENGHEM. Move complete 2 pm. Good billets but dirty.	
"	29-9-17		Bn marched in the morning to Arques where they entrained 6 pm and went by train to Abeele, where they detrained 11 pm and marched to camp near Reninghelst getting into camp 4 am. Transport entrained at Wizernes at 6 pm and detrained at Godewaersvelde at 10 pm reaching camp half an hour after the battalion.	
	30-9-17		Resting and cleaning up.	

Effective strength 48 off 1024 O Ranks. Killed, Wounded, Missing NIL. Sick off. 2, O Ranks 46.

[illegible] Capt & Adjt 8th Devon Regt.

2449 Wt. W14957/M90 750,000 1/16 J.B.C. & A. Forms/C.2118/12.

EDITION 1.A
BECELAERE
German Trenches corrected to 21-9-17.
Part of Sheet 28.
APPROXIMATE BRITISH FRONT LINE
APPROXIMATE FRONT LINE
INTER DIVL BDY
INTER BDE BDY
NORTHERN CORPS BDY
1ST AUST
7TH DIVN
21ST DIVN
Zonnebeke
Broodseinde
Westhoek
Nonne Bosschen
Glencorse Wood
Becelaere
Molenaarelsthoek
Droogenbroodhoek
Keiberg
Polygon Wood
Molenhoek
Zwarteleen
Juniper Wood
Scale 1:10,000

7th DIVISION.

20th INF BDE.

8th DEVONSHIRE REGIMENT.

OCTOBER 1917.

APPENDICES ATTACHED.

Instructions regarding War Diaries and Intelligence Summaries are contained in F. S. Regs., Part II. and the Staff Manual respectively. Title pages will be prepared in manuscript.

WAR DIARY
or
~~INTELLIGENCE SUMMARY.~~
(Erase heading not required.)

Army Form C. 2118.

30/1

8th Durm Regt.
October 1917

Place	Date	Hour	Summary of Events and Information	Remarks and references to Appendices
Camp near RENINGHELST	1-10-17		Bn moved in the afternoon to Bivouac camp near Chateau SIGARD. Correctly billeted 7 pm.	
Trenches near POLYGON WOOD	2-10-17 to 7-10-17		SEE APENDIX No. 1. and attached casualty [illegible]	
ZILLEBEKE.	8-10-17		Bn moved in the afternoon to bivouac camp west of ZILLEBEKE Lake. Correctly billeted 6 pm. Very wet.	
CHATEAU SIGARD	9-10-17		Bn moved in the afternoon to tent camp near Chateau SIGARD. Correctly billeted 7 pm. Cold & wet.	
Camp near WESTOUTRE.	10-10-17		Bn moved in the morning to Hut camp near WESTOUTRE. Very wet. Correctly billeted at 2 pm.	
"	11-10-17		Cleaning up & refitting. Wet & cold.	
"	12-10-17		Classes of L Gun & R. grenades. Box respirator inspections etc. Very wet.	
"	13-10-17		Classes as above. Very wet and difficult to do anything.	
"	14-10-17		Divine service in the morning. Baths for all. In the afternoon A & B Coys & Transport moved to huts at camp 50 ½ mile away.	26 +
"	15-10-17		Battalion training classes etc. same.	

A7092). Wt. W12839/M1297 750,000. 1/17. D. D & L., Ltd. Forms/C2118/14.

Instructions regarding War Diaries and Intelligence Summaries are contained in F. S. Regs., Part II. and the Staff Manual respectively. Title pages will be prepared in manuscript.

Army Form C. 2118.

WAR DIARY
or
INTELLIGENCE SUMMARY.
(Erase heading not required.)

8th Devon Regt.

Place	Date	Hour	Summary of Events and Information	Remarks and references to Appendices
Camp near WESTOUTRE	16.10.17		Classes as before – very wet –	
"	17.10.17		Classes in the morning. very wet – A & B coys returned to THUNDERER Camp.	
"	18.10.17		Baths for all near RENINGHELST in the morning. In the afternoon & evening Bn practised in forming up on a tape in the normal formation. 5–8 pm – OC coys reconnoitred training "theatre".	
"	19.10.17		Bn marched out to a training theatre representing neighbourhood of GHELUVELT & practised over it by companies, and went over it with all officers & NCOs.	
"	20.10.17		As on the 19th only over a new & improved "theatre".	
"	21.10.17		Bn paraded for Divine service at RENINGHELST. Weather fine and warmer. Lt H.A. ROBERTSON rejoined BN. 2Lt F.K. AYERS	joined batt n.
"	22.10.17		Baths near RENINGHELST for all in morning. Gas helmet inspection of draft in afternoon.	
"	23.10.17		Bn moved in the morning to huts and tents near VIERSTAAT. Very muddy but tents dry – Billeted by 5 pm.	
Camp near VIERSTAAT	24.10.17		Bn moved in the morning to dugouts S. of ZILLEBEKE Lake. There was some delay in getting accommodation, but when obtained was good and dry. Billeted 5 pm.	
Dugouts S. of ZILLEBEKE Lake + Trenches E. of GHELUVELT	25.10.17 to 26.10.17		See appendix No. 2 attached –	

A7092). Wt. W12839/M1297 750,000. 1/17. D. D & L., Ltd. Forms/C2118/14.

Instructions regarding War Diaries and Intelligence Summaries are contained in F. S. Regs., Part II. and the Staff Manual respectively. Title pages will be prepared in manuscript.

WAR DIARY
or
~~INTELLIGENCE SUMMARY.~~

(Erase heading not required.)

9th [illegible]

Army Form C. 2118.

Place	Date	Hour	Summary of Events and Information	Remarks and references to Appendices
Camp near VIERSTRAAT	27.10.17		Bn resting and cleaning up.	
Camp near VIERSTRAAT	28.10.17		Bn moved in morning to hut & tent camp near LA CLYTTE. Will do by 1 Pm. wet.	
Camp near LA CLYTTE	29.10.17		Bn moved in the afternoon to OUDERDOM arriving 4.30 pm. Entrained there at 5 Pm & arrived at EBBLINGHEM at 9. Pm. Moved off from there at 9.15 Pm & arrived in billets near BLARINGHEM at 11.15 Pm. Very scattered area but comfortable farm billets.	
Billets near BLARINGHEM	30.10.17		Bn resting and refitting.	
	31.10.17		Bn resting and refitting.	

Total casualties for the month.

	Officers	ORs
Killed	6	74
Wounded	15	330
Died of wounds	1	8
Missing	4	115
Sick	1	82

Effective strength.
25 officers 506 o. ranks.

R Cameron Capt.
Adjt 9th [illegible]

A7092). Wt. W12839/M1295 750,000. 1/17. D. D & L., Ltd. Forms/C2118/14.

Appendix No 1

8TH (SERVICE) BATTALION THE DEVONSHIRE REGT.

REPORT ON OPERATIONS
FROM 2ND OCTOBER TO 8TH OCTOBER 1917.

Reference Maps:-
BELGIUM & FRANCE Sheet 28
& Special Sheet. BECELAERE.

1. GENERAL OPERATIONS.

(a). At 6 a.m. October 4th 1917, the 10th CORPS continued its share in the general offensive of the 2nd and 5th ARMIES.
The 7th DIVISION attacked on the left of the Corps front with the 21st DIVISION on its right and the 1st AUSTRALIAN DIVISION on its left.

(b). The role of the 7th DIVISION was to seize - in conjunction with the 1st AUSTRALIAN DIVISION - the high ground in the vicinity of NOORDEMHOEK and MOLENAARELSTHOEK and so obtain observation on the HEUTEBEEK VALLEY to the East.
The right flank of the 7th DIVISION was protected by the 21st DIVISION who were to seize REUTEL and the high ground in J.12.a.

(c). The attack of the 7th DIVISION was carried out by the 91st INFANTRY BRIGADE on the right and the 20th INFANTRY BRIGADE on the left. The 22nd INFANTRY BRIGADE were in reserve.

(d). The attack of the 20TH INFANTRY BRIGADE was carried out as follows:-
8th DEVON REGT to the RED LINE (1st objective),
2nd BORDER RGT (right) & 2nd GORDON H'RS (left) to the BLUE LINE (2nd objective) by a leap frog movement.
9th DEVON REGT in reserve.

(e). Objectives are shown on attached map.

2. ENEMY'S DISPOSITIONS

(a). The actual dispositions of the enemy were not known.
It had been ascertained from aeroplane photographs that he was holding the high ground opposite the Divisional front by means of a system of concrete pill boxes and small posts.

(b). His approximate front line opposite the 20th INFANTRY BRIGADE front was J.4.d.5.8. - J.4.d.5.4. - J.10.b.4.8.
A belt of wire ran across the objective of the 8th DEVON REGT from J.4.d.7.8. to J.5.c.0.2. thence at right angles to J.4.d.7.0. and back to J.11.a.5.9.
A strong pill box and dugout had been located in this bend at J.4.d.90.05. Other dugouts and pill boxes were distributed fairly evenly over the Battalion frontage.

(c). The enemy was reported to be holding his line lightly in front and more strongly in rear according to his latest formation.
The following was his supposed order of battle :-
Elements of the 121st DIVISION
As events proved, the enemy had also planned an attack for 6 a.m. on the morning of the 4th and consequently many more troops were present than might have been expected.

3. CONCENTRATION MARCH.

(a). At 4.30 p.m. 2nd October 1917, the Battalion moved off from BIVOUAC CAMP at CHATEAU SEGARD and took over the whole of the 20TH INFANTRY BRIGADE front from the 20th MANCHESTER REGT; (22nd INFANTRY BRIGADE), the line was held by "B" Company on the right, "D" Company on the left, "A" Company in support & "C" Company in reserve.

SHEET 2.

3. CONCENTRATION MARCH (Continued).

(b) During the march in an S.O.S. was sent up somewhere on the right and the enemy put down a barrage in J.19.a. causing 1 Officer and 23 other rank casualties.
The relief passed off otherwise quite quietly, and the relief was complete at 12.30 a.m.

4. ASSEMBLY.

(a) Prior to the Battalion forming up for the assault, a certain amount of wire had to be cut within our own lines.
This was most successfully done by "A" "B" and "D" Companies during the night 3/4th.

(b) At 3 a.m. on the 4th instant "A" & "C" Companies moved up from support and reserve and formed up on a tape from J.4.d. 3.8. to J.10.b.25.80. immediately behind our front line. When they were in position, "B" & "D" Companies moved back from the front line and formed up in rear. "A" & "C" coys; then put out posts to cover their front, which were withdrawn immediately before ZERO.
Forming up was complete by 4.50 a.m.

(c) The forming up of the Brigade was as follows:-

(i) The leading Battalion (the 8th DEVON REGT; for the 1st objective) formed up in the normal formation on a front of 450 yards; - 15 yards between lines, and between lines and moppers up; - 70 yards between waves, and 80 yards between the second wave and reserve Company. They shook out to normal depth during the advance.

(ii) The two Battalions for the second objective - 2nd BORDER REGT; and 2nd GORDON H'RS were formed up on tape 200 yards in rear of reserve Company 8th DEVON REGT; They were in artillery formation 130 yards between waves and 210 yards between second wave and reserve Company. Each Battalion covered half the front of 8th DEVON REGT;

(d) The Battalion formed up with 4th AUSTRALIAN BATTALION on the left and 1st SOUTH STAFFORD REGT; on the right.
When the forming up was complete it was discovered that a gap of 180 yards existed between the right of the BATTALION and the left of the 1st S. STAFFORD REGT;
It was according arranged that, when the advance commenced, the right Company of the 8th DEVON REGT and the left Company 1st S. STAFFORD REGT; should each feel together so as to fill the gap, and that each Battalion should echelon up one Platoon of its reserve Company to cover the gap.

(e) At 5.40 a.m. the enemy put down a barrage in J.10.a. This just fell between the Reserve Company 8th DEVON REGT; and the front Companies 2nd BORDER REGT; and 2nd GORDON H'Rs respectively.
The reserve Company 8th DEVON REGT; moved forward slightly to get quite clear of it.

5. THE ATTACK.

(1). G E N E R A L.

(a) The attack was made under a creeping barrage:-

(i) Artillery barrage. The artillery barrage was put down in depth by guns of all calibres 150 yards in front of the forming up tape at 6 a.m. At 6.3 a.m. it moved forward for 200 yards at the rate of 100 yds in 4 minutes. From there it moved forward to "protective" in front of the RED LINE (1st objective), at the rate of 100 yards in six minutes.

(ii) At 6 a.m. a machine gun barrage opened on the rear enemy positions and continued throughout the attack.

(b) The attack of the 8th DEVON REGT; was made by "A" Company on the right, "C" Company on the left, "B" Company mopping up and "D" Company in reserve.

5. THE ATTACK (continued.
   (c) Contact aeroplanes were working with the attacking troops. All men of the leading Companies carried flares to show for the contact aeroplane on arrival at the first objective.

(6). (a) "A" COMPANY. CAPTAIN J.C. FROOD. (Right Company). At 6 a.m. 4th October 1917, "A" Company advanced under the barrage to the attack. Touch was gained with the 1st S. STAFFORD REGT; after the first 100 yards or so. From there to the 1st objective a re-action was felt, and the tendency was to go to the left. This was however adjusted when the first objective was reached.
Very little resistance was met with. In only two places did the enemy show fight.
(i). At about J.4.d.85.00, the enemy left their pepper box and took cover in a small dugout beside it from which they threw bombs, covered by a machine gun just in rear. This was engaged by a Lewis gun, the position rushed and the garrison killed.
(ii). At about J.5.c.2.3. a Granaten-Werfer was in action from behind a pill box. One Section worked round this flank and the position was taken with 20 prisoners.
Captain J.C.FROOD was wounded during the assault on this second pill box but continued in command of his Company until consolidation was complete. The objective was reached at about 6.20 a.m. At J.5.c.0.8. a large concrete dugout was discovered which was the enemy aid Post, and contained a German Medical Officer and a fair number of wounded Germans.
This dugout was entered close up under the protective barrage in front of the first objective
Touch was gained with the 1st S. STAFFORD REGT; without difficulty at J.11.b.1.9.

(b) "C" COMPANY. CAPTAIN W.F.COOPER. (Left Company). At 6 a.m. 4th October 1917, this Company advanced under the barrage. Some slight hesitation was shown at first as the men did not quite realise apparently that operations really had started. They very soon closed right up under the barrage however.
Very little resistance was met with. The enemy showed no desire to contest the ground, and was only too ready to come out of his pill boxes and put his hand up. The tendency in this Company also was to bear to the left. Touch was maintained throughout with the AUSTRALIANS, however, and the frontage was soon re-organised on reaching the 1st objective.
Some trouble was caused by enemy snipers in the houses 150 yards in front of the objective at about J.5.b.1.9. and just inside the protective barrage in front of the RED LINE. Our men went forward to attack these positions but owing to their proximity to our barrage, found it difficult to clear them entirely of the enemy. The objective was reached about 6.20 a.m.
Touch was gained without difficulty with the 4th AUSTRALIAN BATTALION at about J.5.a.5.1.

(c) "B" COMPANY. CAPTAIN H. ROPER. (Mopping up Company). At 6 a.m. "B" Company advanced in rear of the two assaulting Companies. The following areas had been allotted to the Company:-
(i) Moppers Up attached to first wave:-
The area between the tape and a line J.5.d.0.9 - Road junction J.5.c.1.6. - Light Railway and Road junction J.5.c.25.45. - J.11.a.1.9.
(ii) Moppers Up attached to the second wave:-
The area between that line and the first objective.

5. THE ATTACK. Continued).
(c). – (iii) A special section was told off to deal with strong point at J.4.d.90.05.

A considerably number of the enemy were found still left in isolated Strong Points. About 20 men and a machine gun were left in the Post at J.4.d.90.05. These were dealt with by a Lewis Gun and killed.
50 men were found in the butments at J.5.a.3.0. of which about 30 were taken prisoners.
The majority of the men found however, were simply sitting outside their pill boxes, shell holes and dugouts waiting to be taken prisoners. One machine gun opened fire at J.5.c.3.7. and the crew were at once killed by the moppers up attached to the second wave.

(d). "D" COMPANY. 2ND LT R. GIBBONS. MC., (Reserve Coy).
At 6 a.m. October 4th 1917 the Reserve Company advanced in rear of the leading waves. They were not called on as a Company to deal with any situation. Two pepper boxes only were found that had not been dealt with previously both of which showed fight. One was at J.4.d.85.70. the other at J.11.a.1.7. These were outflanked by Lewis guns and captured without much difficulty.
The Reserve Company suffered more casualties during the advance than any other Company, mainly from the enemy barrage opened before ZERO.

(3). ENEMY RESISTANCE, PRISONERS & ETC.

(a). To sum up the resistance offered by the enemy, – it amounted to very little. The enemy was holding his line a great deal more strongly than was anticipated, as he had arranged to attack on a broad front at 6 a.m. on the 4th October 1917.
His men were competely non-plussed by our barrage and suffered very heavy casualties from shell fire, and particularly from our machine gun barrage.
The first line advancing closely under our barrage found very little resistance from the Posts and Pill boxes which they encountered.
Any pill boxes that were missed by the first waves were dealt with quite easily by the Moppers Up and Reserve Company. These garrisons appeared simply to wait until they were taken prisoners, and made no attempt to fire after the first line had passed them except in one or two places.

(b). Prisoners captured are estimated at 250 and 7 machine guns and 5 granaten-werfers.
The number of prisoners is accounted for by the presence in the front line of his assault troops, in addition to the usual garrison.
Prisoners were mainly from the 72nd, 73rd, 92nd, 93rd, 123rd, Reserve Infantry Regiments and the 4th GUARDS RESERVE DIVISION.

(4). LEAP FROGGING.
The leap frogging movement of the 2nd BORDER REGT; and the 2nd GORDON HIGHLANDERS with passed off without incident, and they passed on to their objective under the barrage at 8.10 a.m.

6. **CONSOLIDATION.**

(a). As soon as the two leap frogging Battalions had passed through, consolidation and re-organization began.

(i). "A" Company consolidated on the line of the first objective from J.5.c.8.6. to J.5.c.8.3. with one Platoon near JAY BARN – in touch with 1st SOUTH STAFFORD REGT; at J.11.b.1.9.

(ii). "C" Company consolidated with a line of Posts from J.5.c.5.9. to J.5.c.8.7. and one Platoon in the neighbourhood of J.5.c.5.7.

(iii). "B" Company withdrew their Mopping up Parties when their work was completed and garrisoned the area on either side of a line running from J.5.c.2.9. to J.5.c.4.0. as had been previously arranged.

(iv). "D" Company consolidated with a half Company at about J.4.d.8.6. and a half Company at J.4.d.2.1. During the night of the 4th/5th, the whole Company was withdrawn to trenches in the neighbourhood of J.4.d.2.1.

(b). There was a certain amount of mixture of Units on the first objective, and it took some little time to re-organise into Companies. Re-organisation when complete was very satisfactory.
There was no shelling of our positions for 1½ hours after the objective was taken. Then, finding from aeroplane observation, the enemy started to shell them with guns of all calibres up to 21 c.m. and continued intermittently during the time we held the line.

(c). BATTALION HEADQUARTERS and REGIMENTAL AID POST both during the attack and subsequently remained at the BUTTE at J.10.a.70.75.

7. **HOLDING THE LINE.**

(a). The 20th INFANTRY BRIGADE continued to hold the line they had captured with 2nd BORDER REGT; on the right, and 2nd GORDON HIGHLANDERS on the left, 8th DEVON REGT; in support, in dispositions shown in para 6 (a) above, 9th DEVON REGT; in reserve, from the morning of 4th October 1917 to the night 6th/7th October 1917.
Throughout that time our positions were steadily shelled with considerable accuracy, and frequent barrages were put down by the enemy.
His main barrage lines were roughly J.5.b.4.0. to J.5.a.6.0., J.4.b.4.0. to J.10.b.3.8., J.4.c.8.8. to J.10.a. central. Certain minor adjustments of position were necessary to avoid the main stream of shelling. There was also a certain amount of desultory rifle and machine gun fire. The direction of all fire was from South East.

(b). On the night 6th/7th October, the 20th INFANTRY BRIGADE took over the right subsector of the DIVISIONAL front in addition to the left subsector, – Relieving Battalions of 91st INFANTRY BRIGADE, The whole DIVISIONAL LINE was then held by 2nd BORDER REGT; on left, 9th DEVON REGT; on the right, 2nd GORDON HIGHLANDERS in reserve near the BUTTE as counter attack Battalion and 8th DEVON REGIMENT in support.
The BATTALION moved as follows :-

(i). "A" & "C" Companies held their original line with half their Companies, the other half of each Coy; taking over the support positions previously held by "B" Company.

(ii). "B" Company moved to support position in JOLTING TRENCH SUPPORT from J.11.a.8.9. to J.11.a. Central.

(iii). "D" Company moved to support position in JOLTING TRENCH from JAY BARN to J.11.b.2.5.

(iv). BATTALION H.Q. R.A.P. remained at the BUTTE.

(v). Relief was complete at 1 a.m. with few casualties.

SHEET 6.

9. G E N E R A L. (Continued).

(D). MEDICAL.

The evacuation of wounded to REGIMENTAL AID POST worked very satisfactorily. There was, however, frequently a great congestion of wounded at the R. A. P. who could not be cleared.

(E). BARRAGE.

Our barrage, and particularly our machine gun barrage, inspired the greatest confidence in the men. No difficulty was experienced in keeping them close up to it. At times they kept too close and got right into the fringe of it.

One point that was noticed was that the dust and mud thrown up by our shells got into the working parts of Lewis Guns and rifles, making the problem of keeping them in working order still more difficult.

(F). DIRECTION.

The greatest problem was to keep direction, in an area entirely destitute of land marks. There was only one easily recognisable land mark - the conical mound at J.8.c.5.7. It is thought that men tended to left incline towards this. It is difficult for one man with a compass to guide a whole line, and compasses with so much iron about, are not very reliable. More distant landmarks are invisible in the smoke.

(G). MOPPERS UP.

The problem of direction is more acute still in the case of Moppers up, who have to recognise an area. The tendency is for the Moppers up attached to the first wave to overshoot their area.

In this connection the importance of mopping up was clearly brought out. Even in a very successful attack, the Moppers up had a lot of work to do that had escaped the Assaulting Companies.

(H). CASUALTIES.

A list of TOTAL casualties is attached.

Nearly all of these occurred from shell fire before and after the attack, and very few during the attack itself.

Lieutenant Colonel,

12th OCTOBER 1917. Commanding 8th (Ser) Bn DEVONSHIRE REGIMENT.

COPIES TO:-

Headquarters, 20th INFANTRY BRIGADE.
WAR DIARY - (Two copies).
FILE.
SPARE.

-:-o0o-:-

8. RELIEF.

(a). On the night 7th/8th October 1917, the 20th INFANTRY BRIGADE was relieved by the 22nd INFANTRY BRIGADE in the DIVISIONAL Front.

(b). The 8th DEVON REGIMENT was relived as follows:-
"A" & "C" Companies in the RED LINE by one Company 20th MANCHESTER REGIMENT
"B" Company in JOLTING SUPPORT by one Company 2/1st H.A.C.
"D" Company in JEALING TRENCH by one Company 2nd ROYAL WARWICK REGIMENT.

(c). The enemy put down a fairly heavy barrage on his usual line from 6 p.m. to 8 p.m. and intermittently throughout the night, which somewhat interfered with the relief. Relief was however reported complete at 12.30 a.m. with few casualties.

(d). On relief, the Battalion moved back to [illegible] Camp near CHATEAU SIGARD, getting into Camp about 5 a.m.

9. GENERAL.

In addition to the points brought out in paras: 1 and to 8 above, the following details of general interest are noted:-

(A). WEATHER. - The attack took place at the end of a long spell of fine warm dry weather. The weather broke during the night of the 2nd/3rd instant, and throughout the time that the BATTALION was in the line was cold with a moderate West wind and intermittent rain. The ground got very muddy but never impassable, as, excepting places where the ground was definitely swampy, the soil was light and fairly sandy. This also facilitated digging in.

(B). RATIONS. - Three different methods of bringing up rations were tried :-

(i). Bringing them up by pack train by night up to BATTALION H.Q.

(ii). Bringing them up by Pack train for a certain distance by night, and thence to BATTALION H.Q. by carrying party.

(iii). By Pack train and carrying Party to BATTALION H.Q by day.

Of these, the third proved by far the most satisfactory.

(i). Most of the shelling in back areas was by night.

(ii). On dark nights the difficulty of negotiating bad places in the track for animals is increase 100 per cent, and also the difficulty of finding the way.

(iii). As regards the distance to which Pack animals can be taken.

If the number of men with details permit, a carrying party is far more mobile and able to cope with shelling, bad tracks of the last part of the journey.

(C). COMMUNICATIONS.

Communication as usual formed a difficulty.

(i). Communication forward of BATTALION H.Q. - The Policy of sending forward intelligence men with the leading waves to bring independant information, was completely justified. These men brought back early, reliable and most valuable information. It proved quite impossible to maintain a line to Companies, though frequent efforts were made.

(ii). Communication with BRIGADE. - The only means of communication which proved reliable throughout was pigeons. The power buzzer and lamp were unsatisfactory and Relay Runners were continually becoming casualties owing to the enemy's barrage fire.

8TH (SERVICE) BATTALION THE DEVONSHIRE RGT.

TOTAL LIST OF CASUALTIES.
2nd OCTOBER TO 8TH OCTOBER 1917.

O F F I C E R S.

2nd Lieutenant	GARNETT	V.	Killed in Action	4-10-1917.
2nd Lieutenant	CORNELIUS	F.S. MC.	- do -	3-10-1917.
2nd Lieutenant	[illegible]	T.H.	- do -	4-10-1917.
2nd Lieutenant	[illegible]	W.G.	- do -	4-10-1917.
Captain	BROOD	J.G.	Wounded in Action	4-10-1917.
Captain	DRAKE	A.H. MC.	- do -	7-10-1917.
2nd Lieutenant	[illegible]	[illegible]	- do -	2-10-1917.
2nd Lieutenant	HARDING	L.C.E.	- do -	4-10-1917.
2nd Lieutenant	BAKER	E.J.	- do -	4-10-1917.
2nd Lieutenant	KING	T.N.	- do -	4-10-1917.
2nd Lieutenant	[illegible]	E.	- do -	4-10-1917.
2nd Lieutenant	RUDDICOMBE	E.C.	- do - (and admitted to Hospital on 8-10-1917.)	7-10-1917.
2nd Lieutenant	GIBBONS	R. MC.	Wounded in action and Continued at duty	4/10/7
2nd Lieutenant	MARSHALL	R.	- do - - do -	do.

	OFFICERS.	OTHER RANKS.
KILLED IN ACTION:-	4.	53.
WOUNDED IN ACTION:-	8.	181.
WOUNDED IN ACTION, (SHELL SHOCK)	-	17.
DIED OF WOUNDS:-	-	4.
MISSING:-	-	11.
WOUNDED IN ACTION, (G. A. S.)	2.	2.
T O T A L :-	14.	268.

Appendix no 2

Copy No ...3...

9TH (SERVICE) BATTALION THE DEVONSHIRE REGIMENT.

Reference Maps:-
SHEET 28,1/40,000.
Village of
GHELUVELT 1/5,000.

REPORT ON OPERATIONS - 26/10/17.

1. GENERAL OPERATIONS.

(1). At 5.40 a.m. on 26th October 1917, the Xth Corps carried out an attack on GHELUVELT and POLDERHOEK Chateau in co-operation with the main attack further North.

(2). (a). The attack of the Xth Corps was made by the 7th DIVISION on the right and the 5th DIVISION on the left. The 39th DIVISION were in close support to the 7th DIVISION.

(b). The role of the 7th DIVISION was to capture GHELUVELT and ZANDVOORDE spur and to secure our hold on the TOWER HAMLETS ridge. The role of the 5th DIVISION was to capture POLDERHOEK Chateau and Wood.

(c). The attack of the 7th DIVISION was carried out by the 91st INFANTRY BRIGADE on the right, and the 20th INFANTRY BRIGADE on the left. The 22nd INFANTRY BRIGADE were in reserve.

(d). The attack of the 20th INFANTRY BRIGADE was carried out as follows:-

(i). 1st OBJECTIVE.- 9th DEVON REGIMENT on the left.
2nd BORDER REGIMENT on the right.

(ii). 2nd OBJECTIVE:- (Leap-frogging movement).
8th DEVON REGIMENT on the left.
2nd GORDON HIGH'RS on the right.

(iii). 1st R.WELSH FUSILIERS attached from 22nd INFANTRY BRIGADE were in reserve.

(iv). Boundary line between Battalions was the YPRES - MENIN Road.

(e). Divisional and Brigade boundaries and objectives are shown on the attached map.

(f). 1st R.W.KENTS, (13th INFANTRY BRIGADE) were attacking on the left of 20th INFANTRY BRIGADE on a one Company front and were going through to both objectives.

2. ENEMY DISPOSITIONS.

(a). Considerable information as to the enemy's dispositions had been obtained from aeroplane photographs. He was holding the whole sector opposite the Battalion front by a system of pill boxes and consolidated shell-holes.
He was known to be holding strongly the cellars and pill boxes in GHELUVELT and the ruined Chateau in J.22.b.65.10. He was holding the Railway cutting in J.22.a.5.0. in force, and the Railway line from J.21.d.90.85 to J.22.c.45.95. by a system of consolidated shell-holes.
Known pill boxes were also at J.22.c.8.8. - J.22.d.1.3. - J.22.d.55.40. There were Headquarters in concrete dugouts at J.22.c.7.5.

(b). His approximate front line on the left of the MENIN Road was J.22.a.8.8. - J.22.a.7.4. - J.22.a.5.0.
On the right of the MENIN Road his line was further advanced and ran from J.21.b.5.0. to J.21.c.8.1.

(c). The suspected enemy order of battle was 10th BAVARIAN DIVISION in the line opposite our front and the 15th PRUSSIAN DIVISION in reserve at DADIZEELE. This order of battle was confirmed.

/d.

(d). Owing to the information obtained from captured documents, the enemy was expected to be holding his forward positions strongly with a number of machine guns.

3. ASSEMBLY MARCH AND FORMING UP ON TAPES.

(1). On the night 24th/25th October 1917, the 9th DEVON REGIMENT and 2nd BORDER REGIMENT took over the attack frontage of the 20th INFANTRY BRIGADE.
9th DEVON REGIMENT on the North of the MENIN Road.
2nd BORDER REGIMENT on the South of the MENIN Road.
relieving Battalions of the 117th and 42nd INFANTRY BRIGADES.

(2). Owing to the fact that our line on the North of the MENIN Road was considerably in advance of our line on the South of the MENIN Road, a withdrawal was necessitated on the part of the 9th DEVON REGIMENT in order to bring their forming up tape into line with the 2nd BORDER REGIMENT.
Accordingly at dusk on night 25th/26th October, the 9th DEVON REGIMENT withdrew and formed up in the normal formation on the line running from J.21.b.8.3. obliquely on to the MENIN Road at J.21.b.35.05.
The 2nd BORDER REGIMENT formed up on their original front line from J.21.b.35.05 to J.21.c.95.75. - This line running obliquely to the MENIN Road.

(3). The two assaulting Battalions were formed up on a depth on 140 yards - 15 yards between lines and between second line and moppers up; 40 yards between moppers up of the first wave and the first line of second wave; 40 yards between moppers up of second wave and reserve Company.

(4). At 7 p.m. 25th October, 2nd GORDON HIGHLANDERS moved up from dugouts South of ZILLEBEKE Lake and formed up in rear of 2nd BORDER REGIMENT on a front of 200 yards at right angles to the MENIN Road from J.21.a.5.5. to J.21.a.3.0.

(5). (a). At 6 p.m. 25th October 1917, the 8th DEVON REGIMENT moved up from dugouts south of ZILLEBEKE Lake and moved to their assembly positions by VERBRANDEN Road - MIDDLESEX Road - PLUMERS Drive - 'E' TRACK - MENIN Road, (See attached track map).

(b). The Battalion moved off as follows:-
"D" Company, "B" Company, "A" Company, Headquarters, two platoons of "C" Company, (Mopping Up Company), ~~xxxxxxxxxxxxxxx~~"C" moved with "D" Company, and two platoons with "B" Company.

(c). The Battalion arrived at its forming up positions at 8.30 p.m. and was in position by 9 p.m. There was little shell-fire on the way in, or during the process of forming up, and there was only one man slightly wounded.

(d). The Battalion formed up on a 200 yards front on a line at right angles to the MENIN Road from J.21.b.1.3. to J.21.b.2.6., 70 yards in rear of 9th DEVON REGT and in advance of 2nd GORDON HIGHLANDERS - Leap-frogging Battalion on the right.

(e). The Battalion formed up slightly in advance of the line originally intended and was closed up to a depth of 100 yards instead of 140 yards, with intervals between lines etc reduced accordingly. This was rendered necessary by the fact that the ground immediately in rear was very wet and also the enemy barrage line was immediately in rear of the final position of Reserve Company, and the barrage would therefore have fallen directly on the Battalion. This closing up process undoubtedly saved casualties during the waiting period, and avoided some very difficult and boggy ground.

(f). The following tapes were put out:-
One for 1st line of first wave.
One for 1st line of second wave.
One for rear of Reserve Company.
The forming up of the Battalion in the confined space passed off without a hitch, and Companies were correctly distributed and in immediate touch with Reserve Company of 1st R.W.KENTS on the left.

(g). As soon as the Battalion was in position, all ranks dug in. The ground was easy to dig in, but water was near the surface, rendering ~~occasional~~ frequent change of position necessary. This however helped to keep the men warm.

(h). From 10 p.m. to ZERO hour there was intermittent enemy shelling of assembly positions with H.E. but very few casualties resulted, as the men had had time to dig well in.

4. THE ATTACK.

(1). FEATURES OF THE GROUND.

From the forming up tape the ground sloped upwards nearly to the first objective then dipped and rose again up to the Church in GHELUVELT, which was in a comparitively commanding position. From there it fell away rapidly to the final objective and from there, dropped down into low ground.
South of the MENIN Road, a Valley which was very wet and boggy, ran South through J.21.d. and J.27.b.
On the left there was a stretch of boggy ground running from J.22.d.0.8. along the Divisional boundary to the Chateau at J.22.b.65.05.
The only prominent landmarks were the MENIN Road, which was clearly marked by stumps of trees, the Chateau at J.22.b.65.05, and the Church and Mill in GHELUVELT.

(2). GENERAL.

(a). The attack was carried out under a creeping barrage. This was put down at 5.40 a.m. in depth by guns of all calibres 150 yards in front of the forming up line. It remained there for 4 minutes and then moved forward by lifts of 50 yards, as follows:-
First four lifts 50 yards in 4 minutes.
Next four lifts 50 yards in 5 minutes.
There after 50 yards in 7 minutes to RED protective (150 yards in front of RED line).
The barrage remained on this line for one hour and then moved on at the rate of 50 yards in 7 minutes to the final objective and went to protective 200 yards in front of the BLUE Line.

(b). ZERO hour was at 5.40 a.m.
At ZERO the 9th DEVON REGT and 2nd BORDER REGT advanced under the barrage towards the RED line. Almost immediately the 2nd BORDER REGT on the South of the MENIN Road must have met with very heavy opposition ~~almost at once~~, as the right flank of the 9th DEVON REGT was soon in the air and exposed to very heavy rifle and machine gun fire from LEWIS HOUSE and the pill boxes on the South of the MENIN Road at J.21.d.8.8. and also to frontal machine gun fire from the village of GHELUVELT.

The 9th DEVON REGIMENT then suffered very heavy casualties indeed and their right flank was compelled to hank back as being the most exposed.
They finally reached a line running roughly from J.21.d.9.9. just in rear of light railway line to J.22.a.7.1.
They had by this time lost practically all their Officers. One organised party under Captain FRIDHAM, dug in along a bit of old trench running along 55 contour line from J.21.b.95.05 to J.21.a.8.1.

(3). ATTACK OF 8TH DEVON REGIMENT.

(a). The attack of the 8th DEVON REGIMENT was made by
"B" Company on the right,
"D" Company on the left,
"C" Company Mopping up,
"A" Company in reserve.

(b). (i). If the attack had progressed according to programme, the following would have taken place:- At ZERO the 8th DEVON REGIMENT would have advanced immediately in rear of 9th DEVON REGT to a point 400 yards in German territory where they would have halted and reformed. They would then have advanced again to the 1st objective, passed through the 9th DEVON REGT and laid down as close as possible underneath the barrage. The advance ~~xxxxx~~ to the final objective would then have been continued at ZERO plus 130.

(ii). What actually occured was that soon after the advance commenced the leading Companies of the 8th DEVON REGIMENT began to merge with the rear of the Reserve Company 9th DEVON REGIMENT. This was partly due to the fact that the advance of the 9th DEVON REGT was impeded by enfilade fire and so caused them to lose the barrage. In the earlier stages it may have been caused by the slow rate of the barrage, the tendency being for troops in rear, not regulated by the barrage, to push on too fast.

(c). While the 9th DEVON REGIMENT was still advancing, the 8th DEVON REGIMENT was also suffering from the heavy enfilade and frontal rifle and machine gun fire, (mentioned in para: 4. (2), (b) above).
Shell fire was negligible, as our men were able to get clear of the enemy's barrage before it opened.
By the time the 8th DEVON REGIMENT had reached the line on which the 9th DEVON REGIMENT had halted, (see para: 4 (2), (b) above), the Battalion was very reduced, and for purposes of further advance the barrage had of course been lost.
Formation had still been kept however, at any rate in all cases in which leaders were left, and as many columns as were able advanced straight through the 9th DEVON REGIMENT in an attempt to continue the advance and catch up the barrage. They carried with them a number of the 9th DEVON REGIMENT whose leaders had been killed, and also some men of other Battalions. They made little headway however, for as soon as they got clear of the 9th DEVON REGIMENT they came in for the full force of machine gun and rifle fire that had previously ~~being~~ been felt by the 9th DEVON REGIMENT. The details of these forward movements are shown in para 4 (3), (d) below.

(d). DETAILS OF COMPANY ADVANCES BEYOND LINE OF 9th DEVON R.

(i). "B" Company - Right front Company, (Captain F.J.C. MARSHALL, MC,).

(i. The majority of the second wave, who had lost their officers, made an attempt on the pill boxes South of the MENIN Road, which were holding up our advance, at J.21.d.8.2. under an officer of the 9th DEVON REGIMENT. All the party were hit except one Sergeant who sniped from a shell-hole for some time, and eventually collected some stragglers and attached himself to Captain PRIDHAM's party, (see para: 4 (2).(b), above).

ii. Right attacking platoon was seen going on into GHELUVELT and nothing more is known of them.

iii. The remainder of the Company under Captain MARSHALL, including two other Officers of the 8th DEVON REGIMENT and a number of men of the 9th DEVON REGIMENT, some of the 2nd GORDON HIGHLANDERS and the remains of a Platoon of 2nd BORDER REGIMENT pushed on beyond the Railway line, taking several pill boxes in JOHNSON TRENCH and reaching apparently a point about J.22.a.9.7.

They had completely failed to catch up the barrage again and were suffering very heavy casualties from machine gun and rifle fire both from the right flank, as already stated, and from the front.

Then about 10 a.m. the enemy counter attacked the troops on their left rear, down the railway cutting in J.22.a.6.0. Captain MARSHALL found himself surrounded on three sides and in imminent danger of being cut off and suffering heavy casualties all the time. He accordingly withdrew to a crater where the Railway track joins the MENIN Road at ~~[illegible]~~ J.21.d.85.90. which position he held until relieved, gaining touch with Captain PRIDHAM on his left, and later with 2nd BORDER REGIMENT and 2nd GORDON HIGH'rs on his right. This position was very important, as for some time it covered an exposed flank. Captain MARSHALL's party was the only important formed body of men of the 20th INFANTRY BRIGADE North of the MENIN Road, when the situation became clear, except Captain PRIDHAM's party on his left.

Both parties were formed of a mixture of Companies and Battalions.

(ii). "D" Company - Left front Company, (Captain F.W. GIRVAN).

1. The two right platoons kept touch with "B" Company on the right. They advanced to some distance beyond the Railway (probably not more than 50 yards), where they met very heavy fire and had heavy casualties. They appeared to have divided to the right and left, and to have been merged in either "B" Company or the two left Platoons of "D" Company. Captain GIRVAN was wounded early in the advance.

/ii.

ii. ~~The~~ 2 left Platoons, realising that they had to bear to the left to follow the Divisional boundary, while making for the Chateau in J.22.b.65.05 apparently went too far to the left and got the wrong side of the marshy ground on the Divisional boundary. They found themselves isolated and exposed to fire from J.16.d. as well as from the front and the right. 2nd Lieutenant R.V. EVANS pushed forward with two sections in the direction of the Chateau at J.22.b.65.05, but was wounded almost immediately. The two sections went on and nothing more was heard of them.
The survivors of the two left Platoons were ralied by two N.C.Os, one party falling in with 15th R.WARWICK REGIMENT in a trench at J.22.a.4.9. the other coming under the orders of an Officer of the 1st R.W.KENTS in JOHNSON TRENCH at J.22.a.2.4.

iii. "C" Company - Mopping up Company, (2nd Lieut; W.J.WYATT).
Areas and special objectives had been allotted to the mopping up Company between the first and second objectives. These of course were never reached, and the Moppers up became amalgamated with the Companies to which they were attached. One party of this Company acting as a separate party captured and held the pill box at J.22.c.5.8., but were driven back by the enemy counter attack down the Railway cutting in J.22.a.5.0. at 10 a.m. (see para 4 (3).(d).(i). iii, above), and became amalgamated with Captain PRIDHAM's party.

iv. "A" Company - Reserve Company, Captain G.E.JUPE.
"A" Company set out disposed as follows:-
Left Platoon under 2nd Lieutenant A.MONK with orders to follow up the left of the attack and to be prepared to deal with the Chateau at J.22.b.65.05, if the original attack failed.
Centre Platoon under 2nd Lieutenant LORD prepared to watch the centre and to fill up any gaps that might occur between the two assaulting Companies.
Right Platoon under 2nd Lieutenant PERKINS to form an extra Mopping up Platoon for the cellars in GHELUVELT.
One Platoon moved under Captain JUPE's orders, prepared to deal with any emergency, and in particular to watch the right flank from which most trouble was anticipated.
This Company moved by Platoons and therefore kept more intact than other Companies.

i. Not a single survivor has come back from the right or the reserve Platoons, and Captain JUPE was seen to be killed. It is however clear from other evidence that these Platoons in succession tried for the pill boxes on the South of the MENIN Road, which was holding up our advance, and in the absence of a barrage were annihilated.

ii. The centre Platoon, after 2nd Lieutenant LORD was killed early in the advance, dispersed, suffered heavily in the enemy counter attack from the Railway cutting at 10 a.m. and became amalgamated with Captain PRIDHAM's party.

/iii.

iii. 2nd Lieutenant MONK's Platoon (left Platoon) followed the left Platoons of "D" Company, and lost direction with them. They eventually attacked the pill boxes at J.22.a. 85.95. and suffered heavily. The remainder became amalgamated with 13th R.WARWICK REGT at J.22.a.5.9.

(4). SUMMING UP.

To sum up the details in para 4 (3).(a).(b).(c).(d) above, as affecting both 8th & 9th DEVON REGIMENT.

(a). One mixed party under Captain PRIDHAM consolidated along an old trench from J.21.b.90.05. to J.22.a.2.1.

(b). One party, composed of the survivors of those who had gone forward, under Captain MARSHALL, consolidated in a crater at J.21.d.80.85.

(c). Details of the survivors of both Battalions amalgamated with 13th R.WARWICK REGT in a trench at J.22.a.4.9. and with 1st R.W.KENTS in a trench at J.22.a.1.4.

(d). Elements of both Battalions and of 2nd BORDER REGIMENT reached GHELUVELT but were unable to maintain themselves against hostile fire and the counter attack at 10 a.m. down Railway cutting in J.22.a.5.0.

(e). There was no other formed party of 20th INFANTRY BRIGADE except Captain PRIDHAM's party and Captain MARSHALL's party left north of the MENIN Road by 11 a.m.

(f). BATTALION H.Q. 8th & 9th DEVON REGIMENTS remained throughout at pill box J.2?.b.03. Regimental Aid Posts at J.21.b.18.25 and J.21.b.2.2.

4. C O N S O L I D A T I O N.

(1). At about 12 noon the situation was critical. The extent and strength of the enemy counterattack was unknown. Touch on the right and left had not been gained and the ~~situation~~ general situation was obscure.

(2). 2nd Lieutenant S.A. LACEY, MC, 8th DEVON REGIMENT and 2nd Lieutenant ~~[illegible]~~. EVANS, 9th DEVON REGIMENT were sent up to find out the situation.

2nd Lieutenant EVANS was wounded and 2nd Lieutenant LACEY established connection between Captain PRIDHAM's party on the right and the R.W.KENTS on the left, by putting out two posts at J.22.a.20.15. and at J.22.a.2.2.

(3). At sometime during the morning the pill boxes at J.21.d.80.85. were taken by the 2nd GORDON HIGHLANDERS which relived the situation, and the 2nd BORDER REGT and 2nd GORDON H'RS formed a defensive flank on the south of the MENIN Road from about J.21.d.8.9. running south west through J.21.d. central.

(4). Before this, touch was finally established between Captain PRIDHAM's party and Captain MARSHALL's party (now under the command of 2nd Lieut R. MARSHALL).

(5). The situation was still critical however, as all Lewis guns and Vickers machine guns were out of action from shell-fire and mud, and rifles had become unworkable owing to the mud.

(6). Two Companies of 1st R.W.FUSILIERS were accordingly called on, and came up with the greatest steadiness and determination through the most difficult conditions. Three Platoons remained in reserve at about J.21.a.central with special instructions to watch the right of the MENIN Road.

One Company and one Platoon took over the line of 8th and 9th DEVON REGIMENTS forming one continuous line just in rear of the positions held previously, and linking up with 2nd BORDER REGT and 2nd GORDON H'RS on the right and with the 1st K O S B

KENTS on the left

(7). When matters looked at their worst at about 11.30 a.m. O.C. 1st R.W.KENTS collected and formed a support line composed of elements of all Units of 20th INFANTRY BRIGADE and of the 13th INFANTRY BRIGADE running at right angles to the MENIN Road immediately in front of his Battalion Headquarters, which were at J.21.b.4.3. These were not however called on.

(8). Dispositions of the line North of the MENIN Road at 3 p.m. are shown on the attached map.

(9). At about 3 p.m. 26th October 1917, our barrage was brought back to the original protective barrage line in front of our old front line of the 25th October, and the situation was in hand.

5. ENEMY RESISTANCE & ETC.

(1). The enemy's resistance was very determined. He held tenaciously to his pill boxes, and showed that it is almost impossible to dislodge an alert and determined enemy from a pill box without a barrage.

(2). The enemy counter attack at 10 a.m. from the Railway cutting in J.22.a.5.0. was very determined and was made in strength; but it is doubtful if it was ever intended to be more than local.

(3). A few prisoners were taken who confirmed the enemy order of battle given in para 2 (c).

(4). The enemy barrage was practically non-effective as a means of stopping our advance, as it opened in rear of our troops.

(5). The enemy relied mainly on rifle and machine gun fire, which he used with great effect.
He must have had a number of machine guns in forward positions in accordance with his latest defensive schemes.

(6). Enemy aircraft flew low over our positions at about 3 p.m. opening machine gun fire on our men.

(7). The enemy was seen to fire a message rocket from about J.21.d.80.85. at about 10 a.m.

(8). At the commencement of operations, the enemy barrage was on a line - J.21.b.0.3. - J.21.a.9.5. - J.21.a.8.2. At about 3 p.m. when the situation had settled down, the enemy changed his barrage to a line running obliquely across the MENIN Road from J.21.a.central - through J.21.b.0.3. - J.21.d.central.

(9). It is noteworthy that the enemy's troops in the counter attack at 10 a.m. were lightly equipped, and many of them were armed with revolvers. This gave them an advantage over our men, who were many of them stuck in the mud, and most of whose rifles had become unserviceable.

(10). It appears clear that the counter attack at 10 a.m. down the Railway cutting in J.22.a.5.0. was the only organised counter attack made by the enemy, though throughout the day there was a considerable amount of enemy movement and sniping activity.

6. R E L I E F.

At 8 p.m. 26th October, orders were received that the 1st R.WELCH FUSILIERS was to take over the front of the 20th INFANTRY BRIGADE.
This as far as the 8th & 9th DEVON REGIMENTS were concerned was a simple process, as one Company of 1st R.W.FUSILIERS had already taken over the line North of the MENIN Road.
Our men were withdrawn and relief was complete by 9.30 p.m.
On relief the BATTALION went back to a Camp near VIERSTRAAT.
There were no casualties on the way out, and Camp was reached at 1 a.m.

/7. GENERAL.

SHEET 9.

7. G E N E R A L.

(1). WEATHER.

The weather for the assembly march was fine and dry, and a clear moon, which made the march and forming up a simple process.
About 3.30 a.m. however on the morning of the 26th October, rain set in and a high wind and continued throughout the day.
Coming on top of the heavy rain of the preceeding fortnight it made the ground exceptionally boggy, and the going was very bad.
It was possible however to advance North of the Road as far as our men went. It is impossible to form an opinion of the low ground near the final objective.
Although progress was possible, the conditions were very bad, and rifles and Lewis guns became rapidly unworkable. Any attempt to make use of old trenches ended in many men being stuck in the mud.
For this reason the task of repelling a counter attack presented the greatest difficulties. The conditions of the tracks in rear was at all times good, and the MENIN Road invaluable.

(2). COMMUNICATION.

Communication both forward and in rear of BATTALION H.Q. was, considering the conditions, excellent. Pigeon, visual and runners only were used.

(3). R A T I O N S.

It proved quite practicable and eminently desirable to carry up rations for two days.
The forward dumps of water etc; were well placed, and would have been of the greatest value and a great economy over carrying parties.

(4). MEDICAL.

The evacuation of wounded to the Regimental Aid Post worked satisfactorily. There was, however, at one time a great congestion of wounded there who could not be cleared. They were cleared by evening, but largely by Regimental stretcher bearers.

(5). CASUALTIES.

A list of total casualties is attached.
Nearly all of these occurred from rifle and machine gun fire and there must have been a large number of killed.
Of the missing, there must be a certain number of prisoners but there must also be a large number of killed lying in German territory. Of the men previously reported "missing", 45 have been traced in Hospital "Wounded". also 2 other ranks previously reported "Wounded" have since Died of wounds.

Lieutenant Colonel,

1st November 1917. Commanding 8th (Service) B. DEVON REGT.

Copy No 1, To H.Q. 20th Infantry Brigade.
2 & 3 War Diary.
4,5 & 6. Spare.

8TH (SERVICE) BATTALION DEVONSHIRE REGIMENT.

T O T A L   C A S U A L T I E S,

28th OCTOBER 1917.

OFFICERS:-

Captain	JUPE	C.E.	Killed in action.
2nd Lieutenant	LORD	H.G.	- do -
Captain	MARSHALL	F.J.C. MC.	Wounded in action.
Captain	GIRVAN	F.W.	- do -
2nd Lieutenant	FALKEN	N.E.	- do -
2nd Lieutenant	FARLEIGH	J.S.	- do -
2nd Lieutenant	ASHPLANT	W.R.	- do -
2nd Lieutenant	EVANS	R.V.	- do -
2nd Lieutenant	PERKINS	E.H.	- do -
2nd Lieutenant	WYATT	W.J.	- do - Died of Wds 29/10/17.
2nd Lieutenent	MONK	A.	Wounded and Missing.
Lieutenant	BUCKINGHAM	T.N.	Missing.
2nd Lieutenant	DREW	C.A.	do.
2nd Lieutenant	REED	W.J.	do.
2nd Lieutenant	MARSHALL	R.	Wounded and Continued at Duty.

	OFFICERS.	OTHER RANKS.
Killed in action	2.	20.
Wounded in action	7.	131.
Died of Wounds.	1.	2.
Missing	4.	105.
Wounded and (C.A.D).	1.	---
T O T A L :-	15.	258.

-oOo-

7th DIVISION.
20th Inf Bde.

8th DEVONSHIRE REGIMENT

NOVEMBER 1917

Army Form C. 2118.

Instructions regarding War Diaries and Intelligence Summaries are contained in F. S. Regs., Part II. and the Staff Manual respectively. Title pages will be prepared in manuscript.

WAR DIARY
or
INTELLIGENCE SUMMARY.
(Erase heading not required.)

8th Devon Regt

Vol 26

Place	Date	Hour	Summary of Events and Information	Remarks and references to Appendices
~~[illegible]~~	1.11.17		Reorganisation, Coy parades.	
BLARINGHEM	2.11.17		Lewis Gun and bombing classes. Coy parades.	
La Belle Croix	3.11.17		The Battalion moved in the morning to La Belle Croix area. Good barn billets but so scattered. Correctly billeted 1pm.	
"	4.11.17		Divine Service 10.30 am.	
"	5.11.17.		Lewis gun and bombing classes continued.	
"	6.11.17		Baths for all in the morning. N.C.O.s class.	
"	7.11.17		Practise for Divisional inspection.	
"	8.11.17		The 7th Division was inspected by HM the King of the Belgians. Brigades formed up in line of masses. March past in close column of platoons. Marched off 9.30 am. Inspection 11.30 am. Home by 1.30 pm. A very fine day. The C.O. and [illegible] [illegible] [illegible]. Divisional Commanders conference in the afternoon.	
	9.11.17		Very wet – no parades.	
"	10.11.17		Classes as usual. Route march for remainder.	
"	11.11.17		Divine Service in the morning. Very wet.	
"	12.11.17		The Battalion moved in the morning to St PIERRE. Good billets but very scattered. Correctly billeted by 5 pm.	
St PIERRE	13.11.17.		The Batn. moved in the morning to billets at THEROUANNE. Good billets. Correctly billeted 2pm.	

26

A7092). Wt. W12839/M1297 750,000. 1/17. D. D & L., Ltd. Forms/C2118/14.

Instructions regarding War Diaries and Intelligence Summaries are contained in F. S. Regs., Part II. and the Staff Manual respectively. Title pages will be prepared in manuscript.

WAR DIARY
or
~~INTELLIGENCE SUMMARY.~~ 8th Devon Regt

(*Erase heading not required.*)

Army Form C. 2118.

Place	Date	Hour	Summary of Events and Information	Remarks and references to Appendices
THEROUANNE	14-11-17		The battalion moved in the morning to Billets at FRUGES correctly billeted 1.30 pm. Good billets. 2Lt. A.F.R. SUTTON joined battalion.	
FRUGES	15.11.17		The Battalion moved in the morning to billets at WAVRANS. Correctly billeted 3 pm. Scattered billets. 2Lt. W.D. TRAYLER rejoined battalion. 2Lt's W.G. WELSH. L.A. DUGDALE R. GARNSWORTHY W.C.G. DREW joined battalion. Draft of 162 O Ranks joined battalion. Mostly young soldiers from England. KSLI (trained) and casuals of own Regt.	
WAVRANS	16-11-17		Battalion organising for move. Drawing stores &c. Drill for Drafts. 2Lt AUDSICOMBE rejoined Batn. Draft of 36 O.R. from Wiltshire Regt (trained) joined battalion.	
"	17-11-17		Drill for Drafts etc as on 16th. Draft of 23 O ranks (ACC & ASC) joined battalion.	
"	18.11.17 to 23-11-17		The battalion entrained as follows at WAVRANS. No. 1 train 6 am. AB & HQ ½ transport under Lt Col St Hill. No 2 train 9 am CD & HQ ½ transport under Major CRIPPS MC. No 1 train proceeded via ~~[illegible]~~ St POL AMIENS PARIS DIJON LYON AVIGNON MARSEILLES NICE GENOA PADUA to LEGNAGO where they detrained at 4 am 24-11-17. No 2 train proceeded via St POL AMIENS PARIS DIJON MONTCENIS [illegible] MILAN to LEGNAGO.	

A7092). Wt. W12839/M1297 750,000. 1/17. D. D & L., Ltd. Forms/C2118/14.

Instructions regarding War Diaries and Intelligence Summaries are contained in F. S. Regs., Part II. and the Staff Manual respectively. Title pages will be prepared in manuscript.

WAR DIARY
or
~~INTELLIGENCE SUMMARY.~~ 8th Devon Regt.

(*Erase heading not required.*)

Army Form C. 2118.

Place	Date	Hour	Summary of Events and Information	Remarks and references to Appendices
			where they detrained at 6 am 22nd inst. 8 days rations in bulk were carried on each train and issued daily. There was an average of two long halts per day for rifle inspection cleaning out trucks washing &c. Accommodation on each train 1 first class coach 2 3rd class coaches 22 trucks 13 flats. Entraining strength of battalion 29 off 678 o ranks. Supply & baggage waggons accompanied the battalion. 22nd 23rd 24th were taken up in cleaning up, inspection & steady drill &c. Drafts on 23rd Draft of 27 O Ranks joined Bn (with attached ASC & AAC)	
LEGNAGO	25-11-17		Bn moved to billets at VO. Long march of 22 miles. Half men of last drafts found difficulty over their feet. Halt at 1 pm for dinners. Good billets on arrival. Correctly billeted 7.30 pm. LT. S.Q. WHITT. 2 LTS A.F. FROST. S.A. ROCK. A. JENKIN. H.G. LUDFORD. C.H. ATKINSON. (with RAF) joined battalion	
VO	26-11-17		Rest. foot inspections &c. 33 O Ranks joined Bn. (with attached)	
"	27-11-17		Steady drill musketry &c.	
"	28-11-17		Bn moved to [illegible] Galda. Correctly billeted 2 pm. Good billets. Many men still suffering from sore feet.	
"	29-11-17		Steady drill marching &c. Normal formation drill.	
"	30-11-17		Bn moved to Marsango. Correctly billeted 3 pm. Road march. Men's feet much better. Good billets.	
			Total Casualties for month: Officers killed, O ranks wounded, O Ranks missing NIL. Officers sick 2. O Ranks sick 35. Effective strength 35 off 778 ORs	R C [illegible] Capt & Adjt 8th Devon Regt

A7092). Wt. W12839/M1293 750,000. 1/17. D. D & L., Ltd. Forms/C2118/14.

7TH DIVISION
20TH INFY BDE

2ND BN BORDER REGT

OCT 1914-~~FEB 1919.~~
NOV 1917

www.ingramcontent.com/pod-product-compliance
Lightning Source LLC
Chambersburg PA
CBHW080849230426
43662CB00013B/2054